DUQUESNE STUDIES

Spiritan Series

9

The Spiritual Letters of
The Venerable Francis Libermann

Volume Five

LETTERS TO CLERGY AND RELIGIOUS
(Nos. 185 to 274)

The Venerable Francis Libermann, C.S.Sp.
(1802-1852)

DUQUESNE STUDIES
Spiritan Series

9

The Spiritual Letters of
The Venerable Francis Libermann

Volume Five

LETTERS TO CLERGY AND RELIGIOUS
(Nos. 185 to 274)

edited and translated by
WALTER VAN DE PUTTE, C.S.Sp., L.L.D.

1966

DUQUESNE UNIVERSITY PRESS
Pittsburgh, Pa.
Editions E. Nauwelaerts, Louvain

DUQUESNE STUDIES

Spiritan Series

Library of Congress Catalog Card Number 62-12768

Printed in the United States by
THE AD PRESS, LTD., *New York, N. Y.*

Volume Six, Francis Libermann, C.S.Sp., SPIRITUAL LETTERS. II, *Letters to People in the World*. IX and 307 pages. Price: $4.95, cloth only.

Volume Seven, Francis Libermann, C.S.Sp., SPIRITUAL LETTERS. III, *Letters to Clergy and Religious*. Nos. 1-75. X and 322 pages. Price: $5.00, cloth only.

Volume Eight, Francis Libermann, C.S.Sp., SPIRITUAL LETTERS. IV, *Letters to Clergy and Religious*. Nos. 76-184. X and 420 pages. Price: $5.25, cloth only.

Volume Nine, Francis Libermann, C.S.Sp., SPIRITUAL LETTERS. V, *Letters to Clergy and Religious*. Nos. 185-275, IX and 336 pages. Price: $5.00, cloth only.

IN PREPARATION:

Francis Libermann, C.S.Sp., *Spiritual Letters VI*
Spiritual Writings
A Spiritual Commentary on
the Gospel of St. John

DUQUESNE STUDIES comprise the following series:

African Series—Philosophical Series—Spiritan Series— Philological Series — Psychological Series — Theological Series.

TWENTY PERCENT DISCOUNT IS GIVEN ON CONTINUATION ORDERS FOR ALL SERIES

Imprimi Potest

Very Rev. Vernon F. Gallagher, C.S.Sp., Provincial.

Nihil Obstat

Rev. William J. Winter, S.T.D.
Censor Librorum

Imprimatur

+Most Reverend Vincent M. Leonard, D.D.
Vicar General—Chancellor

Pittsburgh, Pa., August 12, 1965

CONTENTS

PREFACE

The present volume contains many letters showing Father Libermann's spirituality in action. They were addressed to holy priests and religious and to others who were not so holy, to angry subjects complaining about unreasonable superiors and to saddened superiors discouraged by recalcitrant subjects. For each one Francis Libermann had appropriate words of advice.

Throughout the letters we can hear a voice that is often surprisingly modern in its plea for freedom from anxiety and tension, for the holy liberty of the children of God, for total self-commitment in a joyful surrender to God, for respect for each one's own personality.

"Be in God's hands like a toy in the hands of a child," he counsels an anxious soul. "Don't be harsh; always lean to the side of mercy and gentleness," is his advice to a rigid character. "Don't be so anxious to have God move in the direction of your own ideas," he admonishes one who would like to make his own desires those of God. And his counsel to superiors in general is: "Allow everyone to follow his own ideas and accomplish the good in his own way, and encourage them in doing so. . . . If we let everyone act according to his personal ideas, his character, mentality and his whole make-up, great good will be accomplished."

More than a century old, these gems of spiritual wisdom retain their originality and freshness, they continue to appeal even to the new generation's search for a personal identity.

HENRY J. KOREN, C.S.Sp.

DUQUESNE UNIVERSITY, November 23, 1965

ix

1. LETTERS TO FREDERIC LE VAVASSEUR

Frederic Le Vavasseur (1811-1882) was a native of the island of Reunion. In 1829, he went to France, where he unsuccessfully studied engineering at the *Ecole Polytechnique*. He next studied law and then entered the Sulpician House of Philosophy at Issy in 1836. He was ordained to the priesthood in 1841.

As a seminarian, he conceived the idea of christianizing the slaves of his native country. He and another seminarian, Eugene Tisserant, who had similar missionary ideas, were thus led to consult their common friend Francis Libermann. Both also especially invoked the help of "Our Lady of Victories" in Paris. This resulted in the formation of Libermann's Congregation of the Holy Heart of Mary.

After his ordination in 1841, Frederic entered Libermann's novitiate of La Neuville and, having made his apostolic consecration, spent seven years as a missionary in his beloved Bourbon (Reunion). Having returned to France, he in turn fulfilled the functions of superior of Holy Ghost seminary, novice master, provincial, and Superior General of the Holy Ghost Congregation (1881). He died on January 16, 1882.

This brief sketch fails to reveal the extraordinary life of this truly extraordinary man. Frederic was both endowed with great intellectual power and strongly impelled by a fiery temperament. In his early religious life he gave frequent proofs of impetuosity, of immoderate zeal in the practice of penance, of extremism in his pursuit of perfection and in his direction of others. But he gave a chance to grace to mold him, and in the end his character mellowed and he was enabled to crown a saintly life as religious priest and missionary with a saintly death.

1

185

The need to struggle against nature is a valuable grace. Total surrender to God in distrust of self. Remaining with Jesus in utter uselessness. Advice regarding mental prayer and spiritual friendship.

Letter One　　　*Rennes, Pentecost, 1838*　　　*Vol. 1, p. 474*

Praised be Jesus and Mary

Dear Confrere:

> *[I am Happy to See That You Still Have to Struggle Against Nature]*

May the Holy Spirit superabound in your soul as He did in Mary our good Mother. I rejoice before our Lord in seeing that you are still a poor man, struggling constantly against his natural activity and vivacity. It is certain that this activity is a great treasure for you, and I consider it a special favor on the part of our Lord that those combats still continue in you. You may rest assured that, if you had overcome that wretched activity from the very beginning, you would never have accomplished much for your interior life.

In such a case you would have entertained a good opinion of yourself. You would have taken pleasure in considering your spiritual condition, and you would thus have lost everything. You would at least have entered upon the road to perdition by thus contemplating yourself, and it would have proved calamitous for you. But now you have no time to consider yourself with complacency and you are forced to be always on your guard. You see that whatever you may possess does not amount to very much, and you constantly feel a certain apprehension and a fear that you

may not attain the desired end. This will probably make
you conceive a little distrust of yourself.

[Total Surrender to God Requires Self-Distrust]

You ought to know that if we desire to give ourselves
to God by way of total surrender, we need a good dose of
self-distrust. Otherwise we run the risk of falling into an
abyss, or of building a castle in the air, or using a foundation
of straw and dust. This is why I tell you that God is bestow-
ing a true favor upon you by leaving you in your wretchedness. Be satisfied, therefore, with your present condition.
Be little and poor since this is what our Lord desires.

When the hour of your deliverance has come, accept it
gratefully, but preserve an attitude of lowliness, poverty and
mistrust of self in God's presence. In the meantime remain
meek, reserved and peaceful. You will be able to achieve
this by gently calling your mind back when it has wandered
off, by arresting it quietly and without contentious effort,
keeping it before God and united with our Lord in gentleness and peace.

[Remain Before Jesus in Your Uselessness]

Do not imagine that you are less united to God than
you were formerly and are more dissipated. You may be led
to think that you are in such a condition because you sometimes are deprived of feelings. At least, you are not aware
of all the attention and care you ought to take and of the
care you actually do take to repress that over-activity. You
may even lack a certain sensible attention to the task of
repressing that activity, but what can you do about that?
There is no great evil in it.

You are much more in need of God now than you were
before. You are more aware of your incapacity and the
need of God's support. Endeavor to remain quietly united

3

with this beloved Master, so that He Himself may take up all the wretchedness for which you know no remedy. Remain constantly in His presence in your extreme poverty, incapacity, and uselessness.

Never indulge in anxious desires to be "somebody" or to accomplish something. Your only desire should be to lie crushed and prostrate at the feet of our Lord, to be nothing in your own eyes, before God and all creatures, to forget yourself and to be forgotten by everybody, so that Jesus may be praised, blessed, and glorified by, in and with His Father, and by all creatures. What else ought we or could we desire in heaven and on earth but that?

This is why you should never be satisfied with what you are nor pleased with what you are able to do, nor even delight in the graces which Jesus bestows upon your soul. But let all your complacency and all your mental effort and all the joy of your heart be concentrated on Jesus alone. For to Him alone, in His Father and with the Holy Spirit, belong all homage, all glory, and all love; and to us, all contempt, disgrace, ignominy and confusion. This is the sum total of your life. But all this must be accompanied by great peace, gentleness and tranquility; it must take place without any purely natural effort of the flesh.

[*Do Not Analyze Your Mental Prayer But Follow Your Attraction*]

You can put your mind at rest regarding your meditation and continue in the manner you have adopted. Do not analyze what takes place during and after your meditation. Seek only one thing, for it alone is important: to live for God and in Him alone at the expense and to the detriment of your self-love and all your self-seeking.

The method you use to attain this goal matters little, provided you are successful. This is the only thing that is necessary. Remain quiet during and after your mental prayer. Remain quiet throughout the day, and may your every desire be made in God's presence and for Him alone. It would be well for you to examine the things that attract you in our Lord, the Blessed Virgin, Saint Joseph or in other Saints, but all this should be done without tenseness or worry. If you feel some attraction in that respect and you feel capable of following it, yield to it. If not, remain quiet and live for and in God alone.

[Spiritual Friendship]

You should also distrust yourself in everything that concerns your repugnances or your inclinations, in regard to conversing with various persons. Neither act hastily toward those for whom you feel a repugnance nor act readily against your feelings. I assume that you dislike to speak to such people about spiritual advancement or to be on intimate terms with them concerning such matters. You would run the risk of being gravely indiscreet. If you speak to them in spite of your disinclination, take care to measure and weigh your words. Advance only where the way is clear.

God alone touches the heart. You should not advance too far, but leave always a larger share of the work to Him. Act, but do it with moderation and caution, in a supernatural spirit. If someone does not proceed according to your desires, do not worry or get excited about it. Quietly follow your taste and attraction and constantly mistrust your corrupt nature which is ever putting in a claim for a share even in the holiest things. But you need not discontinue to be intimate friends on that account, for your attraction is not purely natural. There is always an element of the natural, even in true charity. We ought to overcome ourselves in this, but should not reject charity on that account.

Entirely yours in Jesus and Mary,
FRANCIS LIBERMANN, ACOLYTE

186

Libermann encourages his friend in his plan for organizing the apostolate among the Negro slaves.

Letter Two   Rennes, March 8, 1839   Vol. 1, p. 638

Praised be Jesus and Mary

Dear Confrere:

"Act manfully and may your heart be strengthened." I hope that our Lord will realize the project[1] he has prompted you to undertake for His greater glory. Pursue that object with confidence and for the love of our Lord. He has merciful designs for the salvation of those poor souls who have been neglected until now. I advise you to undertake that great work and apply your earnest endeavors to it. Do not trust in yourself nor in your own devices and schemes. Do not try to persuade anyone, but let the Master of the house act. It belongs to Him to choose the laborers whom He wishes to send there. Your great task for the present consists in humbling yourself very much in His sight since you are a great obstacle in the way of what He plans to do for those poor souls that are so dear to Him.

[*Disregard What People Will Say About You and Your Plan*]

At the same time, however, you should entertain great confidence in, and love toward Him, and act energetically. Don't become discouraged by the difficulties you will meet or because of the criticisms and the false judgments that will be made about you, your conduct and anything you will

---

[1] To organize a society for the apostolate among the Negro slaves.

do. People will consider you weak-minded, imprudent and proud. They will say all kinds of things about you, not only in your own country but even in Paris. Even respectable persons will disapprove you, accuse you, brand your plan as the product of a hot-headed youth, as folly. They will say that you are undertaking the impossible. This is what one can expect even from those that are very wise and best intentioned.

When they see difficulties which to natural-minded men seem insurmountable, they declare that the thing is impossible. But, dear friend, all this ought not to discourage you nor ought it to delay you even for one moment. Even when the most devout and the wisest of men oppose such a project, persevere in it before God. Not feeling interiorly the prompting of our Lord for such a good enterprise, they imagine that the difficulties render such a task impossible. This is why you ought to remain always united with our Lord in a spirit of great humility as well as of love. Let Him act in you instead of acting yourself; follow His inspirations and the desires He inspires with all gentleness, peace, love, and the most profound humility of heart. And especially when you are in the midst of difficulties preserve patience, remain gentle, be humble and calm, in God's presence, toward all who cause those difficulties and troubles.

[*To Succeed, the Work Should Be Undertaken by a Congregation*]

I have proposed the project to the Superior of the Eudists. It gave him very great joy and he told me that he would most gladly receive you and that he would be most pleased if the poor Congregation of Jesus and Mary could undertake so great a work and one that is so agreeable to God. Such an arrangement would be very advantageous for yourself and even for the good of the work. It seems almost indispensable for that sort of work that it should be undertaken by a Congregation. If the task were undertaken by isolated individuals, the individual spirit would soon manifest itself and the work would have no stability, for it would lack unity of spirit; and there are many other reasons besides. Moreover, it is absolutely necessary for you to prepare yourself for so important a ministry by a few years of retirement from all occupations.

It is for this reason that I greatly favor the opinion of Father Pinault that those who engage in that work should live as members of a congregation. If the good Lord directs you toward our Congregation, this will give me great consolation and it will at the same time be beneficial to this poor congregation which is now so useless in France; it would at least enable it to procure God's glory elsewhere. Moreover, our Constitutions are good and you will not have to change anything in regard to your project; they lend themselves perfectly to it. Our spirit is nothing but the apostolic spirit, and everything in our Constitutions is intended to form missionaries according to the spirit of our Lord. That is their entire foundation.

[Right Now Your Only Task is to Prepare Yourself for the Work Through Greater Holiness]

I advise you not to occupy yourself as yet with the details of the rule that you will follow. It is enough for the present that you have a general idea of the work. If, at a later date, you come with us, we shall regulate the details according as it is granted to us from above. If the good Lord leads you elsewhere, then similar arrangements will have to be made. However, it would be dangerous for you to busy yourself with such matters at this time, for the moment for such regulations has not yet arrived. Simply aim at present to prepare yourself for so great a ministry. Do this with

8

calm, peace, and interior humility of soul and by leading a life of love and holiness, endeavoring to render yourself ever more pleasing to our Lord and more capable of serving as a faithful instrument in His hands.

I don't know why Father Galais thinks that we ought not to speak about those things; this is why I cannot say anything to you about that. I realize that we ought not to be hasty in the works of God and must allow Him to act instead of acting ourselves. Nevertheless, there is no evil in speaking about it if there are no reasons against it. In certain circumstances it would be necessary to speak about that affair. But, as I have said, Father Galais no doubt has his own reasons for taking that stand, though they are unknown to me. If you ask Father Pinault get in contact with Father Galais regarding that matter, the two could decide what ought to be done.

If I had not been afraid of spoiling things I would have written a few words about it to our friend Mr. de la Brunière, but we should let the good Lord act. I will nevertheless say a little about it to Father Pinault and Father Galais.

Adieu, dear friend. May Jesus be your refuge, hope and love.

> Entirely yours in the most holy love
> of Jesus and Mary,
> FRANCIS LIBERMANN, ACOLYTE

P. S. Do not reflect on the question of the choice of your Patron or of the one to whom your work should be dedicated. Leave this quite simply in the hands of Jesus and Mary. I, too, feel inclined to dedicate it to the Cross, which should be your inheritance.

187

Our plans for the new congregation must mature before we undertake anything. We will need fervent and generous souls, not weaklings. Relying on God alone, we need not fear adversities and human disappointments.

Letter Three   Rennes, October 28, 1839   *Vol. 1, p. 661*

Praised be Jesus and Mary

Dear Confrere:

[We Must Let Our Plan Ripen in God's Presence]

Mr. de la Brunière came to see me last night to urge me to offer Holy Communion to God on behalf of the poor and beloved Negroes, because it was the feast of the Holy Apostles Saints Simon and Jude. We have done so, and the good Lord has given me a little enlightenment. However, I do not want to tell you about it, for I prefer to allow that plan to ripen in God's presence. In this way, if it be agreeable to His goodness and to His well-beloved Son, that small spark will develop and become a more vivid light. Before attempting to spread such plans, we should be able to present them with sufficient clarity so that everybody can weigh them before God.

Pray and ask all our confreres to pray likewise. The matter is important; it is very great; we also will pray for it for some time to come. Always encourage our dear friends in their love for those poor Negroes. Tell Mr. Tisserant to send me his memoir.

I shall give some thought to the constitutions during my free moments. Once more pray for this also. I would have preferred to postpone reflecting upon those things until the affair had passed through the hands of the Holy See. But Fathers Galais and Pinault desire it, and I see some advantage in having the constitutions examined before they are presented to the Holy See, especially in regard to the way in which they should be formulated. I think that my plan will meet with difficulties. I will follow it nevertheless, letting our Lord take care of removing every obstacle.

[*An Apostolic Congregation Needs Fervent Members, Not Weaklings*]

Mr. de la Brunière encourages me, and he is in perfect agreement with me. I should like to have something established that is solid, fervent and apostolic; all this or nothing! But "all" will be much, and weak souls will not wish to give or do so much. This ought to be a source of joy for us, for a congregation that is wholly apostolic should not have weaklings. We ought to have nothing but fervent and generous members who give themselves entirely and are ready to undertake and suffer all things for the greater glory of our most adorable Master.

It seems to me that all who are apparently called to give themselves to God in that holy enterprise are disposed to undertake and suffer anything. They will feel additional spiritual joy when they see that the Rule demands a higher perfection and that it will sustain them in a more perfect holiness and in greater devotedness to God. Encourage them and tell them to make themselves ready before God to undertake anything, to suffer death—even the death of the cross. It is only at this price that we share in the spirit and the apostolic glory of Jesus Christ, the Sovereign Lord and the great Model of apostles.

Please tell Father Pinault that I am almost getting angry with him. He never tells me anything about that great and

11

beautiful work and leaves me entirely to myself. I hope to write to him within two weeks, telling him what the good Lord will deign to make known to Mr. de la Brunière and to me.

[*If We Place Our Hope in God Alone, We Need Not Fear Adversities*]

We have already met disappointment and some hopes have been frustrated, but this ought not to discourage us. We should wait until our Lord and His most Holy Mother develop what is their work. Tell all those who wish to join that they ought not to indulge in excessive sensible joy at the sight of the work's progress, as happened when Mr. de Brandt seemed to desire to become a member. Tell them not to yield to sadness when they meet with adversity and their hopes do not materialize. But let them remain constantly in dispositions of humility, lowliness and poverty before Him who is the Head and Lord of all whom He destines for the apostolate. Let them humbly put all their hope in His goodness and love.

Mr. de la Brunière and I will offer Holy Communion for our dear Negroes on the Feast of All Saints. Unite your intention to ours. Ask Fathers Pinault and Galais to do likewise, if you consider it proper.

Entirely yours in the most holy love of Jesus and Mary,

FRANCIS LIBERMANN, ACOLYTE

188

The Holy See encourages us in our undertakings. Why should we worry about difficulties? The devil may try to sow discord among us.

Letter Four   **Rome, June 12, 1840**   **Vol. 2, p. 82**

Dear Confrere:

I want to reply immediately to the letter that I have just received which contained another letter for Father de Regnier and a cheque.

I was very glad to learn through Father Pinault that the Superior of the Holy Ghost Fathers is so well disposed toward me, for, until today, the good Lord has sent me nothing but contradictions and obstacles, and I was afraid that there would be opposition from that quarter also.

[*The Holy See Encourages Our Undertaking*]

On the very day that brought me the letter of Father Pinault, God gave me an additional consolation that greatly encourages me in regard to our dear undertaking. It is a letter from Cardinal Fransoni, the Prefect of Propaganda. I had not hoped for such a thing nor had I asked for it, as I explain in the letter I am sending to Father Pinault. That letter will perhaps arrive later than the present one, for I have sent it by the ambassador.

His Eminence makes mention of all of you as well as of myself, and he exhorts us to persevere in our vocation and do all that we can to remain faithful to it.

Let us note that his exhortation has very great authority, not only because the Cardinal is a saint and is appointed by the Pope as General Superior over all the missions, but also because he reports everything to the Holy Father and acts only according to the orders of the latter. For all the Cardinals act in this way and nothing is done without passing through the hands of the Supreme Pontiff, except routine affairs.

Moreover, the Cardinal Prefect, before writing that letter, proposed our project to the assembly which has the function of examining such projects. This assembly or "congregation" is composed of the principal Cardinals, several Archbishops, Bishops and Prelates, and some religious who are outstanding for their merit and their piety. The Cardinal says explicitly in that letter that what he writes is in agreement with the "congregation."

You see then, dear friend, that we ought to bless and praise God for the grace He thus grants to us. We should encourage one another more and more in the vocation and in its spirit, for God's will in our regard could not be more clearly expressed.

I don't want to say more about that matter. My letter to Father Pinault will explain why we did not meet with such a favorable reception at the beginning, or rather why [Propaganda] seemed even unwilling to listen to me, and why things have changed since then, without anyone else or myself doing anything to produce such a change.

I assure you that when we consider the circumstances, it is most astonishing that His Eminence sent a letter. This alone is a certain proof of his good dispositions toward us and of the fact that he considers our work to be truly in accord with God's will.

[*Why Should We Worry About Difficulties?*]

Do not worry about the difficulties that were mentioned by the Superior of the Holy Ghost Fathers and will probably be mentioned also by others. It even astonished me that that word "difficulties" is constantly brought up. Is there any work of God that is not accomplished in the midst of difficulties? Have we not been aware at all times that we would meet with obstacles? We certainly have, and the obstacles will be considerable. If we were able to foresee them, we would study them and devise good means for overcoming them; but if this is impossible and we cannot choose such means, let us remain quiet. In any case, we should put our trust in God. When the time comes, we shall do what we can to bear the pains, afflictions and contradictions, and avoid as much as possible or overcome the difficulties that will stand in our way. Above all, let us put our entire confidence in Jesus and Mary alone; they will be our only resource, our only support on this earth.

We have difficulties which, I trust, will sanctify us; this is exactly what we need. Woe to us if we do not have such difficulties! It is by the cross that we ought to sanctify both ourselves and others. We are not made to live in peace and tranquillity, but to suffer for the greater glory of God. . . .

Pray much. Although things everywhere are taking a good turn, I still expect a number of reverses. Let us be always in God's hands, ready to live only according to His most holy will, with a loving and humble heart, willing to accept anything He may have in store for us. Let us bless God for everything He does to us and beg Him to give perseverance to all whom He will send us.

[*The Devil May Try to Sow Discord Among Us*]

Be in peace and do not worry about anything. Be full of confidence in our Lord and His most Holy Mother. Union and charity are precious treasures, and I firmly hope that the divine Master will grant them to all of us.

We should not be astonished if the enemy does his best to sow trouble among us; but let us be courageous, practice

15

patience, and refuse to attach exaggerated importance to such things. You know how great is the happiness that results from peace, charity and union among you; and you strongly and earnestly desire and pursue them. If sometimes, or even very often, contrary sentiments arise, it is not your fault. Never yield to anxiety on their account, but say to yourselves that the devil is trying to play with you. Bear patiently and with a sort of indifference what he does to you, and go on as if he did not interfere. At a later time when we are engaged in our labors those things will surely vanish.

I do not consider it necessary to say more about this matter. Please be satisfied with these few words. Best regards to all in the holy charity of Jesus and Mary. . . .

FRANCIS LIBERMANN, ACOLYTE

Do not worry about your interior life. Continue to walk in all peace. Tomorrow I will pray that our Lord may live in you in all His fullness and maintain in you the spirit of the subdiaconate.

189

Bishop Collier is an exception to the rule that men nearly always tend to interfere with God's plans. We must not rush ahead of God's guidance.

Letter Five   *Rome, July 12, 1840*   *Vol. 2, p. 85*

Dear Confrere:

We owe our Lord and His most Holy Mother a debt of profound gratitude for all their goodness toward us and the consolations they have given us. If we succeed in arranging our affairs in agreement with Bishop William Collier and, as I hope from God's infinite goodness, if we are favored with His grace, everything will go well. We have good reasons for believing that the bishop will try to secure a small foundation for us at Cambrai. If he did not make definite promises, it was because he was not sure that he would succeed.

[*Man Nearly Always Tends to Interfere with God's Plans*]

What seems very nice on the part of the bishop is the fact that he does not appear to make the appeal exclusively for his own interests. He is working for the good of his diocese, but he also takes care not to harm the work that is proposed to him. He wants to benefit by the enterprise, but he does not seem to want things to be done according to his own fancy or ideas. He acts as if he felt that he ought to let things develop according to the good Lord's designs and the ideas our Lord has suggested to us for our project.

This way of acting, which I consider most wise and in conformity with God's will, is something I have not met with anywhere until now. Everyone wishes to change and arrange things according to his own ideas, and such a method is precisely the one that opposes, arrests, and sometimes almost destroys God's works. It is a way that is even contrary to the rules of human prudence, for those who are planning such projects know the requirements much better than a stranger who is not engaged in the enterprise and judges things only according to first impressions. Moreover, those who aimed at giving themselves completely and sacrificing themselves for God's glory in an enterprise which God prompted them to undertake, lose half of that resolution when they are forced to abandon half of their project or are asked to execute God's plans in a way that differs from His designs.

17

We all act alike in such matters. Man has always the tendency to interfere with God's works. Whenever we judge as men, according to pure human reason, such interference will take place. We then find it necessary to change, to modify things; we upset things, for there are no two minds that think alike, but every individual has his own point of view. When, however, we look at things from God's standpoint, we easily agree, for we then prefer to place our trust in what the good Lord desires to do according to His designs. We then yield to others more easily and are not so anxious to scrutinize their plans and find out whether they might not be wrong. We realize that if they are wanting in experience, they will acquire it with the help of God's grace; and if they happen to be men of good will, they will change their views once they discover that they are wrong.

When I visited Cardinal Fransoni he did not say anything about making changes, and I learned that it is the rule with Propaganda not to disturb people, but to allow them to follow their attraction. The Cardinal spoke to me about one country that is very much in need of help, but he suddenly corrected himself and without finishing the sentence, said, "O, I was forgetting that your project is directed solely to the Negro." Everyone, with the exception of the men at Propaganda and Bishop Collier, wished to change the plans, and each wanted to have things done according to his own views.

[*We Must Not Run Ahead of God's Guidance*]

I do not see that it will be difficult to begin the novitiate next year. However, it might be useful for me to take time out, visit some good dioceses, and look for devout priests who are suitable for our work and whom the good Lord wishes to send us. In this way we could form a complete community from the start and would not have to send men to the missions before they have had the benefit of observing the Rule while living in community.

To succeed, I would have to set out very soon, but this is not feasible. We would then have to delay the novitiate until the end of the winter. We must not act with haste, lest we run ahead of the good Lord. The right procedure is to follow Him always faithfully step by step and not to run ahead of Him. Moreover, it will be difficult to make a decision about those matters before two months have elapsed. We shall then know what turn things are taking. Let us always obey the impetus given us by the good Lord as a ship obeys every gust of wind in its sails.

Regarding money, I have no particular need for the present. I think, nevertheless, that you would do well to reserve your alms for us and to save some money. We shall thus be able to pay for traveling expenses and for other things we need. . . .

I am full of joy at the thought of the good dispositions of all our dear confreres. Let us pray constantly to our Lord and the most Blessed Virgin, asking them to make them advance in fervor and sanctity.

May the peace and love of our Lord Jesus Christ grow and increase in your soul and in the souls of those dear confreres.

> Entirely yours in the holy love of
> Jesus and Mary,
> FRANCIS LIBERMANN

190

Father Le Vavasseur's extreme rigorism caused constant conflicts in the newly opened novitiate of La Neuville. Four months after its opening, he departed for his native island of Bourbon (Reunion), but promised Libermann not to sever relations with the Congregation. In the present letter, Libermann stresses the need for unity and harmony, while rejoicing over his resolution to remain in the Society.

Letter Six   La Neuville, February 4, 1842   Vol. 3, p. 126

Dear Confrere:

[*We Greatly Need to be United in the Charity of Christ*]

I am very unworthy of the consolation that our Lord bestows upon me, for I deserve nothing but pain and tribulation. God knows that I do not refuse such afflictions. I ask Him to grant but one thing, that we may have a holy union among ourselves in His divine love. I trust that He has given this great grace, a grace that I would be glad to earn at the price of the most severe afflictions He might desire to send me.

Set your mind at rest. I have no more fears, for I hope that the Holy Heart of Mary will have compassion on us and will not permit the enemy to sow trouble among us, especially at this time when we are so greatly in need of peace and union. The Blessed Mother has granted you a signal grace. It is my hope that I too will benefit by it for the good of my soul. You are making a great sacrifice, and this sacrifice was so much greater because of the violence of your temptation. The reward, I hope, will also be great for this small society and the salvation of numerous souls.

I have done nothing and deserve nothing, but at least I am offering myself to our good Master and our Holy Mother, ready to suffer any sort of pain and affliction according to the wishes of divine Providence for the good of this poor little work. I think that I would feel a most profound joy amidst the most severe pains and, with the help of God's grace, would bear them gladly, if we were well united in the charity of Jesus. That charity is found in such fullness in Mary's Heart, from which we ought to draw it as from a common source.

[*Through Lack of Union We Might Spoil Everything*]

Let me tell you that I have often reflected on the Order for the Redemption of Captives and also on another—I cannot recall its name—that had several founders, and my heart was oppressed with grief because I saw with what perfect union and understanding those saints lived and sought to labor for the glory of their Master within their Order. But we, poor individuals, so incapable of doing anything for God's glory, so much in need of such a union, we do not have it and are thereby losing the sacred trust that was confided to us. However, we are, all of us, children of Mary, as those Saints were.

[*I Trust in Mary's Protection*]

I can tell you now what I feared to mention to you when you were still with us: that thought [of discord] broke my heart, for I thought that the enemy still exercised power over us. The thing that consoled me and gave me great hope was the fact that, in spite of it all, Mary our most beloved Mother had revealed her protection over us on several occasions. This made me believe that it was her intention to destroy the power of the enemy. You know that I have repeatedly mentioned this to you. O the goodness of our dear Lord! That hope has not been frustrated. Mary has given us her hand; she will complete the overthrow of that wretched enemy and will make us triumph over all his wiles and ruses.

Forget the past, dear friend, and rejoice in the present. Be wholly devoted to Mary and to her most Holy Heart and live as a true child of the sweet and humble Heart of Mary, which is so full of love for you.

Adieu, my dear confrere.

> Entirely yours in the most holy love of the
> Holy Heart of Mary,
> FATHER FRANCIS LIBERMANN

191

Your apostolic labor must be based on a love full of humility. Trust in God's providence. Safeguarding the congregation's internal autonomy. Advice concerning the way of handling subordinates.

Letter Seven   *March 4, 1843*   *Vol. 3, p. 202*

Jesus, Mary, Joseph

Dear Confrere:

May the peace and love of our Lord and of our most Holy Mother increase and grow ever stronger in your soul.

I am sending you Fathers Collin and Blanpin, in the name of our Lord, to be your associates in your apostolic labors. "Increase and multiply and fill the earth." This is the greatest desire of my heart. It is by your zeal for the salvation of souls that you will beget a multitude of children for our heavenly Father. Those men, with sinful souls blacker than their bodies, will become white as snow, thanks to your care and the blessings which Christ's grace will pour on your labors.

Always remain gentle, recollected, peaceful, filled with love and especially with humility. The spirit that ought to be the soul of all your works is a love full of humility and a humility full of love. Remain constantly aware of your poverty before God, but at the same time keep alive a filial love and confidence. While preserving that attitude of lowliness in His presence, allow yourself to be carried off by divine love and act vigorously, propelled by the power of grace and the love of Jesus Christ which abides in you . . .[1]

[*Trust in Divine Providence*]

[Regarding the travel expenses and salaries of our priests, the government has] promised to pay for the voyage, but added that our men would not receive any salary. I assure you truthfully and sincerely that I am very glad of this. You see, dear confrere, that we should abandon ourselves to divine Providence. God takes care of everything. It would have been difficult for me to refuse the salary if it had been offered. I even thought that God's will and the rules of prudence dictated acceptance of such money. After that, I abandoned everything to divine Goodness which takes such wonderful care of its poor insignificant servants. I beg you never to relinquish this kind of attitude and conduct. God will bless you as long as you act in that manner. May our ways be identical, especially in regard to acting on true principles; this will be our strength, and it will draw God's graces and blessings upon us. . . .

[*Safeguard the Congregation's Internal Autonomy*]

The Prefect of Bourbon seems to be very fond of us, and he has sought to render us every possible service. We

---

[1]Administrative parts of this and the following letters have been omitted.

must keep this in mind; nevertheless, you should not allow him to become the master of your community. Agreements must be kept. As soon as the Rule and the spirit of the Congregation are involved we should resist, doing this, however, with gentleness, humility and modesty. When they are not involved, we ought to obey and try to satisfy him and give him all possible comfort. This is how God's servants must act towards their ecclesiastical superiors.

[*When Father Collin is in a Stubborn Mood, Allow the Evil Moment to Pass*]

I appoint Father Collin as your first Assistant. He is a good man and very simple, resourceful and devout; he has ardent zeal and is as constant as he is courageous. He has good judgment and much firmness and is very gentle when he is faithful to grace. But when he follows the evil tendencies of his nature, he is very rigid, hard and stubborn and will have arguments with everybody. Do not offer him direct resistance; don't try to make him give up his wrong views immediately nor correct him at the time when he is acting in that fashion. Do not oppose him in a stiff and rigorous manner. Allow the evil moment to pass, and when the storm is over, reason in all gentleness with him. You will then be able to make him accept everything you wish.

[*Encourage Him When He is Downcast*]

Father Collin is also greatly inclined to be angry with himself and to become discouraged. On such occasions you should try to restore his confidence in God and make him abandon himself to our Lord. Let him remain in God's presence like a wretched man who desires nothing but God's good pleasure and that His will be accomplished. When he happens to make a mistake or commits a fault, he should gently return to the presence of God, remain there in all his poverty, and restrain any sentiment of ill will toward himself.

[Lest His Self-Love Increase, Do Not Let Him Play the Theologian]

Father Collin lately earned great success in his studies and his mind attained a great development. This made him feel a certain satisfaction with himself; he was prompted to think well of his talents and inclined to self-sufficiency and presumption, especially in matters of theology. He thus was apt to make peremptory pronouncements. That is why I advise you not to consult him regarding matters of theology or the rubrics. Similarly, I would but rarely discuss questions of theology, especially in regard to positive law. Regarding natural law your common sense knows as much as his does. It would be well not to let him make professional use of his knowledge of theology within the community for some time to come. However, you should permit him to spend two hours or more every day in perfecting himself in theological science, for he studied only the first elements and he did it rapidly.

It would be well also not to launch him directly into preaching, for the same reasons. I believe that he would be perfectly successful, but you should handle this young man with care, lest he fall a prey to self-love. It remains true, however, that he was almost untouched by that vice for a very long time. He is as obedient as a child, is full of faith and good desires. If you act with gentleness, confidence and affection of heart toward him, you will do him much good and will take the lead over him.

He has also worried me lately; he has become prejudiced against me, whereas until now he had been very docile, full of confidence and respect. This change in him pained me greatly. It was occasioned by the relations he had with a novice who suffered temptations for quite a length of time. Those prejudices have done some harm to Father Collin, although they are not of long standing. His presumption, or inclination to it, of which I spoke a moment ago, has contributed somewhat to that. But do not worry about all that; he has great confidence in you and is full of joy at the prospect of working with you and being formed by your counsel. Act unhesitatingly with him, but do it with gentleness, as I have explained.

[*Father Blanpin is Still an Adolescent and Needs Experience*]

Father Blanpin is a saintly "child" in the full sense of the word. In fact, I have never met so much simplicity and innocence. It is easy to direct him. He will give you great satisfaction because of that simplicity and docility. He is somewhat awkward, and this, together with a certain naiveness and his carelessness for all earthly things, makes him sometimes annoying. He has no wide outlook; he needs experience in every field, and it is possible that he will acquire it with difficulty. I believe that he will do very much good; his charity and gentleness will never fail. He will be a tireless worker in behalf of the Negroes.

May Jesus and Mary guide you in your conduct with those dear confreres and the souls you are called to save.

Entirely yours in Jesus and Mary,
FATHER FRANCIS LIBERMANN,
missionary of the Holy Heart of Mary.

192

The Spirit of Christ, as well as human prudence, demand gentleness and charity in dealing with government officials.

Letter Eight   *August 22, 1844*   *Vol. 6, p. 316*

Dear Confrere:

I have read your report with great interest. However, it seems to me that you are making use of a somewhat bitter tone in your reply to the Director of the Internal Affairs of the Colony. It would have been preferable to use more charitable words and expressions that did not hurt anyone. I don't mean that you are actually insulting, but, without saying it explicitly, you imply that there was bad faith on the part of the Director. I do not doubt that there actually was bad faith and a bad intention on his part, but, instead of implying this, a tone of moderation, gentleness, and charity in your reply would have been more in accord with our own spirit. Our Lord sends us as lambs among wolves. A lamb does not bite the wolf that attacks it.

I think that you should have assumed that there had been an error on the part of the Director. You could have told him, for instance, that in all probability he had received wrong information from people who were either ignorant or ill-intentioned; that it was regrettable that a man who was well-intentioned like himself should thwart your good desires and put obstacles in the way of the good you would like to accomplish. After that, you could have shown clearly and firmly, though with calm and gentleness, that the information given him by others in your regard was not correct. This sort of moderate and peaceful language is in harmony with the spirit of our divine Master. A lamb does not defend itself against the wolf by attacking it. Besides, speaking humanly, the kind of language I have suggested is much more effectual than one that is violent and petulant; it tends to make others favorably disposed.

It seems that the Director will return to Bourbon. However, don't worry about the past; we have to make foolish mistakes sometimes in order to gain experience about men and things. . . .

> Entirely yours in Jesus and Mary,
> FRANCIS LIBERMANN,
> missionary of the Holy Heart of Mary.

193

We have suffered severe losses in Africa. Yet I remain full of confidence in God.

Letter Nine   *Paris, October 16, 1844*   *Vol. 6, p. 374*

Dear Confrere:

I received your reports and the one of Father Blanpin concerning the mission of Colimaçon. . . . The knowledge of what you are doing gives me great consolation, and it is a great encouragement for all of us.

We need such consolation greatly because of the misfortunes we suffer in Guinea. The blows struck by our Lord were very severe, and I could not help recognizing them as a singular act of His divine Providence. Everything seemed to point to a success in that vast and neglected mission. The information that I had received from all sides caused us to believe that we would be able to save that country with slight losses for ourselves. God has judged differently: He has tried us in a most painful manner; may His Name be blessed.

I received a letter from Bishop Barron, dated August 6th, in which he announces our new losses, Father Audebert and Father Bouchet. He told me that he would take the necessary steps to save the three that remain; but I feel certain, or at least consider it most probable, that they too have succumbed.

I feel sure that I have acted according to God's will and that I would have committed a fault against Him if I had refused to accept that mission. It was impossible for me to obtain adequate information concerning that country because there are at present no persons who possess such data. I am sure of this; hence my soul remains in perfect confidence and repose before God. Yet my heart is wounded with a sevenfold sorrow as was that of our Blessed Mother, at the thought that we ought to procure the salvation of that vast neglected country. That is why I feel sure that it was God's desire, in His Goodness, to offer our seven missionaries to Guinea, not as apostles, but as intercessors before His throne of mercy.

There are extraordinary features in their attitude. Although our dear confreres realized that the unhealthy climate was unbearable, they did not want to leave because they realized they had been sent there under obedience and they saw the good dispositions of the people.

Bishop Barron, who ought to have forced them to leave, let them remain, and he himself intended to stay with them. As soon as I received the first news of the unhealthy condition of the place, I wrote to them and urged them to leave and go to Goree, which is a healthier spot. I sent two letters in succession, but none reached our confreres. They had been sent to be immolated for the salvation of those countries!

My desire for the salvation of those vast multitudes is stronger than ever. I am firmly resolved, God helping, never to abandon those poor souls, unless God's will points in a different direction and shows that I should give up this work, a thing which I don't think He will do.

Do not worry, however; I will not send our missionaries again [under such conditions]. I will adopt a new method so that, humanly speaking, there will be no more victims. I trust that God's goodness will be satisfied with what we have already sacrificed. . . .

If I were to listen to the pain I feel in this difficult function [of superior], I would run away and hide somewhere in solitude; but there is no danger of my doing such a thing! It is necessary for us to be consumed in affliction and labors for the glory of our Master.

Courage, patience, humility and confidence! With these God will achieve His work using the most wretched instruments. Don't worry; those losses will not harm us.

Adieu.

> Entirely yours in the charity of
> Jesus and Mary,
> FRANCIS LIBERMANN
> priest of the Holy Heart of Mary

194

*Greatly disturbed by the fact that Libermann had sent him
a confrere who did not measure up to his own severe principles, Father Le Vavasseur became discouraged and wanted
to withdraw from the Congregation in order to join the
Jesuits. In a reply, which brings to mind St. Paul's eloquent
description of his trials and tribulations, the Venerable en-
deavored to justify his procedures and to calm Le Vavasseur's
apprehensions.*

Letter Ten   *January 28, 1846*   *Vol. 8, p. 28*

Dear Confrere:

[*You Are Wrong in Entertaining Thoughts of Discouragement*]

I want to reply immediately to your letter in which you
speak about Father Plessis and your desire to send him back
to us. You have my approval to send him back. I was at
fault when I admitted him; so it is up to me to bear the embarrassment he causes. However, you break my heart by your
discouragement and the other unfortunate feelings to which
you have yielded. Your letter shows me that you are deeply
depressed and are worried to death about the condition of
our society. I do not want to reprove you for thus plunging
me into new sorrow, yet your words are a sword with which
God desires to pierce my heart.

God is overwhelming me with this most troublesome work
for which we need so much patience. He even wishes those
who are most firm and more valuable than myself to strike
me, whereas I should wish them to support me in my weakness. May his Holy Name be blessed. Be it so, provided His
humble work may make progress; and I must say that it is
evidently developing more and more.

You talk about abandoning the work to which God called you and of which you were the first to be put in charge. Your words are full of discouragement. I believe that when you wilfully entertain such thoughts you are doing something that is most displeasing to God.

[*Shall We be Able to Face the Sovereign Judge If We Give up the Work Through Discouragement?*]

Be on your guard, dear confrere. You do not know God's designs in your regard. You do not see what function is destined for you; you do not see what God has in mind. God's providential designs are hidden from me also, but I can see that the wilful entertainment of such thoughts is an act of serious unfaithfulness.

Let us suppose for a moment that you abandon this work of God and that, I in turn, become discouraged like yourself. What then shall both us say to the Sovereign Judge to justify our yielding to discouragement? And let me add that, where you could mention but one reason for discouragement, I would be able to muster a hundred. For I am burdened with the duties of superiorship; I bear all the solicitude and responsibility for the enterprise; I bear the brunt of all the most violent attacks, the afflictions and trials which divine Providence deigns to send; I suffer in sympathy with all the worries that accompany the missionary undertakings; I have worries about the novitate, the studies, the various houses of missionaries, the arrangement of affairs, the rules that have to be perfected, and the solid foundation that has to be insured for our society. I am all alone here, having only one confrere able to help me effectively in introducing and preserving proper regularity in this place. I have the full burden of the correspondence; I have to deal with a variety of persons; I have to make the right choice of candidates; and there are a multitude of other things that can become a source of preoccupation and anxiety.

32

LETTERS TO FREDERIC LE VAVASSEUR

[My Heart and Soul Long for Solitude, But I Must Continue to Bear the Burden God Has Imposed on Me]

I have not had one moment of peace and consolation since the time when God placed me in this work. My spirit seems to have become dull and insensitive to everything that could give me pleasure and consolation, but I am at the same time supersensitive to pain; and God's goodness has not spared pain.

Consider for one moment how I suffer and grieve because I find not one minute throughout the day to occupy myself with the salvation of my soul. Yet you know how ardently and constantly my heart longs for retreat and solitude. I greatly abhor the world and sometimes feel an almost insuperable repugnance toward it, but I am obliged to keep contact with it. I find it very difficult to converse with men, but it is my duty to do it at every turn. I must be occupied with giving direction to others from morning till night, in spite of the mortal repugnance I feel for it. I constantly have to give instructions, and the least subject of meditation that I am called to prepare for others upsets me three hours before I have to propose it.

Everything within me seems to go counter to my remaining in my present situation. Every attraction of nature and of grace points in a different direction. There is not one fibre in my body nor one tendency in my soul that does not prompt me to seek solitude. In spite of all that, however, I would consider it actually a crime to entertain such a thought in my mind. God binds me and chains me to that task which is crucifying, yet most dear to my heart. I realize fully that in order to obey His powerful will, through which He has taken possession of me, I must sacrifice my rest, my consolation and my happiness. I must sacrifice infinitely more—namely, my spiritual progress, for which I am now not able to labor; this makes me shed bitter tears. I beg

God to pardon me for my tears and my grief. I fully submit with all my heart to the divine will which imprisons me in those heavy chains. I think I can say truthfully that I have never moved even one finger to loosen those chains. It is better for me to be the last in the kingdom of the heavenly Father, and to go there in obedience to His holy will and for the salvation of so many neglected souls, than to be in the front ranks after having left the way traced for me by that adorable will.

[*I Would Sin Gravely If I Were to Dismiss You as You Desire*]

You are considering abandoning the work that causes you pain. Suppose I die before the work has been solidly established. You would then have taken precautions to gain rest for yourself and the satisfaction of your own desires, but the souls which God prompted you to pity so deeply might thereby perish by the thousands and suffer eternally in hell.

Be careful, my dear confrere. You have not yet learned to suffer for the love of God and to sacrifice yourself for His glory. You want me to dismiss you. By so doing, I would commit a most grievous fault before God and against your own soul. You are bound to God and the most Holy Heart of Mary, your dear Mother. Any thought of breaking that bond is an illusion. Many a servant of God lost everything when he allowed himself to be misled by a false view of seeking a state of higher perfection. If you examine yourself carefully you will see that your imagination and self-love contribute greatly to your trouble.

[*What Would Have Happened If You Had Become Superior of the Congregation?*]

You feel very keenly the burden of superiorship and the difficulties that stand in your way. I don't know how you would have managed if, in accord with Father Galais' ideas, you had been put in my place. Instead of your present ounce of difficulties and solicitude you would have had to bear a hundred pounds! On many occasions, acting upon your present ideas you would have said: "God does not want this work; it will never be successful." And yet it is certain that God does want it, and it is evident that it will succeed. The more I examine it, the more I realize that your yielding to views inspired by trouble and anxiety would constitute a serious infidelity.

I feel certain that all your former ideas concerning myself have returned to your mind. However, I can say truthfully that all this has not caused me grief; it has not even ruffled the surface of my soul. You should not allow yourself to be led astray in such a fashion by your lively mind. Recall the past and you will see that here is one more artifice of the devil and that bitter consequences would result if God's goodness did not grant you its protection.

[*I Have Made Mistakes and Will Make Others*]

To come back to the case of Father Plessis, it was a great mistake on my part to admit him to the subdiaconate and the priesthood. This has been the cause of great remorse and anguish of heart, but it was too late. The mistake was occasioned by my lack of experience and my want of confidence in God. I sent him to you because I was hoping that you would be able to undo the wrong I had done.

Do not hesitate to send him back to me; your reasons for returning him are good; I have to accept my punishment. But don't allow yourself to be trapped by the devil on account of this event. Try to calm your mind and stop entertaining anxious thoughts about the admission of candidates to our society. My own worries about Father Plessis have caused me to be more demanding. I expect nevertheless that we shall make other mistakes; there is no one who is immune from error or from being caught by surprise. Things will go more smoothly once we have established a regular state of affairs; but we shall have to wait two more years before achieving such a condition. Our risks will be lessened from now on, for the greater number of our missionaries will be taken from our own students. We have thirty at this moment. Of these, eight or nine are very solid; three or four are somewhat doubtful, and we have almost decided to send two of these away. The others are good. At the end of the two or three years which they will spend here, we shall know what turn things are taking.

[*Don't Be a "Savage" in Dealing with People*]

You are at war with me and using fighting tactics, so I am going to do the same. (You see that I am once more talking in the gay fashion usual between us and discarding the sad tone with which I began this letter. . . .) I have already fired more than one shot since the beginning of this letter; but I was on the defensive; I now want to take the offensive and attack you!

I find that you are a "rough customer." I trust, however, that you will not be as harsh in your relations with others as you are with me; for otherwise you would spoil everything and upset everybody everytime you met with trouble. Don't be a savage with people. However, you can make an exception in regard to myself. Your thrusts against me produce an effect which you would not understand, but let me say that I will never bear a grudge against you on their account. Remember, however, that everybody will not react in the way I do.

Distrust your sensitiveness and your natural impetuosity. Whenever you are moved by a strong emotion against someone or some object, you run the risk of saying terribly harsh things in a horrible way. In such moments you are the slave of wild exaggerations that obscure grace and reason and rob you of wisdom. You become terribly impatient, not in regard to what concerns you personally, but in regard to your dealings with men and the administration of affairs. This impatience tends to produce such a profound discouragement that if you had been here [to share my burdens] you would have been incapable of overcoming it and would have been crushed over and over again.

[*If I Had Followed Your Principles, I Should Have Dismissed You From the Novitiate*]

You judge that I lack wisdom and prudence. Well, I believe that you are impatient. You want everything to be perfect at once, and you take no account of the troubles and perplexities that attend the beginnings of an enterprise. This results from another thing I want to mention: You do not judge things in a practical, realistic way. You reflect on the old established orders and demand that everything in our society be run with the same kind of regularity. You should realize that this is not possible. Your rigorous way of looking at things prevents you from seeing them realistically. We are just beginning to be settled. But you already are judging, condemning, and drawing conclusions from your own ideas, and this leads you to extreme resolutions. In this you do not give evidence of wisdom.

Practice patience. It is clear that we need time to get established. Wait until things are stable and in shape. Don't ask for perfection from the start. See then whether I ought to have been so severe from the very beginning. The work was too frail and too unstable, and my authority was too weak. Judge all this in view of what occurred in your case and that of Father Tisserant. If I had acted upon your own principles, I would have found it necessary to dismiss you

or to keep you for two years. Do not forget the temptations
from which you suffered. Well, do you think that it would
have been wise for me to act according to your principles in
your case? Don't you think I would have acted imprudently
by following those principles?

[*Flexibility is Necessary in the Beginning of a New Foundation*]

In the beginnings of an apostolic enterprise there are numerous circumstances that forbid the strict application of
general rules. At present, we are already in a much better
position to observe them than you think, but now and then
situations will still arise that prevent us from observing the
letter of those rules. How important is discretion in the
administration of the works of God! You were wanting in
this virtue when you yielded to your ardent temperament.

I do not say that I have not made many mistakes nor ever
acted wrongly. My acceptance of Father Plessis proves the
contrary. Neither do I maintain that I shall not commit
errors in the future. However, I think that as a rule my conduct is wiser and more in accord with the spirit of our Lord
than the course you want me to adopt.

Thanks to my method and the concessions I have made,
the work is established and beginning to develop. Men who
are wise and know the difficulties that accompany the foundation of a society are astonished that we were able to obtain
so great a regularity in such a short time, for we have been
in existence only four years. Several years from now, when
we shall have the personnel we need here in Europe, I feel
confident that our community will possess the same character
as a long established society.

If, on the contrary, I had used the unyielding method
which you want me to adopt "not one stone would have been
left upon another."

LETTERS TO FREDERIC LE VAVASSEUR

[*Men Cannot be Handled Like Puppets*]

Let me say something about the members of our congregation. Well, I can tell you truthfully that all, with the exception of Father Plessis, are very fervent and solid men. There was one who deteriorated because he had remained too long alone in Haiti; but he has now returned to normal. I cannot form an opinion about Father Blanpin, for it is impossible for me to know exactly what his situation is.

You proclaim a principle that is so severe that it is absolutely impractical. You want all the members of a community to be so perfect and so detached that they can be handled as if they were puppets. This, of course, would be very nice, but this sort of thing has never existed in the Church, nor will it ever exist.

[*Your Principles Would Force the Jesuits to Dismiss Three-Fourths of Their Members*]

The Jesuits [you admire so much] are certainly one of the most fervent religious societies in the Church. And yet, if your severe principles were applied to them, at least half of them should be dismissed. More than this; you may rest assured that, at the most, only one-fourth of the members of that worthy society possess the dispositions of renunciation which you desire to require of candidates to our society. I do not know very many members of the Society of Jesus. I have known some who were admirable, but I also know several others who are very weak, very imperfect, very inferior to Father Blanpin. Yet, according to your description of Father Blanpin, he seems to be the member of our society that ranks lowest in perfection.

Refrain therefore from judging matters of such importance like an adolescent. Here, it seems to me, is the general rule we ought to adopt, one which I am trying to follow in the matter of admitting candidates. I will not accept any one who does not offer guarantees, who does not offer moral certainty that he will persevere in a priestly spirit. When I discover faults, I try to correct them or to lessen them as much as possible. If the faults are of such a nature that they point to future trouble, I dismiss the candidate. Until now, with the exception of Father Plessis, I have not accepted anyone without observing the conditions of that rule. If the faults of the candidate are not of a nature to inspire fears for the future, if they seemingly do not spell trouble for a later date, I accept the candidate. Of course, I have already made mistakes and will be caught again and again in the future, but people who are more clever than myself likewise get caught.

If you want me to give proof that I am not always more accommodating than the Jesuits, let me mention Father Maurice, a man who gave me more reason for doubt in regard to the matter of accepting him into our society than anyone else. He was excessively fainthearted and full of perplexity. I have never come across a man who had those defects to such a degree. Besides that, he had a funny streak of mind and imagination that gave him great trouble in the past. Yet he was very pious in the midst of all that. I admitted him with great fears and was always anxious about him. He went to our mission in Guinea, but because of his funny streak of imagination and his lack of courage he returned to us, and I was greatly relieved. He next entered the Society of Jesus and has been with the Jesuits for about eighteen months. Now, they know his condition; they spoke to me about it, and in spite of all that they are retaining him. And yet there are in him major defects and deficiencies, weaknesses that had an unfortunate influence on his conduct during his stay with us, and faults which cannot be eliminated during a novitiate. I mention this to show you that you ought to relax your principles a little. Examine things in a practical, realistic way. I tell you in all truth: if Father Maurice were to seek admission with us now, I do not think I would accept him.

Finally, when I take under consideration the acceptance of a candidate, I examine his community spirit, his obedience, simplicity, and regularity, and I ask myself how much probability there is that he will fit into the life of a religious community.

[*Trust in God's Providence*]

You don't know yet what God has destined for you. Abandon yourself to His providence; in the meantime, continue to do good in the work you have undertaken and wait for God's own moment. . . .

It may be that I say things to you that sound severe. Don't let this grieve you. I have no desire of causing you pain, and I can assure you that if there is severity in the terms, there is none in my heart. May God's peace be with you.

> Entirely yours in Jesus and Mary
> FRANCIS LIBERMANN,
> priest of the Holy Heart of Mary

195

The opposition of the Holy Ghost Fathers should not make us act hastily. True humility does not cause discouragement. The source of your own discouragement.

Letter Eleven   *{Feb.-April, 1846}*   *Vol. 8, p. 99*

Dear Confrere:

I am in Paris, and it is from this city that I am writing this brief note. I hope that my last letter will have reached you before this one and that your discouragement has become a thing of the past.

Not long ago I received a letter from the Minister. He asks us to send four missionaries to Bourbon in addition to those already there. . . . Nevertheless, I have refused to send more missionaries to Bourbon for the following reasons:

1. Your latest letters expressed such deep discouragement that I did not dare to undertake anything before consulting you once more about conditions.

2. I judged that it would be very imprudent for us to engage ourselves seriously in enterprises in Bourbon before the settlement of colonial affairs. I have found the Ministry so variable and vacillating in regard to those affairs that I find it necessary to wait until those matters are regulated.

If full control were handed over to the Holy Ghost Fathers, I sincerely believe that we would be obliged to pack our bags and leave Bourbon (keep this to yourself), for Father Leguay, their superior, is very angry with us. You must have guessed this when I wrote urging you to use certain means of resistance if attempts were made to forbid the exercise of the ministry to you. Father Leguay made terrible threats, and he has carried them out in Goree and Senegal. You see that if he were the master in Bourbon we would not fare well over there.

It seemed at one time that he had won the favor of the Ministry. At the present moment, however, the affairs of Holy Ghost Seminary seem more precarious than ever. It is not possible, however, to foretell how things will turn out. This does not make us anxious, for there will always be plenty of work. However, we should not act hastily. As you realize, it would be imprudent for us to abandon the work of Bourbon at the present time. Let us wait patiently; there is no need for hurry since you are doing good over there. Let us allow divine Providence to act, and try to be faithful and patient instruments in God's hands. Above all, do not let Father Collin indulge in excessive ambition. He is not satisfied with what he is doing because he is so anxious to do more.

[*Genuine Humility Does Not Lead to Discouragement*]

I should like to make an observation to all the confreres in regard to this matter. Humility should never be an occasion for discouragement. When you compare yourselves with others, you imagine that you are not accomplishing anything worthwhile and that you are useless. It is good that you remain very humble in God's presence and consider yourselves useless servants, but you ought to avoid grieving over your lowliness. Humble yourselves with all gentleness before God, but remain in peace, for otherwise such sentiments of unprofitableness might become a temptation. They might even be inspired by the devil. Our best method consists in walking in the Lord's presence in all simplicity, always remaining good-natured and doing the little of which we are capable for His greater glory, without trying to measure ourselves or our achievements in comparison with others. If we wish to make such comparisons, our self-love ought to be perfectly dead, for otherwise we run the risk of falling into temptations and illusions. . . .

[*Your Own Discouragement Springs from Your Inflexibility and Fiery Imagination*]

I have already replied to you in regard to the question of your vocation. I sincerely believe that you will have to render an account to God for infidelity in allowing yourself to be carried away by the thought of abandoning God's plan in your regard. I will never consent to it because I refuse to be unfaithful to my God.   •

I think that the source of your trouble lies in a certain natural inflexibility and in your fiery imagination. From

43

this springs discouragement, though you are not always fully aware of it. I beg you, therefore, to try to be more steady, more calm, more moderate in your interior. Avoid tending towards inflexibility; strive rather to be moderate, for otherwise you will often be unfaithful to God. You will raise obstacles to your work and plunge yourself into a sea of trouble. You ought to remember that we are three thousand leagues apart; hence, when you write, you should weigh your words carefully. If you were with me and became excited, we would reach an understanding and would know what to do the next day. But between Bourbon and La Neuville lies a stretch of six months of trouble before we can find out how things stand.

Let us suppose for a moment that we had decided to undertake the mission of Bourbon on a large scale and had given you eight or ten missionaries as you desired in your *famous letter.* Suppose also that, after that, I had suddenly received your letter so full of discouragement, but that I had already promised the government to send that number of missionaries: do you think that I would then have dared to send you men? We should have been forced to withdraw our offer to the government, and I wonder what reasons we could have given for doing so. What would they have thought of us, and how damaging this would have been to that work.

[*Learn to Distrust Your Demand for Absolute Perfection*]

Believe me, dear confrere, when I tell you that I love you sincerely. I love you cordially and tenderly and I don't want to cause you pain, but believe me also when I declare that there is evil in your complaints. There is evil in your discouragement, in your fears of superiorship, in your desires for change. There is something evil in your demand that your confreres be perfect, although you are perfectly right in your estimate of Father Plessis and probably to some extent also in regard to Father Blanpin. But you are too categorical, too harsh, too violent in your judgments. The spirit of God is not present in such conduct; it could not be. Don't be astonished about this, for we are all wretched men. But learn to distrust everything that urges you to be violent, harsh and rigid. When thus tempted, try to calm yourself before God. Don't say one word; don't act until you have regained mastery over your soul, until you have regained perfect gentleness, peace and moderation. Otherwise your imagination will be in command and be your lord and master. . . .

Soften your heart once and for all in the Heart of Mary, making it peaceful and gentle. Try to overcome everything in you that tends to make you depressed and saddened, or rather give your heart to Mary in order that she may purify it of all those depressing notions.

To help you in recovering your peace of mind, let me prove to you that we have become increasingly severe in our admission of candidates. We recently let go a priest who was ready to leave us his whole fortune of 75,000 francs, and ready also to leave home and parents to whom he was excessively attached. He begged me to admit him. I likewise refused to accept two young men, one of whom was very devout and had made good theological studies. He came from the seminary of Marseille, had received tonsure, and brought good recommendations from Father Perrée who is known to you.

> Entirely yours in the charity of
> Jesus and Mary,
> FRANCIS LIBERMANN

196

*Despite Libermann's letters, Father Le Vavasseur's dis-
couragement persisted and led him to write that his mind
was definitely made up to leave the Congregation. He wanted,
however, Libermann's consent. In his reply, Father Libermann explains why he cannot give him the requested permission.*

Letter Twelve   {*December 3, 1846*}   *Vol. 8, p. 361*

Dear Confrere:

It has taken me a long time to reply to your letter. I
am sorry, although I can say that it was not my fault. Your
letter arrived during my absence, and since then I have been
overwhelmed by most urgent and absolutely necessary work.

*[The Excellence of a Society is Not the Decisive Factor in
Determining a Vocation]*

I have carefully examined the content of your two letters,
the last dated June 29, and reflected upon it in God's presence. It is absolutely impossible for me to yield to your
desires. I believe that I would be failing toward God, for I
think that it is not according to His will that you should
leave the Congregation and enter the Society of Jesus. It
seems to me that there is no need of entering into a detailed
discussion of everything expressed in your letters, for this
would not be profitable.

I shall content myself with stating one thing: You have
a higher esteem for the Society of Jesus than for our own.
I am in perfect agreement with you on this point. Without
attempting to act as a judge and determine which society
now existing in the Church is the most fervent, I would
certainly put the Jesuit Fathers in the first rank, and I do

not know whether any other society is equal to it. But this is not a basis for a vocation. Neither is it something that gives assurance that one will reach a greater perfection in that society, for otherwise everyone called to the religious life would have the obligation of becoming a member of that society. It happens frequently that a person sanctifies himself in a state that is less perfect in itself whereas he might have been a very poor servant of God in another society that was more perfect in itself.

[*God's Will for You Should be the Decisive Motive*]

It is God's will that decides everything, and the divine will manifests itself in a variety of ways. I truthfully believe that God gave very clear proofs in regard to your own vocation. There is no longer any need of trying to ascertain that vocation; the matter is settled. If I had to change my mind now and give you permission to leave our society, I would need much weightier reasons than the ones you have advanced. I shall say more: I assure you that the whole content of your three letters in which you deal *ex professo* with this matter, as well as the others which touch it incidentally, show clearly the presence of nearly all the elements that are usually a source of illusions.

On the one hand, therefore, I find no solid reason for granting you your request; on the other, there are signs that make me fear that I would act against my conscience if I followed your wishes. If you leave the society without my consent, I shall not be responsible for your meeting with anxiety, trouble, mental anguish and perhaps discouragement where you had thought you would find a higher degree of perfection. I have seen that sort of thing happen in cases similar to your own, and it might happen to you also. Your mind as well as your character and temperament have even a predisposition for that sort of reaction.

[Make Your Decision and Let Me Know]

Don't imagine that I am trying to frighten you; God forbid! Neither ought you to think that I am trying to keep you by every possible means; this is not so. My act of resignation is complete. I would be sad, but I have experienced greater sorrows, and I also earnestly believe that it would not be the last of my sorrows. Hence I do not beg you to remain with us, but I refuse to give my consent [for leaving us]. All I ask you is, *"quod facis, fac citius"* [what thou dost do quickly]!

Pardon me for using that expression! I assure you that I have no intention of making an odious allusion. The expression flowed spontaneously from my pen and I do not want to begin my letter all over again in order to erase it. Make your decision and let me know.

All your hesitations cause me embarrassment, and might cause us to lose the mission of Bourbon. Things were going better and I had made plans to send missionaries there. The government had asked me to give missionaries to that colony; it insisted, and I was not able to comply with its request. It is greatly to be feared that if I do not reply within a few months, I shall create a bad impression at the ministry. Answer me "yes" or "no," so that I may be able to make a decision. You are embarrassing me not only in regard to Bourbon but also in regard to Mauritius and Australia, for your decision will unavoidably affect my choice of missionaries. It now appears that we need no longer worry about Mauritius. The difficulties that remain now concern Bourbon, and the next will be that of choosing missionaries for Australia. . . .

It is not certain at all that the Jesuits would accept you, for admitting you might cause friction between several members of our Congregation and the Jesuits. You could not give as a reason that your salvation is endangered by remaining with us, so you could not use this argument to counterbalance the fact that you would irritate the sensitivity of our congregation. As you know, in spite of your faults and weaknesses, you are not just an ordinary member in our society.[1] But among the Jesuits, you would occupy no special position. I trust that your departure would not irritate me, but I cannot answer for other confreres, nor can I foretell what might happen to you at a later date.

May Jesus and Mary watch over your soul in order that you may do only that which is pleasing to God.

> FRANCIS LIBERMANN
> Priest of the Holy Heart of Mary

197

Two months after the preceding letter, Libermann received word that Father Le Vavasseur's "great temptation," as he called it, had passed. He now desired to remain in the Congregation forever. Libermann immediately sent words of reassurance, followed up by this letter.

Letter Thirteen   *Amiens, April 27, 1847*   *Vol. 9, p. 128*

J. M. J.

Dear Confrere:

[*Do Not Fear That I Retain Any Resentment*]

I should have written to you a long time ago. I don't know what kept me from doing it until now. Your poor heart must feel oppressed and it is in need of some words of peace. I can assure you that I retain no traces of grief from

---

[1]Father Le Vavasseur was one of the two seminarians who had conceived the first plan for the founding of Libermann's congregation,

all the things that have taken place. I am, on the contrary, full of joy and consolation since I received the first news of the change which God's goodness deigned to bring about in your soul.

I have frequently felt intense pain at the thought that my second last letter, which reached you after that change, must have caused you sorrow. However, when I reflect on what I actually said in that letter, I see that it ought not to give you much grief, for it goes to show that I considered that terrible squall to be only a violent temptation to which you were subjected, and I never felt any resentment against you. I was merely oppressed by a great burden, but God never permitted me to succumb under its weight.

[*Both of Us Have Gained From Your Temptation*]

I feel certain that all that tribulation has been useful for both of us. We were in need of this sort of thing, and it will in the end be instrumental in giving glory to God. We can readily see how useful that temptation has been for yourself. I trust that the lessons it has brought with it and the very strength it has occasioned will turn to God's glory and sanctify your soul. You may have been guilty of some faults that were more or less displeasing to God, but you will draw profit even from them for your soul. It would already be a great gain if you had merely acquired self-distrust, an awareness of your weakness, and knowledge of your faults as a result of that temptation.

However, I expect more for you from the goodness of the Holy Heart of our Mother. No doubt, she has already given you abundant consolation. You will have more strength to walk in God's way. Helped by His grace you will acquire gentleness, vigor, constancy in His service, true humility, confidence and abandonment to Jesus and Mary, patience with your neighbor, sincere charity toward others. You may also acquire many other graces and virtues that are destined for you from all eternity through God's mercy.

That trial was also necessary for me. For some time our great mission of Guinea had been taking a good turn; new graces were reserved for us, God's blessings upon us here in France increased; there was danger that the sudden prosperity might be harmful to me. I was in need of a counterweight to keep my balance. God's hand put that counterweight in my soul. That affliction was so much more painful to me—I must say this in all truthfulness—because you are the confrere the thought and remembrance of whom gave me most joy and consolation, for I have a stronger attachment to you than to the others. I always felt a special need of conversing with you and pouring out my heart to you.

[*I Want to be "One Heart and One Soul" with You*]

This is why I should have liked to be constantly with you to discuss our plans, our troubles and our consolations. It was my desire that in every circumstance nothing should be undertaken without our previous mutual understanding and agreement. I should have liked to be "one heart and one soul" with you in the charity of our Lord Jesus Christ and His Holy Mother. It is precisely at this point that the good Lord was waiting for me; He broke us like so many reeds. But I see that His mercy remains with us. The most lovable Heart of our good Mother has maintained God's favor in our behalf. God's goodness will not abandon us. We shall henceforth be united in the grace and the charity of the divine Master and, helped by His light and love, we shall construct our work according to His merciful designs. It will not be our work, but His and that of His Blessed Mother.

We shall live in perfect union. We shall try to be more faithful to His voice to enable us to give a solid foundation to the work of God. It is God who has united us for the pur-

pose of establishing that work, and who can separate what
God has joined together? Until now we were not in a condition to be perfectly united by divine charity. Our minds were
not sufficiently ready to receive the spirit of God who would
enlighten us with His light and cause us to be perfectly
united in mind.

[*We Can Now Work Together at Giving Our Work a Stable Form*]

The work had not developed sufficiently to enable us to
be perfectly united by grace and to be used by God as if we
were but one person, and the work could not be moulded according to the Heart of His Holy Mother and the will of her
divine Son. But the time is now approaching; things are
clearing up; the time for perfect union has come and divine
Providence has not remained behind.

You cannot imagine what consolation I draw from the
consideration of the kindness with which God has acted toward us and how he unites our minds and hearts for the
accomplishment of His designs at the exact time He has
destined for them.

I fully realize that we ought to be together to speak of all
the things that preoccupy us in regard to the firm establishment of the work of God, to discuss all these things
peacefully, with interior silence of soul, with humility, gentleness and the charity of Jesus. We ought to agree on fundamental principles, draw practical conclusions from them,
apply them to the existing conditions of our society. We have
the task of forming its spirit, regulating its administration
and insuring its existence. How many things we have to do!
How numerous the ideas we have to communicate to each
other!

I know very well that the time has not yet arrived to
give the work a stable and absolute shape and form, but we

must prepare the materials for it. This requires that we be together. It seems to me and has always seemed that, in accord with God's plan, we ought to do those things together; and we should be guided by God's spirit alone in all prudence and wisdom. This requires that we be perfectly united; we are then but one mind and one heart, animated and guided by the Spirit of light and charity, and we would then direct the work toward the goal which God had in mind when He united us. We would give to the work the specific shape and form willed by God.

[*I Want Your Views, Not Blind Obedience*]

Please examine this in God's presence. Consider whether you are all that is required in order that such a perfect union may exist among us, whether we can be faithful instruments in God's hands. In such a case I trust that God's goodness will bring you back here and make you stay with us. We shall live together, at least for some time—that is, for the time that will be necessary to accomplish our object. With God's help and the protection of our most lovable Mother, we shall be faithful to divine inspiration in constructing a work according to her Heart. Give me an answer as soon as possible. . . .

Do not reply: "I am ready to do all that you command me to do." I want you to tell me how you feel about it. It is not sufficient in this case that you practice blind obedience. We need perfect, full, complete union so that God may use us both as if we were but one person and thus fashion His work. There ought to be no prejudices, no repugnances; we should be one heart and one mind; otherwise I shall have to come to the conclusion that God's moment has not yet arrived. In such a case we should have to wait a little longer, but I feel certain that God's moment will come, if it has not yet arrived. . . .

Adieu, dear confrere. I hope that henceforth a permanent peace will reign in your heart. Abandon yourself to Jesus and Mary in regard to anything that might take place.

> Entirely yours in the charity of Jesus and Mary,
> FRANCIS LIBERMANN,
> Priest of the Holy Heart of Mary

198

Libermann sends confidential information regarding two confreres. In the process he reveals his way of dealing with human frailty.

Letter Fourteen   *Paris, June 15, 1847*   *Vol. 9, p. 190*

Dear Confrere:

I am sending you Fathers Blanpin and Jerome Schwindenhammer. Here are a few remarks concerning these confreres.

Father Blanpin

[*His Religious Ideal Has Changed for the Worse*]

I noticed at the time of his return from Bourbon how much he had changed. He had acquired totally different ideas about religious life. At present things are even worse. His throat trouble has embittered him. He is still very sensitive and needs to be handled with much care and tact. Besides this he has developed a certain dislike for regularity, obedience and, in general, for all the religious virtues. He has very inaccurate concepts about such things and prejudices concerning a number of points.

LETTERS TO FREDERIC LE VAVASSEUR

His stay in Rome caused his [spiritual] condition to grow worse. I was obliged to leave him there alone, because I could not have brought him to Amiens, for this would have caused his ruin. His illness had taken a dangerous turn and the cold and dampness of Picardy would infallibly have led to tuberculosis. I thus felt obliged to leave him in Rome for a whole winter, and our Lord seems to have approved my action, for He worked a miracle in his favor.[1] It was after his return from Rome that I noticed how greatly his ideas had changed even in comparison with those he had when he returned from Bourbon; and the change was once more to the detriment of his religious life

I would have greatly preferred to keep him here or send him to Guinea, but for reasons which I am not able to reveal, I found it necessary to send him back to Bourbon, although I knew this would cause you grief and perhaps also cause pain to Father Blanpin. Don't blame me for it and don't yield to discouragement. Be faithful to God and suffer in peace. The evil is not as great as you think. Father Blanpin alone will suffer from it and you together with him, but the community will not be affected; this I know for certain. Our own community has not been affected and it scarcely noticed even that anything was amiss. The trouble existed only between him and myself.

Here now is the thing that is wanting in Father Blanpin. I shall try to express it as clearly as possible although a headache is now bothering me. My remarks are intended to help Father Blanpin and to assist you in your conduct toward him.

Father Blanpin has a very strong prejudice against the Jesuits, and I believe that this is the principal reason for his prejudice against the rules of religious life, against poverty

---

[1]Cf. Libermann, *Letters to Religious Sisters and Aspirants*, pp. 52 ff.

and obedience and, in general, against the very name of "religious." The friends he met in Rome only served to aggravate those prejudices, and yet these companions were very pious and zealous. However, they were greatly opposed to the Jesuits and hence also somewhat set against religious societies, although the latter opposition was not deliberate. I need not name those persons; you know some of them.

[He Wants to Be Independent]

Our dear confrere is somewhat ashamed of his past simplicity, and yet this was his most beautiful virtue. He thinks that he acted too childishly and allowed himself to be led too much by others. Now he wishes to have money at his own disposal in order to be able to give alms. I told him plainly and formally that I was unable to give him such permission; that no member can without the superior's permission have anything that belongs to him or even is at his free disposal; and that, as a general rule, the Superior cannot and ought not to permit this, except for a limited time when there are serious reasons. I showed him the dangers and the inconvenience of a missionary's having money at his free disposal while his confreres lack similar privileges, and the evil that would result if all were given free disposal of money. I think that he understood and that he has given up this idea.

[The Way I Deal with His Difficulties Regarding Obedience]

He has become very sensitive. He suffers pain from the least want of attention and the slightest fault committed against him. He easily yields to anger and attributes wrong intentions to others in his regard. We ought to act in all simplicity with him, but also with gentleness and tact. He finds it very difficult to obey when one does not show great gentleness and when one seems to impose on him or to force him. I must add however, in all truth, that I have never experienced any difficulty with him in this respect. I have had more difficulty in regard to his sensitiveness.

I always spoke to him in my usual way, without sternness, using nothing that could suggest that I was assuming authority or wished to give him a command, but I used gentleness and simplicity. He always did what I asked him to do, without offering objections, even when what I wished him to do was contrary to his liking. I had tried to analyze his particular likings in my own mind and did my best not to contradict them. Hence he has always been docile with me and also asked permissions from me for the most insignificant things. If I had frequently refused those permissions, he would have acted differently. When I refused something, I gave him my reasons for doing it. Father Blanpin complained that you wanted to busy yourself with every detail of his ministry, that you directed him like a child, and he was afraid that he no longer saw eye to eye with you. I beg you to handle him with prudence and consideration.

[*The Source of His Troubles*]

In regard to the matter of his sensitiveness, I must say that I have suffered a little from it. He often had suspicions about things that never had entered my mind. This should warn you that you can expect difficulties and that you ought to act with circumspection, reserve and gentleness, and treat him as a confrere, not as a child. The thing that pains me most of all is that this poor man, after being cured through an exceptional favor of God, should be expected to be quite a different sort of person. I am afraid that this might be a case of abuse of grace. I mean that our poor friend received a great deal of publicity on account of that miracle, but that he is not sufficiently humble to know how to bear that stroke "of good fortune." It is certain that self-love has played a great part in all this, but it is my hope that this trouble will not last.

Father Blanpin is at present in a state of excitement, but I trust that his emotions will quiet down and that the monotonous voyage will give him a good opportunity for serious reflection. He feels that he is at fault. The Blessed Virgin will not abandon him. Realizing his condition, I have released him from his [private] vows, lest he should sin frequently against them. The evil from which he suffers is not rooted in a bad will, but in his erroneous judgment. He is firmly resolved to behave properly toward you, to keep peaceful relations and union with you, to practice obedience, or rather subordination, by which I mean that to my mind he has no correct notion of perfect obedience. All his trouble springs from a certain self-love that is accompanied by great sensitivity and poor judgment; and he has also an unsteady mind, lack of attention and thoughtlessness.

[*The Way I Intend to Deal with His Suspicion That I am Interested in His Money*]

Now one word about the source of the special difficulty between him and myself. That good confrere seems to think that I am a moneygrabber and that it is because he happens to have substantial revenues that I treat him with mildness and consideration. . . . (You know that he transferred his revenues to our house, to the amount of 3,000 francs per year.) I thought at first that this was just a passing fancy, but I have noticed since that there are still traces of that prejudice in his mind.

For this reason, after considering the thing properly before God, I have thought it preferable to refuse the three thousand francs from now on. I hesitated for a long time, being afraid that my desire to refuse that revenue might be prompted by self-love. This is why I have given the matter prolonged and calm consideration; at the end I felt morally sure that I was not prompted by self-love. I believe that I would be acting against God's will if I accepted that financial assistance under those conditions, and that such acceptance would turn to the detriment of the donor. I have not yet mentioned this to Father Blanpin, but I will explain it to him before his departure. I will not change my resolution, unless I see that he has totally different dispositions in that respect. In that case, I will act only after consultation with the Council. . . .

Father Jerome Schwindenhammer

It might be well for you to call him simply "Father Jerome," which is what we call him here. You will be satisfied with this young man. He is an excellent religious, full of love for the rule, obedient, cherishing poverty, faithful to his spiritual exercises. His intellectual powers are not beyond the ordinary. I feel sure that he will adjust himself well to the sacred ministry. When Fathers Thévaux and Thiersé will have joined you from New Holland, you will, I trust, have a fervent community. The wandering imagination and false ideas of Father Blanpin will not affect or upset the others; for those two Fathers as well as Father Jerome are community men and they have a great love for the religious life.

[*I Have Had to Act Against His Tendency to Mortification and Tenseness*]

Father Jerome spent about three years with me. I had to combat his tenseness and over-eagerness, but this fault has now been overcome. Every winter he suffered from chronic constipation, which greatly depressed his mind. The first winter his troubles were particularly violent because of his habitual excited eagerness and tenseness which he did not sufficiently keep under control. The second winter his troubles were not so strong; he more quickly overcame them and they did not reach the same degree of intensity. The last winter, things went much better and he had greater self-control.

The principal thing against which I had to battle was his intense desire for mortification. I finally took his discipline away from him and forbade him to practice any kind of mortification.

He has already great confidence in you. After he has reached you, do your best to brighten him up, for in all probability he will have suffered from constipation during his voyage, and tenseness and excitement will as usual have been its accompaniment. Provide relaxation for him; take him along on your visits to the Negroes, and you will see that he will soon be all right again.

[*Missionaries Need Readjustment After a Long Voyage*]

This, moreover, is to be a general remark on my part. I have discovered from the little experience I have had personally and from what I have learned from the heads of various missionary societies, that long voyages always produce very unfortunate changes in the dispositions of the missionaries. It would seem that this is something that happens to almost all of them. Only in a few there is a good result. Now, it is most important to take care of a prompt readjustment of those who have been affected by the voyage.

Try also to give Father Jerome a proper formation for his sacred functions. . . .

> Entirely yours in Jesus and Mary
> FRANCIS LIBERMANN,
> Priest of the Holy Heart of Mary

199

How to deal with Father Blanpin.

Letter Fifteen   *Amiens, June 28, 1847*   *Vol. 9, p. 208*

Dear Confrere:

I must send you a short word by mail, although it is only about trifles. I should have written to you on the day of the departure of Father Blanpin or on the day following it, but attacks of migraine have made it impossible. I told you before that I had decided to refuse to accept the yearly revenue which he gets from his property. I had the opportunity to speak to him about it only at the moment of his departure from Paris. He accepted so graciously what I told him and then asked so sincerely that I would accept that income, offering heartfelt excuses, that I was afraid of causing him grievous sorrow at the time of his departure [if I refused his offer]. So I told him to write and make his mind known to me after he had arrived at Bourbon, for I was afraid of refusing right there and then and causing him sorrow. On the other hand, I did not want to give him any occasion for entertaining his temptation of prejudice against me, by accepting his offer. He insisted so much and showed so much concern about having given me reasons to worry that I gave him hope that I would continue to accept that revenue for our community. . . .

[*It is Less a Question of Ill-Will Than a Lack of Judgment*]

I here repeat to you what I told this poor young man. There is in him less ill-will than error of judgment. He is scatter-brained, thoughtless and does not sufficiently reflect on his conduct. He is easily upset and readily becomes

61

the prey of prejudice. Hence the wrong he has done is to be attributed more to erroneous judgments than to laxity; he needs to be handled with consideration.

You told me once that, if he had remained longer in the novitiate, he would have a better religious spirit. I believe that, if Father Blanpin had remained four years in the novitiate, he would have behaved properly throughout that time because he would have kept a childlike spirit, simplicity, a humble opinion of himself and hence a distrust in his own capabilities. But, so it seems to me, as soon as he would have been placed in circumstances similar to those in which he has been since, he would have become the same that he is now in regard to religious life. No one who knew him and his simplicity when he was a novice could have been able to foresee what he would become at a later date in regard to religious life.

[*Be Gentle But Firm and Overlook Little Things*]

Father Blanpin's erroneous ideas regarding religious life are due to the circumstances in which he has been placed and his contact with outsiders. Having him now in this particular state, we should deal with him as with a sick man, handling him with consideration and gentleness. We should not give him orders in an imperious way; we should not appear to be annoyed or troubled when dealing with him; nor should we give the impression that our gentleness is artificial and our attention is forced. Let our conduct with him be natural, simple, truly gentle, and affectionate while at the same time we do not yield when matters of importance are at stake. On the other hand, we must not appear to pay great attention to small things. Of course, again, we cannot permit anything that is not good or that is contrary to the Rule and the spirit of the society; but we should not always appear to take notice of what is not right.

LETTERS TO FREDERIC LE VAVASSEUR

[I am Sorry that I Have to Send You a Cross]

I have sent you a cross! I assure you that this was most painful to me, but I saw myself obliged to act this way on account of the circumstances. I would have liked to keep that cross for myself. After all, the poor man would have done pretty well with me; he did so well in the past that in the novitiate, and at Notre Dame du Gard the others never noticed that there was anything wrong. Of course, they remarked that he was sensitive and that he was inclined to be remiss in regard to the spirit of poverty, but his failures were so small and so rare that he did not scandalize them or otherwise have any bad influence on their minds.

I must confess that this dear confrere is a source of great worry for me. I am afraid that he is abusing graces. If so, this would be very grave, for his cure was evidently miraculous, inasmuch as we are able to judge such things.

If Father Blanpin were to return to the world, he would greatly endanger the salvation of his soul. Don't tell him this, for it would do him harm. But if you notice that he is unable to adjust himself or do things properly over there, send him back to me and it will not cause me any inconvenience. I could either make use of him in Europe or send him to some other mission, if his dispositions seem to permit such a move.

Finally let us pray that God's goodness may redouble its graces in that good soul. I trust that, in spite of everything, this dear confrere will realize his mistakes, at least to some extent. I thought it was my duty to speak to you about it at some length so that you might help him.

[I Greatly Desire Your Company Here]

All is well here. Our confreres live in union, harmony, proper obedience and regularity.

In regard to yourself, I beg of you, for the love of God, be humble, gentle, calm and full of confidence in God, thus practicing great abandonment toward God and enjoying steadiness and equanimity. I also hope that the good Lord will grant us the grace of coming together again and speaking about the things that concern God's glory and the spiritual interests of the enterprise for which He wants to sacrifice us. How great is my desire for your company! But it must be in the peace and union of charity of the divine Master, and our action must be unified in His divine Spirit.

> Entirely yours in Jesus and Mary,
> FRANCIS LIBERMANN,
> Priest of the Holy Heart of Mary.

2. LETTERS TO EUGENE TISSERANT

Eugene Nicolas Tisserant was born in Paris on November 15, 1814. His father was a French pharmacist; his mother a daughter of the Haitian General Louis Bauvais.

Eugene entered the seminary at the age of twenty. He spent a few months at the Grande Trappe, but it was not his vocation to remain there. He returned to St. Sulpice and was ordained to the priesthood on December 21, 1840. In August, he entered Father Libermann's Congregation at La Neuville, near Amiens. In October of the same year he was sent to Martinique in the West Indies for the purpose of attempting to remedy the religious situation of Haiti. Forced to leave this country in 1844, he returned to France and was made Prefect Apostolic of Guinea in 1845. He embarked at Toulon at the end of November of that year and died in a shipwreck at the age of thirty-one.

Together with Frederic Le Vavasseur, Eugene Tisserant was one of the two seminarians who conceived the idea of evangelizing the Negro slaves which led to the foundation of the Congregation of the Holy Heart of Mary.

200

True and false humility. The practice of perfect obedience. Spiritual direction.

Letter One   *September 30, 1837*   *Vol. 1, p. 474*

Praised be Jesus and Mary

Dear Friend:

[*Everyone Talks About Humility, But Hardly Anyone Possesses It*]

I wish that the love of our Lord Jesus and of His most holy Mother may fill your soul. May it accomplish in you what He usually accomplishes in the souls that God invites to walk before Him in great perfection and detachment from all creatures. That is, may He always keep you deeply humble and as nothing before and in Him, so that you see but Him alone in self and in others. May He give you a perfect understanding of true humility and show you that it does not consist in words, or in playing with ideas or fancies.

If you have a real desire to practice this virtue, don't be satisfied with talking about humility from morning until night. Our Lord Jesus said that He does not count among His own all those who cry, "Lord, Lord." The same is true of humility.

I have seen great errors committed in regard to this virtue. Everyone considers it laudable to speak constantly about humility, but hardly anyone possesses that virtue. It is scarcely possible to open one's mouth about any spiritual topic whatsoever without somebody saying immediately, "But there is no virtue like humility."

The right means to acquire humility is not to have the word constantly on your lips. I have often noticed that this word rarely has any genuine meaning when used by the greater number of seminarians. It is for this reason that I rarely named it in our spiritual talks, because the term has been so often misused that scarcely anyone understands its true meaning.

Many who claim to understand it desire to acquire it by natural activity, by strenuous efforts, by troublesome and anxious endeavors. Strange humility! You should take care that your virtues are not merely topics of speech, products of the imagination, natural efforts and anxious endeavors of your mind, which becomes troubled and painfully scrutinizes itself in order to find out whether you are humble and to what extent you possess that virtue.

[The Nature of Genuine Humility]

Genuine humility does not consist in anything of that sort. It does not consist in external activity, in anxiously seizing upon everything that is outwardly humiliating. It does not consist in lowly and humble attitudes or actions in the presence of others. Such attitudes and actions may indeed be, and often are, the result of genuine humility. True humility is an awareness and interior conviction which prompts us to acknowledge, with perfect peace, meekness and love before God, that we are but poverty wretchedness, and incapacity and that we are detestable on account of our many sins.

Such a knowledge that is full of love and silent submission to God makes us preserve peace and meekness in His presence, in spite of our utter baseness. We realize our baseness and abjection and how contemptible we are before God and men. But we are at the same time full of joy, realizing that He alone is all beauty, grandeur and perfection. We cast a peaceful and loving glance at our great wretchedness and even look at our miseries in detail, but far from being disturbed by the sight, we remain before our great Master in loving lowliness.

When this sort of humility has reached perfection, we are delighted to be known and spoken of as the most despicable of all creatures. This degree is very perfect. Those who have reached this love of abjection do things that render them abject in the eyes of men. Examples of that extraordinary external humility are found in life of saints like St. Vincent de Paul and Father Olier. But we should not imagine that everyone who performs outward humiliating actions is always most humble.

[*False Humility*]

There are those who act in this self-humiliating way to satisfy themselves and convince themselves that they are humble, or again to make others believe that they are. They often scarcely notice their real motives. Sometimes the whole thing remains on the level of the imagination. In reality those people would be very much pained if others actually despised them or ill-treated them.

And they would be particularly resentful if others despised them for other reasons than those that have their approval. To give an example, if, in order to parade his humility, a person performed an action that would indicate a low degree of intelligence, he would be very annoyed if someone actually concluded from it that he is wanting in intelligence. To give a second example, a person might feel very sad if he were looked upon as possessing only ordinary holiness or even false notions of sanctity.

This goes to show that all such seeming humility does not have true humility as its foundation. Genuine humility is based upon complete disregard of self, and upon perfect union with God, who alone can give it to us.

[*Perfect Obedience Does Not Require You to Consult Your Director for Every Trifle*]

Now a word about obedience. I tell you frankly in God's presence and in a spirit of charity that, to my mind, you have practiced that virtue very imperfectly ever since I made your acquaintance. You never performed the smallest action nor took the least step, nor did you even desire to entertain the least plan or idea without having it prescribed or determined by your director. You rushed to your director whenever you had the slightest doubt or the smallest difficulty, and you wanted him to solve those problems. In all this you did not act according to proper discretion and prudence according to the mind of God. You acted like the Israelites before Mount Sinai; they told Moses that they wanted to hear the word of God only through the instrumentality of his mediation. This was all very nice, but would it not have been better for them to hear God Himself?

[*The True Practice of Perfect Obedience*]

Let me explain. I should like you to practice obedience in accordance with the following suggestions:

Endeavor to conquer and deny yourself in everything; let the carnal man be dead, let him be reduced to nothing. Renounce yourself and all creatures. Remain constantly united to God in an attitude of profound humility as I have explained above. Be perfectly submissive and abandoned to His pleasure in a spirit of great faith and love. All your actions, all your conduct should be animated by those dispositions. It is in this that you must place your progress, not in the mask of obedience which you formerly put on. Seek all light and spiritual life in God alone and sacrifice at the same time all love and affection for self.

Render a faithful account to your director of everything that takes place in you, but do it peacefully without anxious scrutiny, with perfect simplicity of mind and heart. Carry out promptly and exactly not only his orders but also his counsels. Do not look for another Moses in order to obtain knowledge and the light of God, but expect them directly from God, in an attitude of deep humility, great docility and meekness, and with peace of mind and heart.

Having decided what you ought to do in your difficulties, according to your own lights, tell your director what you believe to be God's will. After that, ask his advice and do what he recommends. But never go to him without having previously consulted God. And don't go to your director for every trifle; accustom yourself to let God's light be your guide.

Visit your director at the time appointed for direction and tell him simply what your past conduct has been. If something comes up suddenly that you believe might be dangerous for you to decide even after invoking God's aid, consult your director. But if you are not in a state of perplexity or doubt, settle the matter with God and speak to your director afterwards. Don't imagine that when you are continually running to your director you are prompted by a supernatural spirit of obedience; this is not so.

[*Spiritual Direction*]

Stick closely to what Father Pinault will advise you in regard to the choice of a director. Let him read this letter so that he may be able to clarify whatever might be obscure.

I don't reply to your other difficulties because I don't have the time. Do everything that Father Pinault will tell you. He will suggest the means that will enable you to avoid the dangers to which you might be exposed and to get rid of the trouble you have mentioned. The latter was but an illusion of the imagination, accompanied by a natural desire to practise a virtue which you greatly admired after all that you had heard about it. Practicing it [in the way which you imagined necessary] would do you harm and you would render yourself incapable of doing anything whatsoever for the salvation of souls and the greater glory of God.

Apply yourself to God; this is your business; but do it in all humility, in perfect submissiveness and obedience of mind and heart.

Best regards in the most holy charity of Jesus and Mary,

FRANCIS LIBERMANN, acolyte

70

201

The life of Jesus in our souls. Peace of soul in God alone. Distractions, external practices, and sundry counsels.

Letter Two   *Rennes, January 14, 1838*   *Vol. 1, p. 475*

Praised be Jesus and Mary

Dear Confrere:

[*We Must Die in Order to Let Jesus Live in Us*]

May Jesus be all things in you and may His Holy Spirit be the only life of your soul. Go forward, or rather follow your divine Guide who dwells in the center of your soul. Always preserve interior peace, love and gentleness. Rejoice at the sight of your weakness, abjection, uselessness and nothingness. Remain thus absorbed in our Lord who is in you and become, as it were, annihilated in order that He alone may exist in you.

Your meditation is all right; continue in that way. Don't worry about distractions and failures; as you know, a stagnant pool does not distill perfume. The fact that of yourself you are only corruption is one more reason for surrendering entirely into the hands of our good Lord. He will know how to cause glory and holy love to spring from your weakness. Die to and in yourself, and the life of Jesus will establish itself in you. When we come to realize how loathsome our own life is, ought we not to desire to be entirely dead so that Jesus might live and reign in us with His admirable love?

How beautiful the life that Jesus leads in our souls! But our souls should be, as it were, reduced to nothing and dead. They should have no proper life or movement. This is why you should continue your meditation in the way you have been doing. Let your faith be pure, without any admixture of self. It is through faith that our divine Master lives abundantly and all alone in us. Don't worry about anything, but go right on.

I am not astonished that you experience spiritual darkness. You find nothing to feed and sustain your sensibility, and your spirit, left to itself, sees nothing. Jesus lives in you through faith—that is, without communicating anything to your spirit that will make it act. He is satisfied with keeping it in a state of death; let it remain dead. May Jesus live in your soul as He wills, in accord with His good pleasure.

I think you will do well to seek habitually the company of the most fervent seminarians; this will enable you to perfect and strengthen your interior life. However, do not entirely avoid others; be open and peaceful with everybody. . . .

[*Forget Self to Find Peace of Soul in God Alone*]

When we are moved by an interior impulse to humble ourselves and unite ourselves with God, we need not have fears that this might be a devil's trick. Hence have no fears; merely continue to distrust self. Keep a peaceful watch over yourself before and in God, advancing always, while humbling and abasing yourself and uniting yourself more and more closely to your divine Master who desires to live fully in your soul.

Be perfectly at peace. Tend quietly, humbly, Godwards in all things, and in all simplicity, without following ideas and imaginations but moved solely by the interior impulse of faith. Aim at denying yourself in all things and always purifying your heart, forgetting self completely, in order that your mind and heart may tend to God alone. This is the basis and source of peace of soul and of that union with God which we must strive for and in which alone our perfection consists.

LETTERS TO EUGENE TISSERANT

[*Distractions in Prayer*]

When saying the rosary, do not try to make your own every thought and sentiment which the prayers suggest. Remain peacefully united with God and the Blessed Virgin without trying to think of everything which the words are capable of bringing to our minds. You could also unite yourself to the intentions and desires of the Blessed Virgin. Union with God is all that is necessary. Do not worry if you have distractions [in saying the rosary].

The same happens here as in mental prayer and the same rule of conduct applies to both. As a rule, let your interior and exterior actions of the day be ruled by the same principles as your mental prayer; this is very important. In regard to reading at table and the particular examen, act likewise, preserving the same spirit as during meditation.

Your mind, [you say], is sometimes less closely united to God. This is of little importance, provided you remain in the above-described attitude of union with God. Do not worry, but proceed with all peace and simplicity before God.

[*External Practices*]

Don't become attached to external practices. Perform them in an interior spirit, that is, keep your soul in the same state as in your mental prayer, united to God. Don't worry about special intentions; if they arise spontaneously, act accordingly; if they fail to come, keep yourself united with God; this suffices.

Best regards in the charity of Jesus and Mary,

FRANCIS LIBERMANN, acolyte

P. S. Pardon me for making you wait so long for a reply. I did not have one moment to write to you; this grieved me, but the good Lord desired it that way.

73

[*Sundry Counsels*]

Don't waste your time with a search for the source of your temptations, asking yourself whether they come from your temperament or are a punishment of God. Fight against them as you have been doing, by casting a look of love and surrender toward God.

External mortifications are very good for those whom God induces to practice them. If your director does not permit them to you, aim at interior self-denial in everything by moderating your spirit and forgetting yourself in all things, so that you will see God alone. . . .

Regarding your meditation, do not crave spiritual consolations; seek God alone and purely in accordance with His most holy will.

Your letter came just now. Write as often as you feel need of it and don't become discouraged because I make you wait for a reply; this will not always happen; I have been very busy and had to neglect a number of things.

Don't say to yourself that God is far away from you when you are in the midst of all those temptations. Your mental prayer is sound, it is even better sometimes in such conditions than when you are full of spiritual consolation. All those imperfections you have mentioned can very well exist after a very good meditation. Always tend peacefully to God. Remain in His presence in an attitude of humility and self-annihilation, and let Him do with you what He pleases.

In regard to recreation follow your inclination in this as in everything else; I mean, remain in the same interior state as during mental prayer. Speak [about pious subjects] when God prompts you to speak, but speak with moderation. Avoid trying to force things. If at present you do not have a good understanding of union with God, count on it that you will understand it better at a later time.

202

Avoid over-confidence in self, as well as over-activity. Humility. Advice regarding preaching.

Letter Three   **Rennes, October 31, 1838**   *Vol. 1, p. 476*

Praised be Jesus and Mary

Dear Confrere:

[*Avoid Too Much Self-Confidence*]

May God enable you to keep the resolutions which you took during your retreat; but don't forget that it is our Lord Himself who must execute the good desires which He has inspired, for you are utterly incapable of engraving them in your heart and fulfilling them. You should therefore place all your confidence in Him alone. Be on your guard against self-confidence. Be docile and humble in God's sight; in your own small way and in all humility fill yourself with the desire of pleasing Him. Don't presumptuously aim at high things, but be satisfied with dragging yourself before the divine Master in all your poverty with the intention of being agreeable to Him in all things.

You know very well that you are miserable, weak and incapable of accomplishing anything worthwhile. Constantly renew before God your desire of acting always with that consideration in mind; this will enable you to become reserved, moderate and peaceful. Remain always prostrate before God; keep you mind constantly turned Christwards or withdrawn in the interior of your soul, in an attitude of perfect lowliness and self-effacement, having no complacency in your actions but in God alone. But this requires constant interior peace and repose and a deadening of the activity of your mind.

[*Moderate Your Over-Activity*]

I don't know your present status in regard to that eager, hasty over-activity, that precipitation with which your mind pours itself out and gets lost in all sorts of things. Once started, your mind was like an engine whose wheels spin around noisily and rapidly until it is stopped by an obstacle or runs out of fuel. I presume that you have not yet been able to overcome the over-eagerness of your mind completely, so I urge you to moderate it. Never indulge in that precipitation and over-eagerness, but seek peace in and before God, and try to act always in a way that is properly weighed and measured. Otherwise you will never attain to solid and permanent prayerfulness. On the other hand, don't let this trouble you in the least, but abandon your soul to your good Master.

If you want to acquire and establish yourself in a spirit of prayerfulness, you need interior solitude before all else; labor also will be required, sometimes arduous labor, and very great tribulations. But all this will receive an abundant reward once the divine Spirit of Jesus dwells permanently in your soul. In the meantime long for Him, labor in peace, be faithful in all things, and live as much as possible for and in Him alone. He will always be in you, but His beneficial and fruitful dwelling in your soul is not yet perfect.

[*Humility*]

Scorn vanity, turn your mind to our Lord every time you experience such sentiments; do it with deep humility and interior self-annihilation. After this, remain peaceful, but try to fortify your will and avoid sloth. Walk energetically in the way of holy love. Jesus is with you; He fights for you; He wants you to walk behind Him with the alacrity, love and vigor He Himself shows.

[*Advice Regarding Sermons*]

Regarding the matter of preaching, you will have trouble, even when you have the best good will in the world, and you will find it impossible to practice the true principles of the art. Don't worry about that, but persevere in your desire of doing everything in a spirit of recollection similar to that which you have during meditation and prayerful union with our Lord.

When it will please God to take you to His Heart, your soul, transformed in Him, will utter nought but His own divine language. Before you reach that stage you will have to purify your words, and you will progress according to your progress in the interior life. "He who is of the earth speaks of the earth." Hopefully long for this great grace, for this gift of Jesus' love. Walk with simplicity, gentleness of heart, and tranquillity of mind. Realize that you are but a wretched man; but do your best with what you are and have.

Adieu, dear friend.

Entirely yours in Jesus and Mary,

Francis Libermann, acolyte

203

Libermann encourages him in his plans to organize an apostolic work for the Negroes.

Letter Four   *Rennes, {March 25} 1839*   *Vol. 1, p. 648*

J{esus} and M{ary}

Dear Confrere:

Rejoice with all your heart at the thought of God's goodness toward you. Who are you, dear friend, that He deigns to cast His eyes upon you, to employ you for the great work that He wishes to undertake according to His merciful designs toward the souls whose salvation is encompassed with so many dangers?

[Humbly Accept the Work God Has Chosen for You]

Humble yourself constantly in His sight and be always afraid of putting obstacles in the way of His merciful designs through your infidelities. It is my opinion, dear friend, that you should accept the mission which God's goodness wishes to commit to you, and you ought to do it with a heart that is full of joy and love. I don't need to enter into detailed explanations; they have no doubt been given you by those whom you have consulted and who know the subject better than I. I merely wish to say that I agree with those Fathers and add that it is God's will that you should engage yourself in that work in union with others whom the good Lord will call. I do not yet know all the present members of that enterprise, but it is my sincere and ardent desire that God will send you many and that they will be fervent **men, men** filled with divine love.

LETTERS TO EUGENE TISSERANT

[*You Need to be Demanding in Admitting Others*]

Please tell Mr. Le Vavasseur not to admit weak and cowardly candidates. You need men truly devoted to God's glory, men who earnestly wish to leave all things for Him, who have already conquered their faults or have at least made great progress in that way, men that give a solid foundation for great hopes and who are capable of enduring extreme troubles and humiliations.

I realize that you will not find many who will be able to suffer such pains and humiliations with patience, but let them at least ardently desire such pains and humiliations of all sorts for the love of God. Let them now learn to bear such pains, to humble themselves and overcome themselves in every circumstance. It is also required of all who wish to undertake that holy work that they have a docile and flexible mind, being willing to submit to any superior and obey exactly his orders as well as the rules prescribed for them. For, whatever your particular work might be, it is necessary that you live in community and that the members be governed by a firm order. Otherwise, if there is one among you who happens to be obstinate and wants to have his own way, it could well happen that he will prevent all the fruitfulness that would otherwise result from the enterprise. It is preferable to have but a few members, and these well united and fervent, than to have many among whom there is no order nor unity. . . .

Belong entirely to Jesus and Mary, and make fervent preparations for the great grace which God destines for you in that holy mission.

FRANCIS LIBERMANN, acolyte

204

Preparation for the apostolate among the poorest of all. Its requirements. Father Laval.

Letter Five   **Strasbourg, March 11, 1841**   *Vol. 2, p. 444*

Dear Confrere:

Be always totally devoted to Jesus in the love of the Heart of Mary. I was glad to get a short word from you, for it was a long time since I had heard anything about you. I know where you were and had heard that Bishop Collier [of Mauritius] wanted to ask the Archbishop of Paris to release you to him, but I am not sure about your actual situation.

[*Prepare Yourself for the Apostolate Among the Poorest of All*]

It is a great blessing for you to be with such a good priest as Father Legras certainly is; I know his zeal and his piety. Our Lord seems to take hold of your cause and give you the means for following your holy vocation in behalf of the poor Negroes. It is providential for you to be in a parish of poor people where you can minister to the unfortunate. This will be a good preparation for the much more painful labors that your adorable Master reserves for you in behalf of souls that are incomparably more wretched.

Be on your guard, dear confrere. Do your best to preserve your interior life, to practice renunciation in all things; avoid attaching yourself to the present life, worldly pleasures of any kind. When we are living in the midst of the world, we are always tempted to give back to nature some of the things which divine grace prompted us to give up when we were living in retreat from the world. We ought, on the contrary, to despoil ourselves of whatever still remains, so that we may belong entirely to God and live wholly in Him.

[*The Apostolic Life*]

The apostolate for the Negro demands complete death and full [spiritual] life. There must be complete death to nature, complete renunciation to natural satisfactions, and, on the other hand, Christ should be given the opportunity to live perfectly and fully in our souls. This is why I strongly urge you to deprive yourself greatly of things. I do not mean in regard to those that are necessary and useful for the body to preserve its strength, for the apostolic life is not precisely a life of mortification but a life of love. Moreover, a missionary needs his body to go wherever the will of God, the glory of Jesus Christ and the salvation of souls call him. The apostolic life is a life of interior deprivation of all that pleases sensibility and self-love. A missionary ought to place his joy in God alone, in God's glory and in His love. You are now in most favorable circumstances; you are with a pastor who aims at living an interior life. He will make it easy for you and give you all the means to practice such a life. This life is the easiest approach to, and the source of that spirit that I explained just now. . . .

[*The Affair of My Ordination*]

It is probable that I shall remain in the Diocese of Strasbourg, for conditions seem more favorable here to our project than anywhere else. I don't know when I shall be ordained, but if it be our Lord's will that I be ordained, I think that I shall receive the subdiaconate on the Feast of the Holy Trinity and the diaconate at the end of the [academic] year, if this be our Lord's holy will.

[*I am Happy That Father Laval Has Joined Us*]

Please tell our dear Father Laval that I rejoice with all my heart in having him as a confrere. I would have liked to speak with him for a while, but our Lord has arranged things in such a way that I ought not to expect to see him in this world. Hence we shall have to wait to embrace each other until we are in the Father's heavenly kingdom, which, I hope, divine mercy will grant us.

Father Laval is fortunate: he is getting the first fruits of the labors which our Lord reserves for all the dear confreres. Let him not become discouraged during this year when he will have to be alone. He will not really be alone, for our Lord and the most Holy Virgin will be with Him. Moreover, we will all be united with him in the bonds of the charity which our Lord will deign to pour into our hearts. I hope that this charity will be very great and that it will never be extinguished.

Father Laval can meanwhile prepare the way for the confreres and arrange things to insure more efficacious work.

Adieu, dear confrere. Best regards in the most ardent charity of the Holy Hearts of Jesus and Mary, in which I am

Entirely yours,

Francis Libermann, acolyte

P.S. Please give my best regards to the Reverend pastor. Thank him in my name for the great kindness he has for us in general and for me in particular. I hope to have the occasion of profiting by his kind and charitable invitation when I shall come to Paris.

205

Advice regarding his conduct in connection with the opposition provoked by his intention to become a missionary.

Letter Six   *Strasbourg, {April 12, 1841}*   *Vol. 2, p. 467*

[*Patience and Fortitude*]

Dear Confrere:

May Jesus, our most lovable Lord, triumph gloriously in your soul as He gloriously rose from His tomb.

Let us be patient and put all our trust in Jesus and Mary, and all will go well for the glory of our adorable Master. I infer from what you have told me that our Lord is making all the preparations in you for your departure and your service of our beloved Negroes. I think that the pastor and the other priests of St. Eustache will soon recognize their mistake and will put no further obstacles in the way of your vocation. Let us give full rein to our adorable Master and refuse to put our trust in our own efforts. All you have to do is to act wisely and prudently according to the circumstances and I feel sure that everything will come to pass according to your desires.

You will need great fortitude in your resistance to the assaults that will be made against your vocation. You will also need constancy and great gentleness in your conduct, especially at times when you meet opposition, disapproval and resistance, for you might then be tempted to yield to harshness. Be on your guard at such moments and try to be more gentle than ever. Show great modesty on such occasions and be full of deference, politeness and charity toward everybody.

[*Prudence and Reserve*]

You will have to practice great prudence. Be reserved in your conversations according to your plans. The other priests will have to show you some respect as long as you do not become too familiar with them. You are by nature inclined to such familiarity; nevertheless, while striving to keep that reserve of which I spoke, avoid becoming too serious. When you have the opportunity to speak with those Fathers, do it with gentleness, gaiety and openness of heart, but not with openness of mind; say pleasant things but don't indulge in effusiveness. When matters of devotion are discussed, do not reveal your own opinions, but seemingly approve the conduct of your interlocutors and in general act this way toward everyone. Speak with equal readiness to all, even to those who are most dissipated and most opposed to you, and do this with a uniform gentleness. Never show preferences, that is, do not seem to have a greater esteem for anyone in particular, and remain always both a stranger and a friend in regard to all.

When the other Fathers attempt to rule your conduct, listen calmly and gently; do not show your disapproval, but afterwards do what you think to be in accord with God's will. Do not reply directly when they reprove you, but sidetrack the question as much as possible, either by saying pleasant things or in some other way. By "saying pleasant things" I do not mean telling funny stories that will produce familiarity with them, for such familiarity will give them a handle for annoying you more easily, but I mean say something to divert their attention, in order to evade the question in a pleasant way, or do something leading to the same result. (Regarding funny stories which make people laugh uproariously, it would not be good to tell too many of them.)

Remain faithful to your exercises of piety and to your resolutions, thus avoiding the foul ways of the world, its likes and habits. At the same time, also avoid wounding charity in thought or in conduct. Act generally so as to give the impression that you are just a good fellow, a poor man who has good will, but is somewhat weak in the head, scrupulous, narrow-minded and without any clear idea of piety. This will worry them; the fathers will sometimes be impatient with you, but you will not violate charity; you will, at least have done what the good Lord demands of you, practicing charity and at the same time serving the well-being of your soul.

[*Be Silent About Your Vocation*]

It is important that you do not speak to anyone, not even to the pastor, about your vocation. It will be fortunate if he believes that you are no longer interested in such plans. However, do not say anything against your vocation, nor do anything that would indicate that you have lost interest in it. It suffices that they no longer occupy their minds with your plans. In due time the good Lord will arrange things for you. But in the meantime we ought to reflect upon it and give ourselves completely to the Lord to be used according to His holy will. If you act in the way I have suggested, the Fathers will lose the desire to retain you.

If the pastor speaks to you about your conduct and tells you that you ought to change it, answer him in a noncommittal way. Do not explain the reasons for your conduct. It is important that you never give details about your conduct and never reveal the principles that govern your spiritual and priestly life. Be always docile and submissive to your pastor in everything that does not concern your conscience and in regard to everything that will not lead you to lax behavior. For the rest, always admit that others are right in opposing you, but remain faithful to God. Preserve peace of soul in the midst of your difficulties.

[*Sundry Counsels*]

In regard to spiritual union with the pious priest you mentioned, you risk nothing in trying it out. However, do not build on such a foundation, for in all probability you will not agree with him on every point. Avoid especially imitating his practices, but follow your own interior attraction.

Regarding meditation, do not worry. Be full of faith and love and strive to unite yourself in all things with our adorable Master through that faith and love; all your actions will then be a prayer of "pleasant odor" before our Lord.

May our souls be devoted to Jesus and Mary and may they be totally consumed by the fire of the holy love of their Sacred Hearts, in which I am,

Entirely yours,

Francis Libermann, acolyte

206

Self-sanctification and the sanctification of souls for a priest working in a parish.

Letter Seven[1]   *June 16, {1841}*   *Vol. 2, p. 472*

[Dear Confrere:]

[*Self-Sanctification and the Salvation of Souls are Interconnected*]

You have asked me to give you a fundamental plan for your ministerial work in the parish. You should take care of two things: your own sanctification and the sanctification of the souls that are entrusted to you. These two are mutually de-

---

[1]Only a part of this letter has been preserved.

pendent. It is not possible to sanctify yourself without laboring with all your power for the salvation of those souls, and you will not be able to sanctify those souls if you neglect yourself.

This is a very important principle. It happens frequently that priests think only of their own sanctification and neglect souls. They more zealously seek the virtue of recollection and other virtues that serve their own sanctification than the salvation of souls. This is a great fault. Once we have become priests we no longer belong to ourselves but to souls, according to God's will; we are in His employ to render service according to His designs.

On the other hand, there are priests who, under the pretext of zeal for souls, completely lose themselves in labors of the ministry and neglect their own sanctification, thus suffering spiritual harm. The latter are doing even more harm than the first. It is the duty of a priest to procure God's glory first in his own soul. Moreover, saintly priests save a greater number of souls and accomplish it with much less activity. Hence we ought to do the one without omitting the other.

[Means of Self-Sanctification]

In regard to your own sanctification, use the means that are necessary to remain faithful; these are your exercises of piety such as meditation, examen, spiritual reading, coupled with habitual recollection. Strive for exactitude in these things and permit exceptions only rarely. Devotions to the Most Blessed Sacrament and to the Most Blessed Virgin are essentials for a priest. If you have an attraction for some other devotion, follow it as long as you feel drawn to it, but in regard to the two devotions I have mentioned, determine upon the practice of regular exercises such as visits, the rosary, etc.

Be on your guard against laxity. We yield a little at one time and always have good reasons, but these are not always as sound as we might imagine, and we end by being quite different from what we used to be. Have few contacts with the world, but occupy yourself with your various functions. You cannot afford to lose time, and you will notice that you have scarcely enough time to fulfill your ordinary duties. If possible, do not pay many visits to confreres of the parish; it is easy to do this in Paris; I don't know how things are situated in San Domingo.[1]

Never reveal your spiritual ideas to those priests [who oppose you], and do not explain to them the conduct you have chosen. If you meet fervent priests, be reserved at first until you know exactly their ideas of piety and their ways of exercising the priestly ministry. Avoid familiarity with anyone and become intimate only with the fervent, not acting hastily in this regard; test the terrain and proceed slowly.

Be gentle and considerate toward everybody. Show great respect toward all, avoiding affectation; limit yourself to what is proper, and act in a way to give pleasure to others. Be humble always, without affectation but also without weakness. Be cordial and open, but do not become effusive, and preserve interior reserve. Say only what is proper and prudent, by which I mean a prudence that is according to God. Avoid weakness; be faithful to your resolutions and do not yield when God's interests and the salvation of your soul are at stake; but do this with gentleness and modesty, avoiding harshness, affectation or trouble. Preserve a free mind in your relations with everybody; avoid timidity while preserving modesty.

[*The Salvation of Souls*]

In regard to the second point, namely the salvation of souls, you should be full of zeal, a zeal animated by love and fervor. But this zeal should not cause constant agitation,

---

[1]Father Tisserant wanted to go to the mission of San Domingo or Haiti.

anxiety or disorder. You will know that your zeal is true and good when you notice that you are becoming interiorly more fervent, more recollected and have a greater desire to please God while you are engaged in those works than when you are not engaged in them.

Thus in the matter of preaching, if you do it with true apostolic zeal, you will be more full of God after than before the sermon. If on the contrary, you are not inspired by true zeal you will then be more full of your self, more occupied with what men are saying about it than with God. When we are animated by true zeal, we are in a state of great calm and peace during and after that particular action. When zeal is faulty, we are excited during and after the function. May you have a zeal that is strong, holy, pure, humble, fervent, animated by pure love for God and the desire of His greater glory, by a true interior spirit.

[*How to Preach*]

Regarding the exercise of works of zeal, seek to perform the divine functions of the priesthood with suitable dignity. You should have great respect, great recollection and a great spirit of faith while administering the sacraments and offering the Most Holy Sacrifice of the Mass. Your preaching ought to be apostolic, after the example of the divine Master and Saint Paul. Do not speak with the intention of delivering an [eloquent] sermon; but speak for the purpose of sanctifying souls. Those who preach intent on eloquence are pleased when their sermons are written and are even happier when they have delivered them; they pay more attention to the way of ordering of ideas and uttering sentences, than to saying things that are able to sanctify souls.

Don't aim then at delivering beautiful sermons, but preach apostolic ones. Remain recollected while learning your sermon, and deliver it in the same spirit. Make a half hour meditation before ascending the pulpit; and when there, forget all creatures; consider yourself as God's ambassador, sent to proclaim His holy will to men, as the representative of Jesus Christ. Represent Him in a worthy manner; act without fear or timidity, but also without self-love. Proclaim the word of God with fervor and with a readiness to sacrifice yourself for the divine truths which you are going to deliver.

Avoid speaking in oratorical fashion, but use the manner of good conversation. Don't say to yourself, "I am now going to preach a [great] sermon," but say to yourself, "I am in the midst of God's children; I have to explain to them what is the will of their heavenly Father and I want to fill them with love for Him." After the sermon, pray to Jesus and Mary, asking them to bless those souls and to make the small seed you have cast into their minds develop and bear fruit. After that occupy yourself no longer with your sermon; don't give it any more thought and above all don't speak about it under any pretext whatever.

[Catechism]

The catechism is taught in the same way with slight changes. Realize to whom you are talking; imagine the little minds of the dear children; try to feel things as they feel them so that you may reach their level of understanding. The principal qualities of teaching the catechism are clarity and simplicity. You ought to prepare your lesson with care but in a spirit of prayer, so that you may speak with unction. For it is not enough that the children know the sacred truths of religion; they should learn to relish them. Nevertheless, you need not say many useless words; everything you say ought to be aimed at explaining things to them; but those explanations, though simple and solely instructive, should at the same time have a certain tone of piety.

90

At the end of the lesson make a short exhortation which is capable of moving their hearts. I believe that this custom of Saint Sulpice is very useful; it is called a "homily," and its purpose is to touch hearts rather than to instruct. You see then that that function ought to be performed according to the spirit of God. If you have to teach small children, make them instruct themselves; after they have recited their lesson, ask them questions which serve to explain matters further, and if they don't know the answer, ask another; when they give a partial answer, help them, adding a word here and there. If you give them lengthy explanations, they will not listen to you. You must seek to catch their interest and to move them. They have good will and their will is very straight; their minds are simple and ready to take the "fold" or bent which we give them; there are almost no obstacles to grace in their souls. The only difficulty is their light-headedness, the weakness and mobility of their minds; you must try to fix their attention; if you succeed in this, there will be no other difficulty.

Treat them with kindness, gentleness and firmness, but a firmness that does no injury to gentleness. Avoid familiarity with them. Inspire respect and affection, but never seek to win their attachment to you; direct their love Godwards. This rule—namely, to make them love God rather than ourselves—applies to all and it should be observed by all.

[*Confession*]

As regards confession, I have little to say to you. Be always united to our Lord and place your confidence in Him alone. Use the maximum of gentleness and tenderness in your dealings with sinners. Never be harsh or rigid. Make them realize the evil of their ways without wounding them; but do this always with gentleness; almost never reprove them with severity. Pray to God and have recourse to Mary

91

in order that you may touch the hearts of sinners. Avoid using severe doctrine. I am not a theologian and should not deal with such matters; nevertheless I dare assure you that severe principles are ruinous for souls. Follow Saint Liguori without hesitation.

[*Simplicity and Gentleness in Dealing with People*]

Be always simple, gentle, considerate, modest, without ever adopting the manners and customs of the people of the world with whom you happen to deal, especially when they are truly worldlings. Be all things to all men; be considerate toward them as much as this is possible. Descend to their level without ever leaving the spirit or the way of the Gospel, for a priest is obliged to preserve them, and shun anything that breathes vanity and worldliness. It is not in the latter way that we are asked to become all things to all men.

Be extremely reserved in your relations with persons of the other sex. Be more modest with them than with other persons; do not pour out your heart to them; speak with them about what may be useful for their salvation but never or only rarely about indifferent things. Leave out of your conversation everything that suggests familiarity. However frequent your conversations with certain persons, retain always almost the same reserve as at your first meeting with them. Never say things to them to make them indulge in excessive laughter; be grave also in your relations with them, without falling into excess. Do not treat them rudely nor talk with them in a dry manner; do not act toward them with a certain indifference, and do not give the impression that you do not care for them. Such ways would estrange them from God.

You have the duty of giving yourself to their souls as well as to others; hence you should act toward them with the gentleness, charity and benignity, which Jesus exercised in

92

his relations with Saint Mary Magdalen and the Samaritan woman. Show that you are interested in their souls and deal with them according to their needs, their weaknesses and the faults you discover in them.

Do not manifest an interest in their persons as such, their personal manners, their character and other qualities, for this is always dangerous; but give your interest generally to their soul. If you meet women who are pious and holy, be more careful than ever. One begins by conceiving esteem for their virtues; next one loves the divine grace found in them and, after that, takes satisfaction in the consideration of their beautiful spiritual qualities; one descends gradually, admiring their character, the pleasant quality of their mind and their ways; and then ends by feeling human affection which may degenerate into passion.

Keep your soul pure and clean; keep your heart free, so that Jesus alone may be at the source of all its sentiments. Do not seek to attach those persons to yourself, but attach them to Jesus Christ.[1]

[Yours in the holy love of Jesus and Mary,
FRANCIS LIBERMANN, Subdeacon]

---

[1]The end of this letter is missing.

207

Libermann advises his friend to face the storm raging around him in a supernatural spirit.

Letter Eight   *Strasbourg, July 9, 1841*   *Vol. 2, p. 485*

Praised be Jesus and Mary

Dear Confrere:

[*In the Midst of Your Troubles, Seek Consolation in God*]

You have probably suffered greatly in those terrible circumstances from which you have now been delivered by the grace of God—if, indeed, you are now freed from them. Your heart probably was in a constant state of agitation.[1]

Try to calm your mind, dear friend; gently repose your heart on the Hearts of Jesus and Mary. Seek consolation in the holy love with which the divine Heart burns for you and for all who belong to Him. Let us hope that our Lord will order everything for His greater glory and that, protected by the most holy Virgin, you will be enabled to fulfill God's holy will. Do not imagine that your difficulties are at an end; I feel certain that those men will not let you off so easily after the scenes through which they have forced you to pass. But do not let your heart be disturbed; those difficulties will only serve to purify and mold you.

It is easy to serve God when we meet nothing but joy in his service; but this is not the way He plans things for us nor the way of which He himself gave the example. Persons who enjoy a peaceful life, who have no crosses and

---

[1]Father Tisserant's great zeal had brought him into conflict with the less fervent among the twenty-one priests attached to the parish.

meet with no contradictions, do not sanctify themselves. They remain more or less immersed in vices; they are full of faults; they do not learn to love God in a pure manner. Thank God and His most holy Mother, then, from the bottom of your heart, because He has allowed you to pass through that storm, though leaving you with its bitter aftertaste.

[*Be Fearless But Prudent*]

I think that [those priests] will do their very best to get you away from the parish and to have you appointed somewhere else. And if this happens you will perhaps meet with prejudice in the latter place, and priests there also will annoy you. Don't grieve and do not become anxious on that account. Let our Lord do what He pleases. Those who antagonize you will be instruments for your sanctification. Be prudent, peaceful and reserved in your conduct. Fear nothing; but also keep a quiet watch over yourself so that others may not find in you any reasons for reproof. They will make use of your least misstep to create a new uproar.

Don't be afraid of their judgments or their vocal thrusts. Who is able to hurt you if our Lord is with you? Be faithful to your adorable Master. He will always be at your side. Their lashes will not wound your soul, but they will hurt those who fling out such words. Do not take those things so much to heart; helped by our Lord's grace you can constantly say to yourself, "We have not here a lasting city." If it pleases God to withdraw you from that mess, you will have had the benefit of tasting a little the bitter fruits that the world produces.

In the meantime remain quietly in God's hands and be faithful to our Lord. Whatever your circumstances, do not give up leading an interior life. Don't worry about the opinion of others; the thing that matters is that our Lord have not too bad an opinion about you. After all it is He, not

they, who will be your judge. Nevertheless, try at the same
time to accomplish your work without harshness, sternness,
rigidity; labor with gentleness and kindness in the sight of
our Lord.

[*Do Not Judge Your Opponents and Remain Full of Charity to Them*]

Take care not to judge those who judge you, for if you
judge them, you thereby lose your defense before the Sovereign Judge. Don't be too eager to excuse yourself; it is of
very little importance that men should know how wrong they
are in their conduct toward you. Nevertheless, in your conversation with them you must tell the truth, but do it without accusing others.

Be gentle, peaceful and reserved in your conduct toward
them. Love them interiorly; pray frequently for them; do
not suspect that they are acting against you or that they
talk about you. Let them act and say what they please. Do
not occupy your mind with them or pay attention to them;
such reflection will serve only to keep trouble in your mind
and agitation in your heart.

You remember that when Semei cast stones and dust at
King David during the latter's flight, and cursed him, the
holy king said to Abisai, who wanted to avenge him: "Let
him do what he likes; perhaps God has told him to curse
David." Say in like manner, "It is our Lord who allows
them to act in this way for my sanctification."

Rejoice when you hear all those things against you and
thank the most lovable Lord for His great goodness toward
you. Although you ought to be full of charity toward those
priests, do not seek their company; approach them only when
it is necessary and then act without familiarity; be modest
and reserved; but above all preserve peace and the charity of
God in your soul and refrain from judging anyone.

LETTERS TO EUGENE TISSERANT

[Do Not Worry About What People Say]

I shall not go to Paris during the holidays; otherwise I would accept your invitation. Don't be angry with Father Carron. I feel certain that he said those things in a casual fashion. It is his habit to speak that way, but there is no gall in his words. Moreover, we should not be astonished that he is taking such an attitude; surrounded by persons who see things from a different angle, he is unable to learn the other point of view.

Once more, dear friend, let men say and think what they please. They are but "flesh": "What is born of the flesh is flesh." Their words cannot add or remove one hair from your head. What is important, very important, is that you be found pure and holy on the great Day when all those who were your judges will be judged together with you.

The great lesson you should draw from your trial, beside the good it will do to your soul, is to realize how wicked and detestable it is for a person to let self-love be his guide in his judgments of confreres, and never to put faith in such judgments, for men generally allow themselves to be misled by their prejudices and their passions.

Adieu, dear friend. I am writing in a hurry, for I have little time. I have to study several courses to make ready for my ordination to the diaconate, which I shall probably receive on the tenth of August, if it be God's holy will. . . .

Praised be Jesus and Mary, in whose love I am,

Entirely yours,

FRANCIS LIBERMANN, subdeacon

208

Let us rejoice now that people calumniate us because we want to live and work for God's glory.

Letter Nine   *La Neuville, October 8, 1841*   **Vol. 3, p. 35**

J. M. J.

Dear Confrere:

I am writing this hurriedly, for I have only a brief moment to give you. We received the packages . . . but you forgot to send me my *Novum Testamentum,* which I greatly need. . . .

Do not grieve because there are people who wish to harm me. I know something about what you tell me in regard to the Bishop of Amiens.[1] It must have made him a little prejudiced or at least given him apprehensions, but he is so good and devout that he certainly will not do anything against us on that account. We must be on our guard; that is all. We live in retirement and silence and shall let men cry out against us as they please. We must leave everything in the hands of our good Mother and rejoice with all our heart when people calumniate us and treat us as wicked.

If we wanted to live according to our [evil] inclinations and our malice, those people would leave us perfectly alone and not cause us any trouble. But we desire to labor for the salvation of souls who are in danger, and we want to consecrate ourselves wholly to the divine love of our good Master and, lo and behold, we are calumniated and perse-

---

[1]The bishop had been warned against Father Libermann's "intrigues."

cuted. This is a good sign which should give joy to our hearts, according to our Lord's command or counsel, "When men calumniate you for my Name, be glad and rejoice."

We are permitted to believe that, since we seek the glory of our Lord and labor for love of Him, we are thus despised, disparaged, ill-treated and calumniated everywhere; for the only reason for this is our desire to serve Him in conformity with His love for us and His zeal for poor and wretched souls that dwell in the shadow of death.

I have written to Father Carbon and explained the situation to him. I have proposed to him beforehand what could be done to overcome the difficulties that might arise on account of the prejudice against myself. . . .

Let us place ourselves completely in the hands of our Lord and His most holy Mother and consider ourselves blessed when we live nailed to the cross. We can then confidently hope to have a small share in the holy love and the ardent zeal that burned constantly in Mary's Heart.

Let us always remain united by this intention and by prayer in that holy love, in which I am.

Entirely yours,

Father Francis Libermann

209

Refused permission by the Archbishop of Paris to enter the novitiate in order to prepare himself for the mission of San Domingo (Haiti), Father Tisserant wanted Francis Libermann to appeal to the Holy See to obtain the desired permission. In his reply Libermann explains the supernatural and natural reasons why he cannot take such a step.

Letter Ten   La Neuville, January 21, 1842   Vol. 3, p. 111

Dear Confrere:

[*I Cannot Agree with Your Proposed Plan*]

I have put off replying to your letter because I wanted first to consult our Lord in regard to your problem. The thing that matters is that we always act in accordance with God's will; and if it is clearly His will, it does not matter that it be according to our own tastes and ideas or not; we can then have peace and assurance. Hence let us place ourselves in the hands of our good Master and allow Him to do in us what He pleases.

You had a great, a burning desire in your soul which was inspired by our Lord; you had besides the advice of men who were full of wisdom and the spirit of God and yet, as I noticed in reading your letters, your soul was not at ease.

Let me now tell you what I think before God concerning that matter, adding that Father de Brandt is in perfect agreement with me. I am afraid of saying this, but it is a fact that we hold an opinion that goes counter to the views of all those priests in Paris. I feel ashamed of having to confess this, for why must a poor man like myself oppose the ideas of so many respectable men who are full of the spirit of God?

Nevertheless, what else can we do? I have examined the matter and considered it from every angle in God's presence, and my mind remains settled. Please explain my reasons to those Fathers and ask them to recommend this affair to the most Blessed Virgin. I believe that I would act against God's will if I already now took the step that you have suggested; it might also prove harmful to our work.

[There are No Signs That God Wants Us to Act Now]

First of all, I see no sign indicating that God wants us to take such a step; and if there is no sign, how can we believe that God wants immediate action? The only result of such action would be that you would stay for [a longer] time in the novitiate; but I do not consider this a sufficient reason for hurrying things.

The miracle which our Lady has worked in our favor does not signify that immediate action is in order. When external graces of that nature are given to make us act, a corresponding interior grace will also be given and will strongly and yet gently impel us to act. Now I do not believe that such an interior grace has been at work. Moreover, I think that I too would have felt prompted to act if such a grace had been at work. If the affair of San Domingo required your immediate departure, we could then take those steps, for God's will would then be evident; but considering things as they now stand, it might be harmful to take those steps [immediately].

We are all blind. Very often when we seem to see things as white they are black. In such times we should let divine Providence be our guide and wait peacefully until God's own moment has arrived. Who knows if this moment is still far off? Let us then continue to wait patiently for a few months.

It would seem that the Blessed Virgin wants us to wait. It is clear to me that the favor she recently granted us was

101

meant to encourage us while we were waiting, for she has taken the work in hand, while at the same time she has not urged us to act [immediately].

[*Your Immediate Entrance into the Novitiate is Not Desirable*]

If you were to come to us now, you would in all probability leave for Bourbon at the end of the year. Suppose then that at a later date we had to try to send men immediately to San Domingo: we would be forced to wait for at least six months. But if you were not able to go to labor in San Domingo before the coming year, what would you do in the novitiate for such a length of time? There are great disadvantages in keeping inactive for two years in a novitiate those who are destined for the missions—that is, for a very active life.

You tell me that you are afraid that you will not be able to spend sufficient time in our poor little "nest" of La Neuville. I personally entertain no such fears. Moreover, if that were to happen, I don't see that great harm would result. The "novitiate" you are presently making under the auspices of the most Holy Virgin and her beloved servant [Father Desgenettes] will be as profitable to you as our own, especially if it be God's will to have it that way.

[*Harm Could Result from Precipitation*]

Secondly, your coming to us now might do much harm to our work. If I were to write to Rome at this time, I would not be able to say anything about San Domingo, and if I nevertheless spoke about it I would be told that I am starting too soon on such a project, for the Roman authorities would think that I am acting hastily. . . . Rome might easily think of us as men who are wanting in prudence and experience, young men who want to win a battle with a bishop through violence. They would think that we are acting hastily, prompted by an inflamed imagination which refuses to wait until the time determined by divine Providence has arrived.

It is difficult to foresee all the disadvantages that might result from taking those steps. If they once judge it premature and disapprove of it they might be led to conceive other unfavorable ideas in our regard. My Jewish origin and the fact that my ordination to the priesthood was postponed will be additional reasons for thinking ill of me. . . .

Adieu, dear confrere. May the peace and the love of our Lord Jesus Christ fill your soul.

Your poor servant in
His holy love,

FATHER FRANCIS LIBERMANN

3. LETTERS TO IGNATIUS SCHWINDEN-HAMMER

Ignatius Schwindenhammer was born at Ingersheim, in the Diocese of Strasbourg, in the year 1818. He was ordained a priest in 1842. A short time after this, through Father Libermann's intervention, he came to Paris and was sub-director of the Archconfraternity of Our Lady of Victories for one year. In this way divine Providence gradually led him to the society founded by that convert Jew; he entered its Novitiate of La Neuville, near Amiens, September 8, 1843. He later became professor of theology and superior of the community of Notre Dame du Gard (1848). After Libermann's death, he became his successor as Superior General of the Congregation of the Holy Ghost (1852). He died in Paris, March 6, 1881.

210

The Holy Spirit, not our personal activity, is the source of holiness. Moderation of self-activity. No self-imposed mortifications. Adoration and mental prayer.

Letter One   *La Neuville, January 13, 1842*   *Vol. 3, p. 101*

J. M. J.

Dear Confrere:

Your letter was most consoling, for it showed me that you are constantly increasing your desire to live solely for our divine Master. May it continue to grow and entirely fill your soul.

[*The Spirit of Jesus*]

You are right, dear friend; if we want the spirit of Jesus to animate all the powers of our heart, we have to be dead to self and to every other creature. As I probably told you on another occasion, our great task is that of dying to self. This is the essence of all that we ought to do and strive for, helped by the all-powerful help of divine grace; and this grace is very strong in us through the mercy of our good Master. We ought always to follow the promptings of the divine Spirit who dwells in us.

The divine Spirit wants to be the soul of our soul, and we should let Him be absolute master over it, enabling Him to communicate to it His life and action. We should allow Him to act in us just as our body allows itself to be activated by the soul. Allow Him to give our soul whatever movement He desires to impart. But there is one difference: our body is necessitated by the actuation of the soul, whereas our soul has freely to accept the holy impulse of the Spirit of Jesus which dwells within. Our soul should be as it were lifeless, as our body is dead without our soul.

How blessed our condition and how great our holiness if we were thus dead to ourselves but alive through the divine Spirit! If our soul had no longer any taste except the one that is given by the divine Spirit! If it had no other desire, love, action than those given to it by the Holy Spirit! If we no longer loved anything, sought no more glory, felt no longer any joy or satisfaction, had no longer any will of our own, or any life but in and through Him! In such a condition no obstacles would block the way to perfection and the sanctification of our soul. On the contrary, if we let our own affections, volitions and activity be our sole guide and motive power, we obstruct and prevent the action of divine grace in our souls; we live a purely natural life.

105

[*Holiness is Not Attained Through Personal Efforts
But Comes Only from God*]

This, then, dear friend, is the essential principle for your conduct. Avoid violent efforts; do not rely on your own efforts to unite yourself more perfectly to God. The task of uniting our souls with God is not our task but that of our Lord. It is the Holy Spirit who has the role of developing greater or lesser perfection in us according to the divine plan and the degree of our correspondence with grace. Without His help, all our striving and labor will be useless and even be harmful; for the more you exert yourself in a natural way to cement that union with God the more self-willed you will become, and the activity of the Holy Spirit will be smaller as your natural activity increases. Yet it is the divine Spirit alone who can produce that holy and admirable union in its various degrees; our natural action and effort, on the contrary, can achieve nothing for that purpose.

Hence in the practice of the holy "presence of God" avoid tenseness and strain. Do not seek to propel your soul Godwards and to unite it with Him unless you feel within you a divine impulse that pushes you and, as it were, carries you off. In the presence of such an impulse, yield to it, but do not seek to run farther than the impulse prompts you to go. You will thus avoid acting by natural activity and will be obedient to divine direction.

I think that you understand in what sense you ought to avoid striving for divine union by personal efforts. Your task consists in facilitating the divine action of grace and keeping your soul in a constant readiness to obey the divine impulse with perfect fidelity. You will facilitate that divine action when you use the means ordinarily employed to remain recollected and thus expose yourself better to divine grace—for example, by observing the [seminary] rule, keeping silence, paying peaceful attention to God, thinking often of things that

106

will move your heart, and considering our Lord and the most Holy Virgin in the various mysteries.

You will dispose your soul to divine action when you increasingly moderate your desires, curb and control your vivacity, gently confine yourself to supernatural sentiments, or at least carefully avoid yielding to natural affections, when you renounce wilful enjoyment of creatures, that is, refuse to surrender completely to the joys created by your relations with them, when you watch carefully over the pleasure which self-love finds in itself or in the excellent things which you discover in yourself, or in the esteem in which others hold you.

Be particularly on your guard against the various forms of self-love. Be indifferent in regard to things that concern yourself; forget yourself as much as possible so that the attention of your mind and the intention of your will may be truly "in God." If these are self-centered, they are not "in God."

[*Moderate Your Self-Activity*]

Another fundamental disposition which you need is habitual moderation of the activity of your mind. I spoke about this last year; hence I need not say much on this subject. Always preserve great mildness and gentleness of mind. Never permit your mind to become sour, rigid, tense. Remember the words of Holy Scripture: "He reaches powerfully from end to end and disposes all things gently."

March on, do things without being too much preoccupied with the work you are engaged in; give it only the attention which it requires; but your attention should not disturb the depths of your soul. Your soul should be only superficially affected to the degree of attention you have to give to the work in hand. It makes no difference how important any particular work may be; it ought never to disturb your interior life. Your interior must belong to God alone and not to any external thing, whatever its nature. God alone must be the driving force in you, and He alone ought to act in you.

Remind yourself of the truth that the works of God are indeed His works. They are not ours. The thing we are expected to do is to take the proper steps according to the impulse and direction given us by God. Hence we ought to avoid all haste, agitation, all preoccupation and anxiety. Never act with precipitation. Wait for God's promptings, and if God postpones giving them, remain peacefully in His presence. Don't be so anxious to have God move you in the direction of your own ideas and likings. God can and will wait; why can't you? And why shouldn't you also desire to wait? Otherwise your eagerness will merely prove that you are self-seeking.

Rely always greatly on God and very little upon your own efforts. When you undertake something for God and for His holy love, conceive a strong desire to procure His glory by means of that work and to establish His reign in souls. May your soul be ablaze with fires of divine love. But do not crave success. Let this thought not enter into your mind and let no such ambition be the motive or end of your actions. Success will be pursued indirectly, but it is the glory of God and His divine love that must animate your desire, and this desire should be gentle and peaceful. I hope that our Lord will grant you the grace to deaden more and more your excessive eagerness and impetuosity of mind.

[*No Self-Imposed Mortifications*]

Lay down a rule for yourself and determine what precautions you ought to take for the good of your health. Avoid excess; be moderate in this care. You ought to know by this time what is truly harmful to your health; [in taking precautions] act, as it were, mechanically. When you happen to be ill, rejoice before God because you are able to suffer something and do not become troubled. If trouble comes of its own accord, humble yourself before God and try to calm your mind rather than endeavoring to remedy that evil. Let such agitation then be considered a cross.

I do not advise you to practice bodily mortifications; our Lord does not demand them; moreover perfection does not consist in such things.

Accept joyfully the burden of the Seminary rule and the sufferings that are caused by men. Practice sobriety, poverty, that is, be indifferent to the possession of nice things. Do not seek things that will give you comfort; try not to relish keenly the pleasures occasioned by creatures.

[*Adoration and Mental Prayer*]

In your mental prayer pay special attention to adoration. If your adoration of God is fervent, the rest will also be fervent. Meditate on the mysteries as you have been doing. Nevertheless, if you have some particular taste for one or other mystery, dwell on it at greater length. Do not change the subject of your meditation every day. . . .

The news you sent me makes me very happy. I will pray with all my heart for your intentions. Tell Mr. Burg that I do not forget him before the good Lord. My best regards to MM. Acker, Freyd and Kobès. Tell the last that his soul is particularly dear to me in our Lord, although I have never had the pleasure of seeing him in Strasbourg.

In the charity of Jesus and Mary I am,

Entirely yours,

FATHER FRANCIS LIBERMANN

109

211

Faithfulness to God will give you control over your emotions and result in perfect peace. Advice regarding his vocation.

Letter Two   *La Neuville, May 9, 1842*   *Vol. 3, p. 189*

Jesus, Mary, Joseph

Dear Confrere:

> [*Faithfulness to God Will Give You Control
> Over Your Emotions*]

I wish I had a little more time to reply to all your questions, but I am very busy and a full answer to those questions would make this letter very long; so please don't be angry with me for being relatively brief.

Thank our Lord for showing you what He wants you to do for your sanctification and what is the chief obstacle that stands in its way. It is true that your physical condition affects your moral dispositions and is the major cause of your agitations of mind; but this does not mean that you ought not to make peaceful efforts to calm yourself. You must aim at giving your soul more and more completely to God. You are capable of diminishing those agitations and attaining to a condition in which your soul will no longer be disturbed. You will attain this state of peace by interior renunciation and progressive curbing of your fiery emotions.

The greater your fidelity to God, the stronger your adherence to His love and the more perfect your detachment from the things that affect your sensibility, the easier will be your control over the emotions that are aroused through the senses. Organic agitations will then cease or at least

110

become much weaker, for they are occasioned or caused by a certain amount of susceptibility. When the soul is thus aroused, it gets away from its foundation, which is God, and although He is not far away, the soul allows itself to become agitated as soon as an emotion arises. This agitation takes place in the mind, although the will continues to tend toward its sovereign Love. The troubled mind then no longer sees its foundation in God and lets itself be carried away and cast into anxiety. If, on the contrary, you accustom yourself to flee to God in the midst of such agitation, your mind will have a support. Trouble and darkness will then no longer overcome it so easily, and the organic agitation will gradually vanish.

[*Perfect Peace Results from Pure Love*]

This, dear friend, is why you should always try to act in a gentle way and deaden all passionate movements. Purify the sentiments of your heart and establish your interior life on the foundation of perfect love. If you sincerely wish to acquire perfect peace, you need a love that is pure and free from all self-love.

The two vices that usually put the greatest obstacles in the way of our spiritual progress are self-love and a sort of tenderness toward ourselves. The latter is frequently a considerable impediment, and it prevents us from loving independently of sensibility. If it pleases God to reveal to you the nature of pure love, you will then realize how harmful it is to entertain self-love and that sort of tenderness toward self.

Aim at a life of prayerfulness, but strive for it in all gentleness, avoiding natural effort and strain. You recall what I told you regarding that matter, and you say rightly that we should not look beyond the present moment. Always endeavor to sanctify yourself in your present situation, and do not seek to leave the particular spiritual state you are in, unless the good Lord demands it. . . .

[*Advice Regarding His Vocation*]

In regard to your vocation, it is my opinion that you should not remain in the world, for I feel certain that you are not made for such a life. On the other hand, you should not go into solitude either [by joining a contemplative order], as you proposed last year. Seek rather to join a group of fervent men who desire to serve God and labor for the salvation of souls. . . . The thing that still needs to be decided is whether you should join the Jesuits or come to us in order to go to the missions. You need not hurry that decision, for you are not yet leaving [the seminary]. . . . The good Lord is not telling me anything at this moment in regard to what choice you ought to make; wait and the matter will be settled later on. . . .[1]

> [Yours in the holy love of
> Jesus and Mary,
> FATHER FRANCIS LIBERMANN]

---

[1]The end of this letter is missing.

212

Thoughts about the approach of the priesthood and the death of his parents.

Letter Three   **La Neuville, August 4, 1842**   *Vol. 3, p. 247*

Praised be Jesus and Mary

Dear Confrere in Jesus Christ:

[Jesus, Priest and Victim, Living in You]

The greatest day of your life is getting nearer, for the Lord will soon raise you to His divine priesthood. Fill yourself therefore with a perfect love of sacrifice. The priestly spirit requires that he who offers the sacrifice should also offer himself together with the divine Victim. Jesus is the Victim whom you will offer, but the same Lord Jesus should also be a sacrificing priest in and through you. You ought, as it were, to disappear and the Son of God should take your place in you.

Jesus, thus "living in your soul," desires to share with you His divine life of sacrifice, which is inherent in His priesthood. Hence, just as Jesus never exercises the priestly function without immolating Himself to His Father—since there is not nor could there be any other victim that is truly pleasing to His eyes—so ought you not to immolate Jesus without immolating yourself together with Him.

[God Took Away Your Parents That You May be Entirely His]

And now what must I say to console you for the loss you have suffered [through the death of your parents]? Since you are to become a priest, our Lord will become your *All* and you will no longer need earthly consolations or support. It seems that God's goodness has desired to take everything away from you before you ascend to the priesthood in order that you may no longer possess anything on earth, in order that you will no longer be attracted to any wordly thing, but your life may be a life of sacrifice like that of Jesus in the Eucharist. For He is there to immolate Himself constantly for men and unite them intimately to Himself in order that, through Him and in Him, they may fulfill the highest duties of religion to His heavenly Father. This is what you will do at the holy altar.

Now, in order to accomplish this perfectly, you should no longer be a man according to the old Adam, a creature of earth and mire; but you should be a man according to Jesus Christ, a heavenly man. Hence our Lord wants you to forget your origin from Adam and all those [natural] desires and affections. Your soul must cling completely to God. No other principle should animate your thoughts, feelings and love than your new origin; you must now live only in, for and through Him who imparts and perfects in you that new conception and birth.

The Lord took away from you those who connected you with the tainted stock of Adam, in order that you might become a true priest according to the order of our great divine Melchizedec. You must be "without father, mother and genealogy; and have neither beginning of days nor end of life."

You ought no longer to have any personal views or tastes, no affections for the perishable things of this world. You must be immersed and, as it were, lost in the eternal Jesus without ever returning to a beginning or tending to an end. "Former things have passed away"; the reign of nature in you must come to an end. You have been a weak child long enough, living, at least partly, under the influence of nature. You must henceforth become a man, a man in Jesus Christ through the divine priesthood with which He will clothe you. . . .

Don't worry about the interior condition of your soul. When you unexpectedly commit a fault, restore peace to your soul and gently continue your way before God, as if you had not been at fault. Put all your confidence in Jesus and Mary, in whom I am,

Entirely yours,

FATHER FRANCIS LIBERMANN

213

Let God act in you as He pleases. By sending trials, He destroys your self-love. Patience in the matter of his vocation.

Letter Four La Neuville, November 25, 1842 Vol. 3, p. 346

Jesus, Mary, Joseph

Dear Confrere:

May God's will be the soul of your life.

I am not astonished that you do not get along well with Father Tisserant; he is not cut out to give you direction or to be useful to you. He told me almost nothing about your state of soul. I asked him to give me news about you; he replied that you had still some difficulties but that they would gradually fall away.

[*Remain Before God Like Clay Before the Potter*]

I am grateful to our good Master because He is giving you a little peace. I realize that it is not your vocation to

115

remain at your present post, and I have always thought that you would not remain there. But allow God's hand to lead you. Please, dear friend, do not seek to hasten things that concern God. You should remain in the Lord's presence like clay before the potter. The workman does what he pleases with it: he beats it, presses it, and beats it again to make it supple. The clay offers no resistance; it leaves the potter perfect liberty to do with it what he wishes. The potter fashions a vase and it often happens that when it is half finished he breaks it up and reduces it to a shapeless mass. He then starts anew to make of it the particular vase he wants. The more the clay has been battered and crushed, the easier it is for the potter to achieve his purpose. That kind of clay is used to make the most beautiful vases. But clay that has not been sufficiently kneaded, serves only to make cheap pots and it will sometimes be put to common uses.

This parable is easy to understand and can readily be applied to spiritual things. Allow God full liberty to handle you; wait peacefully in a spirit of gentleness and patience until "God's moment" has arrived. If you were immediately in a position to fulfill your own desires, this would be harmful to you, even if what you do is in accord with God's will. Entertain a love for pains, crosses, and opposition on the part of others. Blessed is he whom the Lord tests and tries a little. You recall St. Paul's words; we spoke about them when we were walking in the garden of the Seminary of Strasbourg: "Tried virtue works out hope. And hope does not disappoint, because the charity of God is poured forth in our hearts by the Holy Spirit."

[*Trials Destroy Our Self-Love*]

When divine charity fills our hearts we are happy in the midst of contradictions, for such temptations put us to the test. We are in need of being tried, otherwise our self-love will destroy that divine charity, or at least it will injure it and mingle imperfection with it.

In times when everything runs smoothly and nothing prevents our interior repose, we walk in peace, but this is but a peace of the senses which happen to be undisturbed. Meeting no opposition, our self-love is not aroused. We feel joy in belonging to our Lord, and follow therein our own desires. But self-love and affection for self which accompany the impulses of divine grace mingle their poison with that divine stimulus. In this way our works are a mixture of good and bad things; they are imperfect. The more we act in that way, the more our self-love and affection for self may develop. We may even permit them to become stronger than those impulses of grace. If that happens, we are in a bad way and almost incapable of regaining the upper hand.

Generally speaking, we can say that souls that are tranquil and exempt from the sort of opposition which you presently suffer remain in their imperfections, and their faults eventually take the upper hand. I repeat therefore that you are fortunate because God deigns to put you in a state of embarrassment and trouble like a dislocated limb. I call that situation a "test" or "trial", for it tests and tries your soul. If you are faithful, you will greatly increase your strength, you will make constant acts of surrender to God, of humiliation before your Lord, of recourse to Mary, of gentle and peaceful submission to your present condition. Patience will be the fruit of your trial, an interior patience which will gradually make you impassive in God's presence: "Patience has the perfect work."

Let me assure you that patience constitutes the great perfection of souls that belong entirely to God. Such patience works out hope, which is based on the divine charity with which those souls are filled. For, seeing ourselves in

117

affliction, oppressed by contradictions on the part of men, we cast ourselves at the feet of our Lord; infused charity does its work in us; self-love and tender affection for self have to yield, and gradually disappear; and charity finally gains the upper hand. Our soul then finds no longer any support in self; it is driven by interior charity and it surrenders to our Lord with complete confidence; it places all its hope in Him. And this hope never confounds, for the charity that fills our soul overpowers it and plunges us into Jesus, thus causing us to possess all that we hope for.

Be firm, then, in the way of the Lord. Surrender to Jesus and fear nothing. You belong to Him and He to you. What, then, can you possibly fear? Don't reason, don't examine, but give yourself to Jesus, permitting Him to destroy in you the old structure of nature and gradually to establish His reign in your soul.

[*Avoid Haste in the Matter of Your Vocation*]

You are in no way doing wrong when you occupy yourself with the question of your vocation. This, in fact, accords with the order of God's will; but you should do this peacefully and lovingly and avoid acting hastily. I do not think that the time for making a decision has already arrived. Don't be afraid of Father Desgenettes. If the delay in the decision will cause him, at a later date, to feel your loss more keenly, the good Lord will compensate him for it. Father Desgenettes has had many troubles far more severe than that [of losing a good assistant]. Moreover, we must not take men into consideration in regard to such matters; the good Lord will make up for everything. When we are too anxious to prevent one difficulty we usually cast ourselves into greater ones. On the contrary, if we wait for God's "own moment," His goodness will arrange things in such a way that all obstacles disappear.

So remain in peace and say, "I have waited for the Lord and He has taken care of me." Wait for the Lord, and at a later time He will attend to the matter. Your various "attractions" are genuine, and I know that you have had them for a long time: the attraction for retreat, for becoming a guide of souls, for relations with simple people, for being away from the world. But wait for God's own time, full of gentleness, peace, humility of heart, and confidence that is saturated by love. I hope to be able to visit Paris soon; we shall then speak at length about those questions. . . .

Adieu, dear confrere.

Entirely yours in the
charity of Jesus and Mary,

Father Francis Libermann

214

If your irresolution continues, you should not join our Congregation. It is against God's will to worry about what kind of work you would be expected to do if you were to join us.

Letter Five   **August 2, 1843**   **Vol. 4, p. 297**

Dear Confrere:

[*Your Indecisiveness Makes Me Hesitate to Admit You to the Novitiate*]

I am sorry to have caused you grief and anxiety. This affair is certainly important, very important, but this is precisely the reason for my delay. It is true also that I have been very busy, but it is not on this account that I have waited so long. The true reason was my embarrassment, for I did not see things clearly, although I had had a clear view before, as I explained to you in detail.

I sought counsel from our good Lord to find out whether I should spend two days in Paris, and it seemed to me that this was not in accordance with His will. Again, I have not been well for a few days, and this is why you did not receive my reply yesterday or this morning.

The thing that embarrasses me in regard to your vocation is that you have had additional hesitations since the time I gave you a considered opinion. I would not want you to come and join us for anything in the world if it were contrary to God's will. . . . You know well, dear friend, that I did not act hastily. I waited several months before stating my opinion. And now, in spite of all that, your uncertainties have reappeared, and it is this that embarrasses me. If you are uncertain now, must we not expect that you will have such uncertainties at a later date? Ought we not to expect that you will be uncertain at the end of your novitiate?

[With such an attitude] you will suffer during your novitiate and will not advance in perfection, and at its end you may have to begin all over again, a thing that is forbidden by our Rules. We are not permitted to let you commit yourself and to admit you into the Congregation if those hesitations are still present. The general rule is that before one enters the novitiate one is already decided. This ought to be so especially in your case, for we have to expect that your irresolution will still exist at the end of the novitiate as well as at its beginning.

This now is what seems to me in accord with God's will: make a novena to the most Holy Heart of Mary. If at its end your irresolution is gone, pursue your vocation. If your hesitations remain, follow the ordinary way of divine Providence, [that is] remain in your diocese or in Paris. . . .

LETTERS TO IGNATIUS SCHWINDENHAMMER

*[Your Worry About the Work You Would be Asked to Do
is Not in Accordance with God's Will]*

I received a letter from Father Pinault regarding your problem. Judging from his letter, he misunderstood your problem; at least, this seems to be the case. The life which you would lead here would be quite normal. You would live in retirement; you would occupy yourself with your own sanctification, and help in the formation of our little society, its direction, and the formation of its novices. Besides this, you would have a certain amount of ministry in the neighborhood; its extent would depend on God's will. You have tried to foresee the kind of ministry that you will have to exercise; such an approach is irregular, as I have already told you. It is not possible to foretell such a thing regarding any place to which you might be sent.

You should abandon yourself to God's guidance. He alone is the Lord of the vineyard. He chooses His laborers when and in the way He wishes. Your worry [about the sort of ministry you will exercise] is not in accordance with God's will. We should always remember our incapacity, but on the other hand we must always be ready before our Master for any work that He might wish to give us. After He has given us a task, we must apply ourselves fully to it to cultivate the small portion of the vineyard entrusted to us and make it produce fruit. This is a fundamental lesson I want to give you; woe to him who fails to follow it! He runs the danger of following his own mind and doing harm both to himself and to the souls in his charge.

You "feel an attraction for the work of direction in seminaries," etc., but you are not permitted to tell your bishop that you prefer this or that. It is not good and not in conformity with good order to state your likings unless the bishop asks you to manifest them. You should deliver yourself blindly into his hands if you desire to remain in his diocese, or if he judges it proper to retain you in it, and you ought then to go where you are sent without offering objections.

This I call acting according to the ordinary way of divine Providence. I know well that, unfortunately, there are many priests who do manifest their likes and wishes; but this is also one of the greatest difficulties in the administration of dioceses, and it must be a source of great embarrassment for bishops. I don't think that this is merely a matter of perfection; rather it seems to me that it is actually a fault when a priest proposes his own likings to his bishop without being asked to reveal them. Examine all this in God's sight; it belongs to Him to tell you in the depths of your soul what He wants of you. . . .[1] *Adieu,* dear confrere. Pardon me for delaying my reply.

Entirely yours in Jesus and Mary,

FATHER FRANCIS LIBERMANN

215

The bad news we are getting from Africa shows that God does not want us to rely on ourselves but solely on Him.

Letter Six   *Paris, November 20, 1851*   *Vol. 13, p. 379*

Dear Confrere:

We have just received another piece of very bad news from Galam. Father Arlabosse, who became ill at Bakel, was taken to Saint-Louis in Senegal and died there. I do not know exactly when he became ill nor the date of his death. . . .

---

[1]Father Schwindenhammer entered the novitiate a few weeks after this letter.

You know that I have had constant anxiety about that mission since the departure of Father Arlabosse. This fervent confrere had formed wrong ideas about that country; he told us that it had a very healthy climate. He had scarcely left when I learned that Galam is the most unhealthy spot in Africa. Hence I am not surprised to receive that bad news, but this has filled my heart with sorrow. . . .

The thing that astonishes me most in all that has happened to us in that holy and crucifying mission [of Africa] is that the blows are always struck at the confreres that happen to be outstanding in ability. Father Arlabosse is the twelfth missionary whom God has seen fit to call away from us on those African coasts. Well, ten of them were the most capable men we had, and I am not including Father Allard, who nevertheless was not without talent.

This thought might seem to give us good reason for deep sorrow, but if we consider it properly we shall on the contrary feel greatly consoled, for the hand of God is clearly seen in all this. He is not here acting according to the ordinary ways of His providence, but in view of special designs that are hidden from our eyes, and we have the duty to adore and bless Him.

One thing, however, stands clearly revealed in His manner of treating us: He wants to maintain us in lowliness; He does not want us to indulge in lofty ambitions. He does not want us to base our works on ourselves and on the means that are in our hands. God alone must be the foundation of the work He desires to accomplish with the use of instruments that are indeed poor but generous, full of self-renunciation, and persevering amidst all sufferings, opposition and dangers. We must be docile, obedient and full of the religious spirit, full also of unshakable confidence in God alone. I feel certain that He will cause us to adopt such an attitude even if for this purpose He has to tear our hearts to pieces.

If anyone of our beloved students seems to lose heart on account of that bad news and other news that might follow, do not hesitate to reassure him. Tell him that we will never send any one to Guinea whose heart is not full of fortitude and courage, ready to meet the greatest dangers. . . .

In Jesus and Mary,

Francis Libermann, Superior

4. LETTERS TO JEROME SCHWINDENHAMMER

Jerome Schwindenhammer, born on November 25, 1822 at Ingersheim, Alsace, began his ecclesiastical studies at Saint Sulpice, finished them at La Neuville, which he entered in 1844, and made his consecration to the apostolate in 1847. He left for the island of Reunion in the same year, and became superior of that community. He was called back to France at his own request in 1855, and taught at Blackrock College, Dublin, until 1869. He then returned to France, where he worked in the archives of the Holy Ghost Fathers. He died there in 1899.

216

The value of temptations. Obedience should not be based on personal esteem but on God. The special grace I have for spiritual direction does not benefit me personally.

Letter One   **Avignon, June 21, 1846**   **Vol. 8, p. 176**

J. M. J.

Dear Confrere:

[Temptations Teach Us Self-Knowledge]

When I read your description of your temptations, I did not feel sorrow or worry, but on the contrary I experienced joy and consolation in the Lord. I consider it a great grace and source of happiness when you undergo from time to time those painful experiences that are so humiliating for one who wishes to belong to God and has some appreciation of the value of divine grace. Those temptations will make you realize the evils that are latent in your evil nature.

Having such intimate knowledge, you will have a proper evaluation of yourself and will be led to be faithful to divine grace; you will lean entirely on God's good pleasure and appreciate your great need of His assistance. You will at the same time be grateful for His kindness toward you; you will moderate the emotions that spring from your temperament and will avoid becoming self-centered. During the temptation remain, as it were, motionless before God in an attitude of humility; realize how wretched you are and sacrifice yourself to His love and His good pleasure.

You should never be astonished because you undergo such temptations. Remember that the evil is rooted in your nature, but that, on the other hand, Christ's grace is in the depths of your soul. Despise those disorderly movements; remain in your lowliness before God and fully abandon yourself to Jesus, our divine Liberator; your soul will then resist the wicked promptings of the flesh. It will reject them and attach itself more and more to the grace of our Lord; and grace will constantly increase your strength. . . .

[Obedience Should Not be Based on Personal Esteem]

Do not put your confidence in my words, in my direction of your soul, but seek to obey God alone and to follow His guidance. Never base yourself on what you might think to be good in me. Feel sure that there is nothing good in me, or almost nothing, and that there is in me much that is evil. This, I assure you, is most true. But this should not trouble you as far as obedience is concerned, for you ought to give obedience to God and not to the virtue, the holiness or the talent of any man.

I repeat that there are no serious difficulties in those things, but it would be unfortunate if you obeyed simply because you have a mistaken esteem for your director, for sooner or later you will find out the truth. Truth cannot remain hidden, especially since I do not seek to appear different from what I am. If I am a hypocrite it is only in little insignificant circumstances and when I am taken by surprise. Hence great evil could flow from that [mistaken esteem you have for me personally.]

[*The Special Grace God Has Given Me is Not for My Personal Benefit*]

You can perfectly trust, without any fear, everything pertaining to the spiritual direction which I give you. It is a general principle that one should not be afraid to trust one's director. But there is a special reason: I believe that God has been pleased to grant me a special grace in regard to the truth of salvation and the direction of certain souls. It is just this matter that fools people and makes them take me for what I am not nor ever have been. It is a grace that is purely for the benefit of others, one from which I draw no personal benefit. It is like the case of telegraph operators: they send very important messages over the wires, but draw no profit from them and receive only a small pay for their services in matters they fail to understand.

I am telling you this for yourself only. Others might be scandalized if they heard this, but you will understand now why you do not cause me pain when you tell me about your temptations [against me]. Far from it, dear confrere! Your soul is always precious to me and it is precious in our Lord Jesus Christ.[1]

[Entirely yours in Jesus and Mary,

FATHER FRANCIS LIBERMANN]

---

[1]The remainder of this letter is missing.

217

*Libermann explains why his correspondent's "temptation"
to have a high regard for his virtue, has no basis in reality.*

Letter Two   *{Rome} August 3, 1846*   **Vol. 8, p. 202**

J. M. J.

Dear Confrere:

I understand your temptation [against me]; it is rooted
in the same interior condition that is the cause of all your
other temptations. Is is absolutely without foundation, untrue and even impossible. I am anxious to console and sustain you during the severe battles you have to wage against
the enemy. This is why I want to tell you something about
myself on the condition that you will never divulge it to anyone else.

I already told you what I think of my present condition,
and I spoke the truth. I have now merely to add a word
about my past, and this will serve to take away the basis of
your temptation.

[*My Knowledge of Virtues is a Pure Gift of Grace*]

I must confess that I have never made a meditation on
the virtues, not even on the virtues of Jesus and Mary. I
have never been able to draw any conclusions or make resolutions at the end of my mental prayer, concerning the practice of certain virtues in order to guide my conduct or teach
others. This I have attributed sometimes to a derangement
of my nervous system, but I have also thought sometimes
that it was due to a native incapacity. I realize that my
mind has acquired a certain vigor, a certain loftiness, and
that my judgment has become more broad and more correct.

But it is certain that it was grace alone that created in me what was not there, strengthened what was weak, and corrected what was defective. This is so true and so evident to me that if I were to become an unbeliever it would be impossible for me to deny the existence and the action of grace in my soul.

[*God Has Given This Knowledge to Me for the Benefit of Others*]

When I spoke about virtues or perfection it was never as a result of previous meditation; but while I was speaking, truths presented themselves to my mind, fell in order and developed of their own accord. At such moments I felt an impression of light on my mind and of strength in my will, but these impressions vanished as soon as I discontinued my discourse. This makes me believe that God gives me grace for the benefit of others, and I fear for my own salvation. But God, I am sure, will have pity on me. In the long run, then, I have not acquired anything either in regard to knowledge for my mind, strength for my will, or the practice of virtues. God has given me everything. He attracted me without asking my leave and He did so with a violence that I have never noticed in any other soul. At the beginning I was very lax, indifferent, worthless for everything that pertains to the supernatural life. Our Lord gave me the grace to resist my father who desired to tear me away from the Faith. I chose to renounce him rather than to abandon my faith. After this, the good Master came suddenly to tear me away, as it were, from my own self. For the space of about five years He held my faculties absorbed and captive, and throughout that time I never had any thought of "working" to acquire any particular virtue. My whole occupation consisted in being with Him, and this was very easy. Throughout that time I had no clear idea of spiritual things.

129

This, I think, will suffice to make you see that your temptation in my regard is groundless. You see that Jesus acts and accomplishes everything in souls. It is metaphysically impossible for anyone to attain to supernatural virtues by natural efforts. One could perhaps succeed in faking those virtues, but it would be impossible to acquire them in reality.

[*Sundry Counsels*]

You may converse with Mr. Plantaz[1] about matters of piety; there is nothing wrong in it but do not give him admonitions unless he asks for them. Never make a deliberate reflection upon him for the sake of sounding his interior life and knowing his dispositions. When he asks you for observations [regarding his conduct] tell him what comes to your mind at that time.

You are right in not desiring anything special. That is what I want. Receive Holy Communion twice a week besides Sundays. Try to forget yourself at all times. Do all things with simplicity, with peaceful confidence in God and in the Blessed Virgin. You will suffer those various temptations as long as you remain alone with your self. You should try to draw profit from them, making use of them to overcome yourself, preventing them from leaving strong impressions on your mind, imagination, sensibility and conduct. Once you will be engaged in an active life, you will have less trouble.

Entirely yours in Jesus and Mary,

FRANCIS LIBERMANN

P. S. Burn this letter three days after receiving it.

---

[1]Philippe Plantaz was one of Father Libermann's most fervent novices. He died at the age of twenty-one.

218

*Do not judge others or worry about their opinion of you.
Self-forgetfulness.*

Letter Three   *{October, 1847}*   *Vol. 9, p. 298*

Jesus, Mary, Joseph

Dear Confrere :

I received the letter written by you while you were
on the high seas, and it gave me satisfaction to see you
calm and peaceful. I hope you have reached your destination [Reunion] and are in possession of the grace and
love of our Lord. You have at long last become acquainted
with our beloved Negroes; no doubt you have already been
able to visit, console and instruct them. Tell me in your next
letter how things are working out in your sacred ministry.

Follow faithfully the advice that Father Le Vavasseur,
your Superior, will give you. Open your heart to him also
in regard to your interior life. You are too far away from
me to receive my direction. You remember in a general way
the advice I have given you; you know in most cases what
God wishes you to do. Be calm, moderate, humble, and gentle. You know that you have a natural inclination to self-love.
Every time you become mentally tense and rigid, self-love
appears at the gate, eager to enter. Self-love will be active
without your noticing it; it will lead you astray and make
you see things from a wrong point of view.

*[Do Not Judge Others or Worry About Their
Opinion of You]*

Remain interiorly humble in God's presence. Refrain from
judging anyone; do not be enthusiastic about the good you

see in others nor become agitated when you think you find evil in them. Remind yourself of the truth that we ought to love our neighbor not on account of his qualities but because of the charity of Jesus Christ that dwells in our souls.

So whether others do good or evil, love them equally. Do not judge them, and never allow yourself to be unfavorably impressed by others. In general, pay no attention to the impression they make upon you which may prompt you to judge them—a thing to which you are too much inclined—and let this be your rule in every circumstance. Distrust first impressions and be on your guard against being guided by them.

Never occupy your mind with what others might be thinking about you. Do not seek to read their interior, to discern their intentions, their ideas, sentiments, impressions. This sort of reflection is very bad and always leads to grave temptations. It stirs up the imagination in all kinds of ways and makes it easy for the enemy to do his work in our souls. Such judgments are based on impressions, and these are developed by our imagination; grace and reason have no share in them.

[*Forget Self*]

Every time you notice that your mind is excited, that it adopts a rigid attitude, becomes self-centered, troubled and agitated, say to yourself. "I am in the grip of a temptation." Aim then at restoring peace to your heart. Quiet the interior movement and remain in a humble attitude in God's presence; be docile to His grace, and abandon yourself to His will.

Aim always at forgetting yourself. The labors of the ministry and your relations with our poor Negroes will make this easier for you. Don't get on the wrong track by making too violent efforts in your fight against nature for the purpose of keeping recollected during your labors. You will find

132

it difficult to preserve recollection on the sensitive level, unless the occupations of your sacred ministry naturally lead to recollection. This sometimes happens, but not to everyone.

In general, be content with the interior perfection that God grants you. Be always satisfied with everything, whether you are able to do much or little good at the beginning. Act with perfect simplicity of heart for the love of God, and leave to Him the care of blessing your holy desires to the extent of His wishes. May God's goodness fill your soul at all times with abundant grace and keep you in a state of peace, humility, self-forgetfulness, and complete confidence in His mercy.

> Entirely yours in the charity of
> the most Holy Heart of Mary,
>
> FATHER FRANCIS LIBERMANN

219

Our nature does not change but through God's grace, we can control it. Peace, humility, and self-denial. Living for God alone.

Letter Four   *Paris, February 20, 1851*   *Vol. 13, p. 43*

Dear Confrere:

I am finally freed, I hope, from the hard captivity that held me bound and pressed on every side and left me no rest nor any instant to write to my dear confreres.[1] This was a source of great grief for me, for I felt certain that my silence was the cause of much sorrow for all of you. But now

---

[1]Father Libermann had spent many months in a successful effort to overcome the difficulties preventing the establishment of the hierarchy in the French Colonies.

the bishops are ready to leave, and that will be an end to that complex and important affair. I shall now belong to you, and your letters will not remain without an answer.

I have not ceased to pray for your spiritual progress, and it is my hope that the good Master has favored you with ever-increasing graces. I cannot properly recall your needs as you have expressed them in your letters; besides these are too old to suggest the counsels I ought to give you. But I know your soul; I did not leave it even for one moment, but have been united with it at all times in the charity of Jesus our Master.

[*Despite God's Grace, Our Nature Remains Always the Same*]

God's grace dwells in you, dear confrere, and it constantly inclines you to self-denial and total surrender to Jesus, in which alone you will find *peace, humility,* and *strength,* and *life.*

I don't think that any radical change has taken place in your nature. At least the roots of our faults and imperfections remain in our souls, I mean that the tendencies remain. Grace weakens and diminishes them, gives us mastery over them, but our nature will not be changed before our resurrection. At that time the qualities and virtues which God's grace has put in our souls will be communicated to our flesh, and our senses will share in those virtues and qualities.

In the present life, when we have the happiness of belonging to God, our flesh, that is, the sensible part of our nature and our imagination which belongs to it, remains always more or less subject to its evil tendencies. This should not frighten us nor trouble us in the least, but we must be full of confidence in Jesus who lives in our souls. He is able to protect us against the evil that resides in our flesh. Hence, beloved confrere, look with indifference at all the wretched

134

things you detect in your flesh, in your senses and imagination. Suffer them with patience, gentleness and peace, as crosses that are laid on you for the glory and the love of God. Be without fears; your soul belongs to God and will always belong to Him. Aim at the four virtues which I mentioned above and which I underlined.

[Peace]

Seek to keep a small "retreat" in the depths of your soul and allow no trouble to enter there. Keep this retreat intact when you feel agitation in your imagination. Look upon this agitation as on a cross which you ought to carry peacefully for the love of God. It makes no difference whether your imagination is aroused by judgments you make about men or by the judgments you think others make about you, or by the troubles of your ministry or the sight of your own imperfections, or from any other cause. You must keep your soul in the presence of Jesus and say to Him: "So much the better, O my God! I want to suffer for love of You."

In regard to the thought that occasioned the trouble and aroused the imagination or was aroused by the latter, try to distract yourself, despise those thoughts and imaginations to the best of your ability, and remain peacefully in God's sight.

[Humility and Abnegation]

This peace is based on humility and abnegation. Although your confreres have a great esteem for you and love you, as I know from Father Le Vavasseur, you are inclined to think sometimes that the contrary is the case. Well, in such cases, try to realize in the depths of your heart the worthlessness of your being. Always remain at the feet of our Lord as a wretched man, but at the same time entertain sentiments of love and humility.

135

Try to be indifferent in regard to men, even toward those who are dear to you, so that you may not care whether they despise or esteem you, love or forget you. But you, on your part, should love them and show them your love and respect because of your love for Jesus, whose poor servant you are. By such a humility we sever the chief root that is the cause of all the troubles we find in ourselves. By means of self-abnegation we become indifferent to joy and pain and in this way protect ourselves against another root—namely, our sensibility, which causes us to feel hurt at every turn. Moreover, we thus acquire the mastery over all our passions and acquire great steadiness; and this severs the last great root, the passionate movement that follows upon the experience of pleasant or unpleasant impressions and stimulates our imagination.

You see then, dear confrere, how great are the resources that divine grace has placed in you to perfect and sanctify you.

[*Draw Life from God Alone*]

You have a sensitive and impressionable nature; hence you have to expect suffering as a constant companion. Sensibility and impressionability are great gifts of God, but one has always to pay dearly for them by way of the suffering of which they are the occasion. Be glad of it. God will give you strength, constancy and perseverance. Be gentle and moderate in the use of your energy; be peaceful and gentle in your constancy. God is with you. Be united with Him and draw all your life from Him alone. May that divine life be poured into your soul in superabundance.

> Entirely yours in Jesus
> and Mary,
>
> FATHER FRANCIS LIBERMANN

5. LETTERS TO LOUIS MARIE LANNURIEN

Louis Marie Lannurien was born March 10, 1823, at Morlaix, Brittany. He first studied at the Seminary of Saint Sulpice and then entered Father Libermann's novitiate in 1845. He was ordained to the priesthood in 1846 and taught dogmatic theology first at Notre Dame du Gard and then in Paris. He became Father Libermann's assistant in 1849, founded the Pontifical French Seminary of Rome in 1853, and died there September 5, 1854, at the age of thirty-one.

220

Your vocation still needs to become more mature and strengthened. Replace your worldly manners by the simplicity of the Gospel. Do not reason with your temptations against the faith, but simply disregard them.

Letter One **La Neuville, October 23, 1841** *Vol. 3, p. 43*

J. M. J.

Dear Mr. Lannurien:

[*Your Vocation Still Needs to be Tested*]

Your letter brought me great joy, for it showed me that the good Lord has touched your heart and inspired you with affection for our poor Negroes. It would give me great consolation if He gave you to the [Society of the Holy] Heart of Mary for the salvation of those wretched souls. So I am far from rejecting your offer. I believe, nevertheless, that we should give your inclination to our holy work

137

a chance to mature. When a farmer casts a seed in the ground, the one who will do the harvesting does not quickly pull out the young shoot that appears above the ground; he waits until there are flowers and fruit. If I were to admit you immediately, your vocation would be insecure and it might be destroyed at the first temptation that you would have to bear. Moreover, it is difficult for me to discern whether it is God who is knocking at the door of your heart and whether the call comes from Him. You must test the spirit that prompts you and find out whether it comes from God or not, and you should not put faith in any suggestion or inclination.

I propose to you a very simple test, one that will surely be useful to you. You remember that our divine Master said: "The tree is known by its fruits." Allow then that fruit to mature during the present year, tasting its sweetness and its strength. Thus you will be able to discern if it is truly the fruit of the tree of life. Have patience, therefore, dear friend, until the end of the year, and do your best to make that good desire bear fruit for the spiritual advancement of your soul. If you persevere in your resolution, this will already constitute a solid proof, for what proceeds only from our nature does not last long, especially when we consider that until now you have had the habit of enjoying comfort and ease, and suffering no want of any kind.

[Practice Internal Renunciation]

I should like you to do even more than that. I should like you to apply yourself to the practice of interior renunciation in view of that vocation, to give yourself to God with great generosity, overcoming yourself in all things and not "bargaining" with our Lord Jesus Christ, but seeking to please Him in everything and everywhere.

Do not imagine that you ought to practice exterior mortifications, unless you feel a strong urge for them; but joyfully seize upon the providential privations that come your way of their own accord; also avoid "letting yourself go," surrendering to the pleasures of the senses in things that bring you ease and comfort. Try to be indifferent in regard to the things that concern your body. Whether your soul feels comfort or not, it should not grieve on that account, but you must abandon yourself lovingly into God's hands.

To sum up, practice sobriety in the use of creatures and do it in order to please God and out of love for Him. Practice interior sobriety, refusing to indulge in keenly enjoyable pleasures; practice external sobriety by not running after what can give ease and comfort and well-being to your body. Besides this, practice submission to God's will, a loving submission amidst all the privations that occur in the ordinary course of divine Providence and on account of the actions of men. Aim at this perfection; do not think that you will immediately reach that goal. If the thougth of that holy vocation makes you efficaciously strive for that perfection, it is proof that your vocation comes from God; for such a perfection is a requisite for those that follow such a vocation.

[*Do Not Cultivate Worldly Manners*]

Again, do not seek to observe meticulously the fine points of etiquette and worldly manners. Abandon as much as possible those worldly ways, and adopt manners that are simple and dictated by the spirit of the Gospel. Practice a "negative" politeness, by which I mean that you should avoid everything in your manners that might be offensive, as also in your words and your bearing. You need not even think of that, for you have an instinct for good manners and have acquired the habit of tact; practice charity, that is, have a true and supernatural affection that makes you act to be pleasant to everybody. This will make you obliging, gentle and humble; it will prompt you to bear patiently your neighbor's faults. But do not reverse that order, as is done by worldly people who boastfully claim to "have religion"; they have an "active" politeness and a "negative" charity. Their politeness exceeds their charity; their heart is not in tune with their lips.

[*Do Not Reason With Temptations Against the Faith, but Disregard Them*]

In regard to your temptation against faith, do not worry. Those temptations have greatly harmed you because you did not handle them properly. They have influenced your conduct and have slowed you up in the way of perfect renunciation. The weakness resulting from your indulgence to the cravings of the flesh, was the reason giving rise to those temptations against the faith.

Act, then, with more vigor; be a little more energetic in the things you do for God, and do not reason so much. When those thoughts against the faith arise in your mind, never seek to convince yourself of the truth of the contrary by your reasoning. It is this habit that has increased and strengthened those temptations; such a method is always perfectly useless. You should not even pay attention to all those things. You do not need conviction; your mind is fully convinced of the truth.

Those thoughts arise in the imagination and merely touch the surface of your mind; and because nature always craves consolation and pleasures, and faith refuses them, it prompts, as it were, a desire to be rid of the faith and its truths because these tend to restrain those pleasures. But in reality you do not desire such a loss. There is question only of one of the many tendencies of the flesh to oppose the spirit. This movement of laxness and heedlessness of the flesh affects the surface of the mind and keeps it, as it were, bound and crushed under the weight of that thought against the faith.

Note well that that despondency touches only the surface and the sensible part of your mind; in the spiritual depths of your mind the habit of faith remains, and the will clings to it. You then want to reason and convince yourself, not because your mind needs to be convinced, but in order to get rid of that thought that causes you despondency and embarrassment. That approach is bad and produces harmful effects, for the evil comes only from the laxness of the flesh, and it is this that you must try to overcome. It is this evil that you ought to attack at its source.

In regard to your temptations of doubt, do not seek to overcome them, but reject them and bear patiently for the love of God the pains and the burden that afflict your soul. The embarrassment that results from them you must suffer lovingly and peacefully as a sort of penance.

In regard to the thought itself against faith, gently distract your mind from it without becoming troubled. Do not become fearful when you feel the oncoming of that temptation; despise it, raise your heart to our Lord, and gently appeal to the Blessed Virgin with great confidence and love.

I think I have explained this matter sufficiently; since you are undergoing those things, you certainly will understand. I leave you, placing you in the hands of Jesus and Mary, in whose love I am,

Your poor servant,

FATHER FRANCIS LIBERMANN

The physician you mention is a bit of a quack, as are almost all the physicians in Rome. His medicine was a mixture of tonics, antispasmodics and a third ingredient whose name I cannot recall but which was supposed to purify the blood. This compound, it is claimed, can cure fifteen kinds of ills! It is powerful stuff, which can do some good when an illness is on its way out, but it might be dangerous to put oneself into the hands of such a medical man. If you want those medicines I shall send them to you; I still have the prescription.

I forgot to mention that it would greatly be to your disadvantage to come here for your studies in theology. You are much better off at Saint Sulpice.

221

Libermann replies to several questions raised by his correspondent.

Letter Two   La Neuville, December 12, 1841   Vol. 3, p. 68

J. M. J.

Dear Confrere:

May the peace of our Lord protect and guard your heart and especially your mind. May it enable you to advance constantly and grow in divine love.

I would be delighted if it pleased our divine Master to give you to our poor Negroes, but I would not want to grab and steal you. Jesus is the one who is to give you to us. Let us wait in peace and love until He judges it opportune to reveal His will to us.

I shall now do my best to reply to your questions, relying on the grace and mercy of our Lord Jesus Christ.

[*The Desire to Save Souls*]

You desire to work for the salvation of souls; this is a good desire. You see directly that souls are lost, and this sight affects your will which thus indirectly desires to work for souls; you thereby aim indirectly at procuring God's glory, and grace is at work prompting that desire. Saint Paul very often showed similar sentiments toward souls. Nevertheless, I should like to see in you from time to time a direct impetus toward God. But let us allow God to do what He pleases; the things I hope for will come about.

[*Self-Detachment*]

The desire for perfection is also good: "Blessed are those that hunger and thirst for justice." Yet that desire is still somewhat beyond you. No matter, keep going. What I mean is this: If you desired perfection solely for God's sake, you would already possess it; but at present you are merely tending toward it. However, keep going and your longing will lead you to the desired goal.

[*Self-Love*]

You speak of your "evil inclinations, especially self-love." This is a quite common disease! It is indeed a very great evil which has to be cured, but it is impossible for you to be your own physician in that respect. Humble yourself, constantly annihilate yourself, as it were, before our Lord, letting Him cure you and adopt that attitude especially whenever you suffer some humiliation. Overcome self-love also in regard to things you do not like to do. For instance, you feel ashamed of leaving a few mouthfuls of food on your plate; well, act against your repugnance; leave some food on your plate, not precisely by way of mortification but in view of overcoming your self-love, and do this in all gentleness, without tension, in God's presence.

[*Unruly Activity of the Mind*]

Your spiritual troubles are not really caused by the diversity of your inclinations, although these may sometimes influence you; it is rather the unruly activity of your mind that is the cause. I don't find the exact terms to define my thought, but let me say that you should pay direct attention to that activity, for you might otherwise suffer great harm. It is possible that your mind acts somewhat in a jumpy fashion, by fits and starts, and that it does not act in a uniform manner; this, of course, favors those disorders.

The second principle that seems to be more definitely at the root of that noxious evil is the fact that your mind is too wide open to all sorts of foolish ideas, too uncertain regarding a general plan of conduct, too vacillating when it ought to reject all that foolishness and act firmly and uniformly.

Now, dear friend, here is the way to combat that great evil through an easy remedy. Try to keep your mind in a state of great calm before God and at the same time avoid all over-eagerness and tenseness in that endeavor. Your conduct in general and in all its details should reflect a gentle peacefulness of mind, motivated by your great love for God. This peacefulness should enliven your resolution and facilitate its execution.

Every time a silly idea appears before your mind, follow the invariable rule of paying no attention to it, whatever the nature of that thought. Make no efforts to reject such ideas. Do not act harshly or impatiently in combating such ideas and don't be impatient with yourself. As soon as you become aware of them, gently raise your mind to our Lord or the Blessed Virgin. Elicit an act of the will, such as an act of offering yourself in sacrifice, an act of love, of self-humiliation, etc. Such acts will help you to restore peace to your soul, try to forget the thought and with perfect gentleness distract your mind from these thoughts. It is important for you to give a larger share of activity to your will, and a lesser one to your mind. And you should curb your mind, not permitting it to act in spurts. Accustom yourself to act with greater seriousness. I think you know what I am driving at.

It is also important for you to prevent your mind from being the plaything of those sallies, those fickle thoughts that arouse your mind from all sides. Act toward them as you do with small flies; pay no attention to them. If you examine and analyze them, you will see that those thoughts are no thoughts at all; they are physical reactions produced on your brain by a habit you have acquired that reacts on your imagination. Such an analysis will reveal that those reactions are more material than spiritual. Hence pay no attention to them, even when doubts enter your mind regarding actions that concern God's glory.

[*Peace of Mind*]

Here is a general rule that you ought to follow most faithfully and as a matter of conscience: every time a thought presents itself to your mind and causes a certain embarrassment or tension, a certain harshness, struggle and trouble, you must treat it as a temptation and reject it, as I told you above. In other words, you must calm your mind in God's presence and sacrifice yourself to His love. Never act otherwise, whatever may be the nature of that doubt.

Do not be afraid that you will be unfaithful to grace and yield to nature. In regard to mortifications that are accompanied by those symptoms [of fear and anxiety], you should always choose the milder course until you have overcome that fault [of anxiety]. Don't be afraid; when something is prompted by grace, there is never any accompaniment of that kind of hesitation, for grace is manifested in the will and puts the mind in a state of great repose.

When a battle is taking place between the flesh and the spirit, it always occurs in your cowardly will. Every time God moves your will, your mind is at rest. Act fearlessly according to my advice. I take full responsibility for any

145

evil consequences, provided you keep your mind calm and do this with perfect gentleness and without violent efforts. Do not seek to clear up the doubts that assail your mind at the time when they tend to disturb you; have then but one intention, namely, to restore calm in your soul at any cost. This, dear friend, is the Gospel's pearl of great price; sell everything and buy it at the expense of everything else. Having that repose of mind, you possess a precious treasure, and I guarantee that you will go forward with giant steps.

Let me make use of a comparison to explain this still more. If the devil makes faces at you, close your eyes in order not to see him; do not run to him and slap his face. Be indifferent to his grimaces. The sallies that bother you so much are but grimaces. Gently close the eyes of your soul and seek to establish great calm in your mind in our Lord's presence. Turn your attention away from those foolish things and with gentle love fix it on the divine object of your love.

[*The Reading of Scripture*]

It is more useful for you than for anybody else to read Holy Scripture with devotion and in a way that will serve to nourish your heart. I cannot now develop this point, for I have not the time. Read with piety and recollection. When reading the Old Testament, dwell devoutly on the figures that foreshadow the various subjects of the New, and meditate on the prophecies that announce our Lord and His law of grace. Never amuse yourself making considerations that satisfy your curiosity or that are merely interesting from the standpoint of human science. If [during the spiritual reading of Scripture] you make reflections, let them be *in doctrina spiritus*. Give food to your soul, considering what spirit animated the ancient patriarchs and prophets.

In regard to the New Testament, seek to nourish your soul with the doctrine so full of love and grace that is found therein. Enjoy it, taste it, relish it, and relish also the knowledge it gives you of our divine Master, but let this knowledge be practical and of a loving kind. . . .

[*The Study of Theology and Church History*]

Study your theology methodically. Try to grasp what you are studying and do not worry about your poor memory; you will end by remembering those things; at least when you have become accustomed to that kind of study. If you have not been advised to study Guénée because of his supposed importance for you, leave that author aside. He will do you harm because of the particular bent of your mind and will offer you little advantage. You will soon forget the substantial things that might be found in him, but will retain only his startling remarks and things that can amuse the mind.

Church history is a useful subject. Do not be satisfied with reading it, but endeavor to get a solid grasp of what you read and put events in proper order. Reflect, compare, make a serious study of the matter. But take care not to lose your interior spirit, do not forget renunciation to self and all other things, and remain in a spirit of abandonment to our Lord.

If you are a bit of a "Gallican," inclined to be prejudiced against Rome, I advise you not to read Fleury, for he has an evil mentality. Read Bérauld instead.

[*Spiritual Reading*]

Regarding spiritual reading, the best book for you is the one you relish most. Read the books you have mentioned; they are excellent, and are especially good for you at this time on account of your state of soul. When you are no longer able to read such things, take a life of a saint, one that produces a good effect on you and gives you fervor and courage.

Bear in mind the principle that you should not read the spiritual authors for the sake of learning the theory about the interior life. I do not want you to know this life in any way other than as a result of personal practice. And you will acquire this practice by always acting with the good will God gives you and trying to do all you can to be agreeable to God and become a man who is truly "renounced" and lives interiorly.

[Follow the Promptings of the Holy Spirit]

You do not need to be aware of your progress, for such progress depends not on you but on the Holy Spirit. He, and not your own spirit, must be your guide. It suffices that the Holy Spirit knows how He guides you. Your only role is to follow His divine inspiration at all times and grow constantly in longings and love for your divine Master, sacrificing to Him all the satisfactions of your soul, seeking to please Him alone and fulfill all He asks of you. And this you must do moved by the sentiments He communicates to your heart and not by the ideas that come into your mind, for it is not by such ideas that grace will operate in your soul. You should be indifferent to any idea of your mind that is not accompanied by a strong impression in your will, as I have already explained to you.

I advise you to put aside the copybook in which you have written all the things you find good in your pious reading. Do not read in order to remember, but in order to be edified and to apply yourself to the practice of what is good. If you are too intent on the task of keeping things in your memory, you will not be edified and will not properly practice those things. Entrust yourself to the guidance of the Holy Spirit, and do not indulge in reasonings about what you ought to do. You should go to God more through the heart than through the mind. If you approach Him with a determined will that is full of love, your mind will have sufficient knowledge for your conduct. . . .

[*Ejaculations*]

When the bell calls, repose for a moment on the Heart of Christ and make acts of the will, few acts of the mind. Your use of "Jesus, Mary, Joseph," could very well be nothing but something that flashes through your mind if it is only a recalling of those names.

Your conduct at the time when you go from one exercise to another is good. Nevertheless, here again be not content with pronouncing those words with your mind, but let them be cries of the heart. At least make those ejaculations with the heart, while keeping your mind calm. Your trouble is that in your acts of devotion you allow your mind to orate when it should keep quiet; let your heart speak, and let it do so only when it is prompted by grace.

[*Meals*]

At meals eat as much as is necessary for your good appetite, but do not stuff yourself. Pay no attention to the quality of the food. "The kingdom of God is not in food and drink."

[*Monthly Retreat*]

The practice of the monthly retreat should not consist in reasoning about what can make you acquire perfection; rather, it consists in putting into practice what the good Lord demands of your heart. Resist the tendency of softness and laxity in your will, and refrain from acting with harshness of mind.

[*Relics*]

Keep the relics that are given to you. If they are not very useful to you now, they may serve a good purpose later on. Do not devise a practice to honor them, but when you feel the need or are prompted by devotion, offer some act of respect, it matters not what, provided this springs from the heart.

[*Examination of Conscience*]

Your examen, even when preparing for confession, should be a simple glance, and not a careful examination of each action; it should not be a labor of the mind. Place yourself peacefully before God; desire that He make known your faults to you and dwell peacefully on your principal actions. When you notice some faults, stop your mind, silence it, and yield to the sentiments of your heart. In examens dwell more on the evil affections that accompanied the evil actions than on those actions themselves. If you forget a few, there is no harm done. Your surrender to our Lord will make up for it.

Adieu, dear friend.

Entirely yours in Jesus and Mary

Father Francis Libermann

222

God must decide the matter of your vocation. The apostolate requires mortification, but only the negative kind.

Letter Three   La Neuville, February 8, 1842   Vol. 3, p. 128

J. M. J.

Dear Friend:

I am very late in answering your letter of January 23rd, but I have been so busy with a lot of things for the past two weeks that I have been unable to read all the letters brought to me by Mr. Bouchet. I think that the good Lord must have given you a little patience, for, as is said in today's Epistle of St. Paul, "charity is patient."

[God Must Decide in the Matter of Your Vocation]

Don't be in a hurry to decide your vocation to the Negro missions. We know of course that the needs of the Negro are very great. Many souls perish because of want of help. That is why I should like very much to have you with us, the more so because this might foster the sanctification of your own soul; at least this is a thing we can hope for.

All such reasons, however, are insufficient. We have to find out if God wants you to be one of us. As I have told you before, whatever my own desires might be, I do not want you to come unless we feel certain, or at least have a well-founded hope, that the Master is sending you. Pray therefore, put your confidence in Jesus who has given you so many graces, and have recourse to Mary, our good Mother.

We should not base our decisions for or against a vocation upon guesswork. Listen to God in your interior; if He wants you, He will dissolve the obstacles that might

stand in your way. Try merely to be faithful in following
only God's will, whatever be the side to which He might
incline you. If He inclines you to work among our poor and
beloved Negroes, have the courage to conquer the obstacles,
aided by God's grace. If on the contrary He destines you
for ministry in France, purify your views and intentions in
order that, when making your choice, you are not led by
your own inclinations.

[*Negative and Positive Mortification*]

Having no desire to influence your vocation, I shall not
reply to the questions regarding your difficulties. I leave
them to the care of Him who has the authority to call you
and for whose love you must offer yourself. Let me say
merely that the spirit of mortification is something that is
necessary for the apostolate. But the only kind of mortification that is necessary is what we would call "negative," one
that makes us detached from earthly pleasures and prompts
us to deprive ourselves of everything out of love for God.

In regard to "positive" mortification which we inflict on
ourselves for that same love, a thing you admire so much in
St. Peter Claver, it is not essential to the apostolic spirit.
It is not on that kind of mortification that the abundant
fruitfulness of a missionary's work depends. Positive mortification is a special grace that God granted to Peter Claver
and to some other saints. When mortification is practiced to
the extent that they practiced it, it is very beneficial; but
such a practice is possible only through an extraordinary
grace. We are not permitted to prescribe such a thing
as a rule that we ought to follow.

Moreover, our rules do not forbid mortifications; they
even suggest them to some extent, although the spirit that
animates our rules is not one of mortification. If you consider
the case of Peter Claver well, you will see that even his spirit

was not one of mortification. It was his great love of God that constituted the spirit, the soul of his entire life, and it was from this source that he drew a desire for mortification. Again, you should remember that our way of life is already sufficiently mortifying in itself. We have no superfluities. Whatever we have is poor and ordinary; our food will be like that of the poor whom we evangelize, but it will be wholesome and substantial. The common rule will be such that all are capable of bearing it, although at the same time we shall be faithful to the rules of [negative] mortification which I explained above.

In regard to the amount of food you should take, examine before the good Lord what is sufficient for you in each meal, and then keep to what you have determined. . . .

Please excuse me this time and pardon me for not saying anything about the virtue of religion about which you questioned me. I am so pressed with work that I hardly find time to finish this letter which, by the way, I began three days ago! Our "Brother" [the cook] has departed and has left everything in disorder.

I also beg you not to feel embarrassed; write to me everytime you desire it and think that it might be of any profit to you. If I have little time, I will reply in a few words.

Speak to me another time about the virtue of religion. My greatest satisfaction as well as one of my chief duties is to serve you in everything that could be useful to your soul.

Your poor servant
in Jesus and Mary,

FATHER FRANCIS LIEBERMANN

153

223

The virtue of religion. No constant self-scrutiny but love of God. Sundry counsels.

Letter Four   *La Neuville, May 5, 1842*   *Vol. 3, p. 182*

Praised be Jesus and Mary

Dear Confrere:

May your heart always belong to God and belong to Him alone. Esteem and love nothing but Jesus, and love everything else for Him and in Him alone. Seek only to please Him in all that you do; this is what your virtue of religion ought to be.

The virtue of religion consists in [1.] giving your whole being so that it may be completely immolated and sacrificed to God's glory; [2.] having a sovereign reverence for Him and for everything that concerns Him; [3.] and in loving Him above all things. All these duties should be fulfilled not by feelings and sentiments but by genuine desires and efficacious will which are translated into action on every occasion.

[*The Spirit of Sacrifice*]

In regard to the first aspect [of the virtue of religion], the spirit of sacrifice, you must remain before God ready at all times to have God's will fulfilled in you, even at the cost of all that you are and possess. Dispose yourself to serve Him in the souls whom He desires to have and reward eternally. Be ready to follow His every wish and disposed to sacrifice to Him your parents, friends, country, pleasures, reputation—in one word, everything which He might wish to ask of you. Be ready in all gentle peacefulness to be a perfectly supple instrument in His hands, even if this means that the vile instrument will suffer harm or be destroyed in the process.

[*Reverence*]

The second aspect of the virtue of religion is reverence. The necessity of adoring God demands that you remain in an attitude of profound modesty and humility. Do not endeavor to accomplish this through violent efforts and tenseness of mind, but let it be more an attitude and disposition than a sentiment. Be full of respect in holy places and toward sacred things.

[*Love*]

The third aspect is love. This should inspire a great desire to please God. When you know that something is agreeable to Him, execute it immediately with a good heart, in all gentleness and peace. The service of God requires great peace and great mildness of us. Also love all your confreres, treat them with gentleness and charity out of love of Him, and for the same love bear your pains, humiliations and afflictions. This, dear friend, is all you need to know in regard to the "spirit of religion."

[*Work Out of Love for Jesus Without Constant Self-Scrutiny*]

It is childish constantly to wish to account for what you are doing and ask at every moment, "How should I do this in order to do it well, or what must I do to make this work useful?" The answer is, "I must do it out of love of my Jesus and with the desire to please Him, and then that work will be very useful." After replying in this way, work, read, etc. out of love of Jesus, and don't worry about the "how" and the way you are doing it.

If that thought of the "how" comes back dancing before your mind, pay no attention to it. Act as when a fly lands on your cheek. Don't become impatient. Gently dismiss that thought with a sort of indifference and continue your work or your reading without stopping. The thought will annoy you for some time; but try to practice indifference and it will finally leave you alone. It is as when a small dog is barking at you. If you pay attention to him and defend yourself, he will bark more loudly and will continue longer; if, on the contrary, you continue your walk without paying attention to his barking, he will soon stop. . . .

[Sundry Counsels]

In regard to the distaste you experience in your spiritual exercises, my reply is, as you have already guessed, to accept this evil with patience. I add: consider yourself most fortunate to be able to suffer some little thing in God's service; have the courage never to yield to what that distaste might suggest and do not shorten your exercises at any time on that account.

Regarding your vocation, consult your director. I can tell you now that if your director prompts you to decide in favor of our poor Negroes, I will not put any obstacles in its way. I will accept you with joy, for the love of Jesus and Mary.

I am not permitted to prescribe anything to you except what you are actually doing, for otherwise I might disturb God's own plans in your regard. I am not sufficiently acquainted with the circumstances to be able to offer suggestions.

Beg Mary to grant you peace, and exercise yourself so that you may attain it, but act with the greatest gentleness. Seek to give great liberty to your mind; don't ask yourself at any time how you ought to do this thing. Act as it were mechanically; merely see to it that you are acting out of love of Jesus. Ask our most holy Mother for the grace of acting in that manner; she knows how to give good lessons in regard to peace of soul.

Don't seek to practice mortifications, but strive to free yourself from your embarrassment of mind, and do it with peaceful love for Jesus.

It is a good thing to recount the holy deeds of men who are still living, of men who are full of the love of God, provided this is not reported to them and they do not learn how greatly they are esteemed on account of their good deeds.

Regarding praising men, I believe that, generally speaking, this ought not to be done except for men who are truly perfect in their participation in the holiness of our Lord Jesus Christ, men who are perfect models of fervor and can be proposed as examples in every part of their conduct. But, if everything is not perfect and worth imitating, it is preferable to praise only their holy actions. Otherwise, although such persons are very pious and very pleasing to our Lord, you may risk having others imitating them in things that are not in accord with our Lord.

Adieu, dear friend.

Entirely yours in
Jesus and Mary

FATHER FRANCIS LIBERMANN

224

Live with the freedom of the children of God, free from anxiety and tension.

Letter Five   La Neuville, October 3, 1842   Vol. 3, p. 295

Dear Confrere:

It was by accident that I failed to reply to your letter immediately after its reception. I just now opened a package in which that letter had been enclosed, and this will make my advice seem out of date, for in all probability your mind has changed since the time you sent your letter.

[*Peace of Soul*]

Accustom yourself to living with the holy liberty of children of God and preserve peace of mind. Bring calm and gentleness into your interior. Look upon those agitations [you experience] as annoying things that you should suffer with patience; and see to it that you do not react violently to them. Don't be astonished that you experience such things, and don't be preoccupied with your interior condition. Accept all those things with patience and gentleness as things that are willed by God's providence, to which you ought to submit with love, and then seek to distract your mind from them. Later on, I hope, those thoughts will no longer invade your mind when you will be engaged in the works of the ministry.

While you are in the seminary you have no such activity and your attention is given to a narrow field. Your mind is somewhat "jumpy," and it does not find there objects that can arouse enthusiasm; and so this "jumpiness" transfers to your interior and you amuse yourself pursuing minutiae. . . .

LETTERS TO LOUIS MARIE LANNURIEN

[Avoid Tension and Anxiety in Your Spiritual Life]

Put your mind at ease in regard to the *manner* in which to perform each action. In general, adopt the disposition of doing everything for God and with submission to His will. Renew this desire and intention frequently; after that, in each action, act according to the first thought that comes to your mind, directing your heart to God. Never hesitate. When you are unable to decide because of your reasoning, put reasoning aside and act according to what suggests itself to you at that moment. Of course, I am supposing that you are observing your particular rule.

In regard to study, determine, in understanding with your director, what subjects you ought to study each day and the amount of time you should consecrate to them. After that preserve a free mind.

Concerning your fears that you might perhaps not be observing this or that rule or regulation of the seminary, it is sufficient for you that you give yourself to the good Lord with the desire of doing everything that is agreeable to Him. Don't complicate matters and avoid worries about those things. If through inattention you sometimes fail in the observance of this or that rule or regulation, there is no evil in that; at least the evil is not great and it will not have bad results for your soul. But that agitation, that constant disquiet, is a real evil in the sense that it prevents substantial progress in the perfect life, in the life of a child of God, a life of peace and love. "Love and do what you please" [St. Augustine]. Be more intent on giving yourself interiorly to God than on striving with that sort of tension to practice those external acts and on scrutinizing your way of doing these things.

[Live with the Holy Liberty of the Children of God]

During recreation entertain genuine love for those who are with you. Preserve a peaceful mind and be at ease. Don't seek to be edified by others nor try to edify them. I mean, don't plan that sort of thing in advance. Go to recreation as to any other exercise, for the sole purpose of pleasing God, and entertain no further thoughts about it. Merely seek to be with those who are good, whether they are "old timers" or newcomers. After that, . . . all you have to do is to give your mind and heart to Jesus and Mary, having merely the pure desire of pleasing the Well-Beloved of your heart.

Having this disposition, remain in peace and follow your inclinations during your conversations with others. Don't ask yourself, "Am I generous or selfish?" but think merely of giving yourself to God during recreation and pleasing Him. When you wish to speak, speak; when you have nothing to say, keep quiet; don't, however, make plans about either talking or keeping quiet, but let yourself go in all that to what is agreeable to God and according to the inclination of the moment.

Avoid tension, and don't try to go beyond what is doing you good, but act freely and with simplicity in God's presence, and don't indulge in examining everything that you do and the manner in which you conduct yourself. Be fully surrendered to God, keep your heart wide open in His presence; enjoy great interior broadness of mind concerning everything; feel very free in regard to external actions. This is the surest way that will lead you to God and will sanctify you.

Eat as long as you feel a need for food. It is God who gives you your craving for food, and you must satisfy it. Don't be fastidious about food; take what is put before you.

Despise the esteem of men; reject in a spirit of indifference the feelings and desires they arouse in you, but do this in all

gentleness. Humble yourself on the occasion of such sentiments in an attitude of peace in God's presence, and distract
your mind from those things.

Prepare yourself for your ordination without trouble,
abandoning yourself in peace to God, with confidence in
Mary, with freedom of mind. Don't seek to do anything beyond that.

Entirely your in Jesus and Mary,

FATHER FRANCIS LIBERMANN

225

*Abstain from constant self-scrutiny and be like a child
with God.*

Letter Six   *February 11, 1843*   *Vol. 4, p. 104*

· Jesus, Mary, Joseph

Dear Confrere:

[*Abstain from Self-Scrutiny*]

Your major difficulty is your habit of self-scrutiny. For
the love of our Lord try to become a bit careless. Let me
explain. When, for example, you stop at some passage of
Holy Scripture which you do not understand very well, you
reflect upon your mental activity and become embarrassed,
asking yourself, "Did I stop long enough to consider this
point, or ought I to read further?" Forget yourself! Walk
with more freedom and don't examine your actions so
carefully.

For the love of our Lord, proceed with a certain carelessness when you are reading or doing anything else. Be in-

different to the "how," the manner in which you should do this thing or another. Be satisfied with performing those actions, that reading, out of love for the divine Master, without worrying about the way you are executing your actions. For you the "how," the manner of doing things, is simply to remain calm and at peace. This applies also to your prayerful way of reading holy scripture: be calm and restful, desire to please our Lord and to have a spirit of faith; such is our method of studying Holy Scripture. . . .

[*Be Like a Child With God*]

You ought to have a sort of indifference of heart in the way you go to God. Keep your heart at peace and do things with simplicity and without too much reflection. Simply desire to please God and have the good will of accomplishing what is pleasing to Him. It is important for you that you do not strive too much for that which is pleasing to Him and do not search for what is most pleasing to Him. Act like a child that loves his father. A child cannot examine and scrutinize what is most agreeable in this or that circumstance. He cannot make that kind of a choice. Now this is your situation. What does a child do? He acts upon the first thought that comes to his mind. This, it seems to him is what will give pleasure to his father; so he does it immediately. Act in a similar way. The child sometimes makes mistakes; you also will make mistakes, but there is no harm in that. He for whose love you are doing those things knows your good will, and this good will is pleasing to Him. This unconcerned way of acting is something that is necessary for you; it will perfect you much more than your method of excessive care and self-scrutiny. . . .

It is good that reflections do not play a great role in your mental prayer. It will be the better for it. If resolutions upset you, don't make them. You will notice that your mental prayer will be just as good if you always make the resolution of preserving peace of soul, while seeking to please God in your actions, without examining the "how.". . . *Adieu*, dear confrere.

Entirely yours in the charity of
the most Holy Heart of Mary,

> Father Frances Libermann,
> Missionary of the Holy Heart
> of Mary

226

Meditate in such a way that your mind has something to do without, however, making meditation a reasoning process.

Letter Seven   *March 28, 1843*   *Vol. 4, p. 166*

Jesus, Mary, Joseph

Dear Confrere:

[Do Not Make Your Meditation an Intellectual Game]

I fully understand the difficulties you experience in your mental prayer. When you reason, meditation becomes an intellectual game or a laborious job. If you do not reason, your mind that is accustomed to activity becomes bored and is in a hazy cloud. It is this vagueness that is burdensome to you and disturbs you. You could perhaps choose a more definite subject for your meditation without, however, choosing one that is metaphysical or that you will reason about.

Take for your subjects of meditation the mysteries of our Lord or of the Blessed Virgin. Consider the divine

163

Savior in His mysteries and His various states of life. Look at Him in His various actions as shown in those mysteries; consider in a practical way How He acts and how perfect is the way He accomplishes those things; finally consider the principles that are the soul of those actions, the interior activities of Christ's soul and how He executes those actions.

Take for each meditation two or three practical considerations which are usually subdivided into various points. Stop from time to time to produce affections if they arise spontaneously. If you have no affections, adhere with will and mind to what you behold in Jesus, not in the sense that you must say over and over again that you adhere to them; but cling to them from the bottom of your heart. When a sentiment does not flow, as it were, of its own accord, remain in silence and adhere [to Jesus] with a certain attitude of faith and desire.

[Example of a Suitable Meditation: Jesus' Gentleness in His Passion]

You could take as your subject, for example, the gentleness and peacefulness of Jesus in the midst of His torments and humiliations during His Passion. How did He act in those circumstances? This is a first consideration. You could consider the various things He did and the various things He had to suffer, and how He accepted his sufferings and the treatment He received. See how He let Himself be placed on the cross; how He extended His arms and permitted His executioners to stretch His body on the Cross. He said not one word, did not cry out with pain but raised His eyes to His heavenly Father. How gentle and peaceful His glance toward His torturers. Consider the sentiments and thoughts present in His interior: His complete submission to the will of His Father; His indifference for what concerned Himself; the generous love that animated His sacrifice; His compassion toward the wretched persons who made Him suffer when He beheld their blindness, the loss of their souls; His desire to save them.

Why did He suffer in that way and with those dispositions? Look at His interior dispositions and consider them in a practical way: His compassion for our wretched condition, His desire to sacrifice Himself for the glory of His Father, His horror for sin, the way He looked upon sin for which He was offering expiation, the will of His Father who wanted Him to suffer in that way.

After each particular consideration stop a moment to produce some affection or act of faith, as I explained above. In this way your mind will have a subject with which it can occupy itself, without indulging in a reasoning process. Try and see, dear friend, if you can proceed more or less in this fashion.

[*Avoid Self-Examination*]

The resolution which [as you told me] you frequently take is very good and is especially useful for you: never to occupy yourself too much with self; not to follow too much the lead of your own mind to get out of the habit of acting upon its lively impulses; to calm yourself gradually. You should never voluntarily entertain ideas that make you think of yourself.

Give yourself to our Lord in peace and gentleness, and quietly calm your mind. . . .

Adieu, my dear confrere. Best regards in the most holy charity of Jesus and Mary,

Father Francis Libermann,

Missionary of the Holy Heart
of Mary

6. LETTERS TO ETIENNE CLAIR

INTRODUCTION

Etienne Pierre Joseph Clair was born in 1818 at Annonay in the diocese of Viviers. He studied for the priesthood in the Seminary of Lyons, and it was there that Libermann first met him in 1839 on his journey to Rome. Father Clair was a relative of Bishop Mioland of Amiens, the prelate who accepted Libermann for ordination to the priesthood and gave him permission to establish his novitiate at La Neuville, near Amiens.

Father Clair felt an attraction for the religious life and particularly toward Libermann's Congregation of the Holy Heart of Mary. Libermann thought much of him at one time and even invited him to join his society and become its novicemaster. When the many obstacles that stood in the way of his religious vocation were removed, Father Clair finally, in 1844, entered the novitiate; a year later he was professed and made his consecration to the apostolate. Unstable, he went in eight years through half a dozen different posts, until in 1853 he left the Congregation. He then sued the Congregation; filled a variety of posts in the diocese of Lyons; was interned in a mental hospital; went to Switzerland; sued his brother, the archbishop of Lyons and the Prefect of the District of Rhone; became an apostate to his catholic faith and his priesthood; and died a pitiful death in Geneva.

Some lines regarding the pernicious fruits of self-love, written to Father Clair, appear to have been prophetic. In his numerous letters to Father Clair, Libermann pointed out the dangers of self-confidence, excessive natural activity and self-esteem. He suggested as a radical remedy a humble docility to God's grace, which is the only way to Christian perfection.

227

Jesus, the "Soul of your soul." Peace of soul and moderation even in spiritual desires. Sundry counsels.

Letter One   *Rennes, October, 1839*   *Vol. 2, p. 197*

Dear Mr. Clair:

You gave me great joy in our Lord writing to me and describing in detail the interior condition of your soul, for I assure you that I greatly desire your sanctification in His love. May Jesus and Mary be the foundation of all your hope and the object of all your love. Relish, enjoy, desire nothing except for and in Jesus. Have no heart, soul, body, and existence except for and in Jesus. When will you allow Him to live fully in your soul?

[*Jesus, the "Soul of Your Soul"*]

I believe that it is our Lord who has inspired your desire, and this gives me very great joy. He will live in you, dear friend; this is my firm hope. Live also in Him. Don't be satisfied with the desire of being always occupied with our Lord Jesus, but have besides a greater and more lively desire to possess Him in your soul and to be possessed by Him. He will then be the life and, as it were, the soul of your soul, so that you have no longer any actions, sentiment, desire, affection, will, or intention of your own, but Jesus Himself will animate you in all your internal and external activities. He will then live in you in "His spirit of holiness, in the fullness of His power." He will re-enact in you all the interior states of His Holy soul, states in which He wants you to have a share.

I tell you all this in a few words, not exactly to point out to you that you do not possess any element of that perfect

167

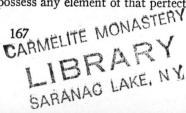

life of Jesus in souls, but rather in order to prompt you and make you enter into those interior sentiments in the presence of Jesus and Mary and attain the summit of a most holy love.

[*Peace of Soul*]

The great means to establish Christ's admirable reign in us are precisely the spirit of constant mental prayer and peace of soul. God's mercy is granting you a great grace in giving you that twofold attraction. Follow that attraction with gentleness and love in the presence of so much divine goodness.

Recall constantly and establish firmly in your mind and heart the fundamental truth that the greatest and even infallible means to possess the spirit of prayer, is peaceful possession of our soul in our Lord's presence.

Note well those words, "to possess one's soul in peace," they are the words of our divine Master. Your soul must always be cloistered within itself, or rather it should be cloistered in Jesus dwelling in your soul; not imprisoned and shut in as with an iron bolt, but held in sweet repose in Jesus' arms. Natural eagerness and tension constrict the soul. On the contrary, it expands by such a sweet repose, by peaceful action, by moderation in its interior activity. I don't think that this practice will be difficult for you, for it is our Lord who is doing this in you and who moves you in all gentleness.

[*Moderation of Spiritual Desires*]

Avoid harshness and rigidity of mind and will. Don't rush with excessive eagerness and violence toward objects that attract you, even if they are most holy. When you feel interiorly drawn and experience holy desires, never run ahead of God's guidance. Don't seek to preserve interior sentiments or pious affections beyond the time that our Lord deigns to give them to you.

Keep always in mind that it is neither your function nor within your powers to form and fashion yourself and make an interior man out of yourself. Neither are you able to undertake or choose what is better or more perfect; this belongs to our Lord alone, and He alone can give it to you. The conclusion you should draw from all this is that you ought to avoid natural activity, excitement, anxious longing to achieve what you consider excellent.

When you experience desires that are lively and yet gentle, humble and full of confidence, you may follow them. But don't use violence and anxious effort, and don't rush beyond the limits of those desires. Open your poor heart before the most loveable Jesus. He knows well what is taking place in your soul and what is wanting to you.

Don't act like a child who wants categorically and absolutely to get the things he happens to see. In all such circumstances repose in Jesus, pour out your soul, as it were, before Him like oil. I say "like oil," that is, without noise or violence, but with gentleness and a most peaceful love. Do not fear then to desire and sigh interiorly for Jesus and Mary; but desire them in the way I have described. Remain thus peacefully in Jesus and all will go well.

[*Sundry Counsels*]

You are permitted to think of yourself, but it should be in God. It is not yourself you ought to consider, but God living in you. Self-consideration which restores peace to the soul and increases interior humility before God is not really a consideration of self but of God.

Don't worry about your shyness or your other faults. Go to God and live in Him in perfect peace of soul. All those faults will then fall away like so many scales. Nevertheless, resist them when they come to your notice, and re-establish peace in your soul in God's presence with the desire of living only in and for Him.

Avoid haste both interiorly and exteriorly, and be even more careful in trying to preserve interior tranquility. Be sedate, gentle, peaceful and grave in and before God in all your actions of mind and heart. Avoid tension and violent efforts; avoid the least affectation; do everything with mildness and with the gentleness of our Lord and His Blessed Mother. I am very glad that you intend to submit my letters to your director [at the seminary]. Not only does this not trouble me, but I greatly desire it, for it gives me more assurance that I shall not do you great harm in the things I may say wrongly, especially at the beginning before I get to know you sufficiently well.

Adieu, dear friend. May the peace of Jesus and Mary fill your soul.

> Your poor brother and servant in their holy love,
>
> FRANCIS LIBERMANN, ACOLYTE

228

We must not scrutinize God's action in our souls. God's graces should not make us self-complacent. Faithfulness in accepting God's guidance.

Letter Two   *Rome, March 4, 1840*   *Vol. 2, p. 202*

Praised be Jesus and Mary

Dear Brother in Our Lord Jesus Christ and in the most beloved Mother of our souls:

Since you desire to be given to Jesus and Mary, I shall not cease to give you to Him, and I don't wish to keep anything for myself that belongs to your soul. This, however, will not prevent me from making always every effort to form our divine Master in you. It will always be my greatest consolation—and one you are not able to fathom—to see Jesus growing in you and attaining to the full stature of a perfect man in you. To reach this goal, you must allow yourself to be led by His divine hand, like a child that knows nothing, that is unable to walk or do anything whatsoever.

[*Abstain from Scrutinizing God's Action in Your Soul*]

Avoid trying to find out or consider what God is doing in your soul. The eyes of your soul should see nothing but Jesus living in you. But if you want to act purely and in accordance with His most holy desires, you should see this dear and most adorable Lord, as it were, apart from your self, so that your joy, consolation and love are in Jesus dwelling, living and reigning in your soul. I mean you should see Him in this way rather than seeing your soul as possessing that great treasure of your love.

This is very important, dear brother. The more our considerations and our views are detached and abstracted from our self, the purer they will be. The more also they will be free from our self-love and the more pleasing to Him who wants to be the sole and complete good of our souls. I do not mean to say that you are guilty of a fault if sometimes you notice humbly and purely the divine graces that exist in your soul and the various operations of our Lord in you. It might sometimes even be inopportune to reject such views and the sentiments that result from them. To show that we ought not too readily reject them, let me point to the fact that such views can serve to humble us; they can lower us in the presence of our divine Master and leave nothing that can serve as food for our self-complacency; they can also

171

make us enter interiorly into true union of love with our Lord.

Such a recollection and such a union are then free from all self-flattery; they are rather accompanied by self-forget-fulness. For our love should not be one that is, as it were, the product of our soul; it should rather be a yielding or outburst of our soul as it rests in God.

When you are in the latter disposition, you can then abandon yourself to that view and to those sentiments, al-though your self is involved in them, but make sure that it is always done with self-distrust, and indulge in it as rarely as possible.

The self-consideration in which you are allowed to in-dulge without fear, when it offers itself to you with relish, love and recollection, is that which reveals your faults, your wretchedness, negligence, infidelity and natural activity, and it should then make you humble yourself before our Lord and the Most Blessed Virgin.

[*Do Not Become Proud Because of God's Love for You*]

I am not displeased because the good Lord sometimes lets you experience worry after He has granted you a grace, for, dear brother, you run great dangers at such times. On the occasion of such graces self-love makes us grow in our own estimation, and little by little you might imagine that you are better than others. You might at least run the danger of indulging in self-complacency, seeing that our Lord appar-ently gives you preference. This is not a way to please Him.

Ask the Blessed Virgin how she acted amidst the im-mense graces with which she was overwhelmed, and then consider what you ought to make of the few farthings which you have received from our Lord's hands. Act like a poor man who realizes that he would drop down exhausted and discouraged if Jesus and Mary did not lend their merciful help.

I have known persons who received very great graces and who at one time gave themselves to God with a most loving and generous heart. I never thought that they would later fall backward; they nevertheless did become lax, and they would have fallen away entirely if our Lord and the Most Holy Virgin had not come to their rescue. I even believe that they will never recover their first perfection, although the latter was only a beginning. I know others who reached the same degree of fervor and who, like the first, caused the admiration of all who knew them, and yet they are now in the most imminent danger. Hence, dear friend, it is not a bad thing that you suffer some troubles and anxieties from time to time. I do not want to give you advice in their regard, but prefer to abandon you to our Lord. He will dispose things according to His divine good pleasure.

[*Follow God's Guidance Whether Pleasant or Painful*]

Be faithful, letting yourself be directed by the divine Guide who wishes to care for your poor soul. You see clearly that He brings you back to the right road as soon as you make a blunder and leave His holy direction either to listen to the flesh or to your own opinion, whether in your words or in your actions.

I confess to you that if I dared to mingle in the affairs of our beloved Master regarding the guidance of your soul, I would ask Him to treat you with a little more severity in such circumstances, whereas He always treats you with gentleness and never gives you severe reproof. But, as I say, I would not dare, for all the world, to interfere with the divine work of our Lord in your soul. I see very well that this is to your liking; you prefer to receive sugar instead of gall. Well, dear friend, eat sugar as long as our Lord gives

173

it to you, but be ready to drink gall and vinegar when, in His own good time, His divine hand offers it to you.

Don't ask anything at this moment except love and a desire for your own abasement, self-forgetfulness, the love of Jesus and Mary, and perfect union of your soul with those two heavenly souls. Ask that that divine Love of our souls may possess your soul, but don't try to interfere, desiring that our Lord would change His conduct in your regard. It is not for you to be involved in the direction of your own affairs, but you should allow yourself to be guided according to the wishes of the good Lord Jesus.

Take care to follow our Lord's instructions most faithfully. Cling to the one that concerns that principal attention to Him, an attention that should be constantly preserved. Regarding the matter of food and material activities, act with simplicity according to the interior promptings of our Lord. Also follow His suggestion in regard to detachment from your parents, in accordance with your present ideas. I shall pray for this at Saint Mary Major's, at St. Peter's, Saint Paul's, at St. John's and in the Catacombs. . . .

> Entirely yours in the holy love
> of Jesus and Mary,
>
> FRANCIS LIBERMANN, acolyte

229

Thoughts about the subdiaconate.

Letter Three   *Rome, July 25, 1840*   *Vol. 2, 206*

Jesus, Mary, Joseph

Dear Confrere:

[*Henceforth You Belong to God Alone*]

You made a sacrifice when you received the subdiaconate. It is my hope that by it our Lord has finally given you the great grace of purifying and immolating your soul and body completely to Him, for His glory and good pleasure.

Making this vow, you took the first step toward the priesthood and you expressed your intention in the presence of angels and saints. This vow in our Lord's hands was like a sword which He used to immolate you to the glory of His heavenly Father. From now on there is for you no longer any glory, self-interest, enjoyment or satisfaction on this earth. Our Lord has seized you, bound and pinioned you, and He reserves for Himself the completion of the sacrifice at the time when you will reach the last step, the priesthood. From now on you are no longer your own master nor the master of your affections. They belong to our Lord; He has the right to dispose of them as He pleases; and He will dispose of them for the greater glory of His Father.

[*You are Beginning to Become Part of the Sacrifice of Jesus*]

By receiving the subdiaconate you died, as it were, and were sacrificed for God's glory. This happened because of the love and infinite goodness of our Lord toward you. This death is not only a death to yourself but death also to all creatures. You are beginning to enter into the adorable sacrifice which Jesus offered for the world. It is a sacrifice of death and of extermination of your self, a sacrifice of divine life in your soul and in the souls of all who surround you.

This makes you understand why our Lord gave you those desires for "interior" death and destruction of which you spoke. He wished to prepare you for the things He desired to do in your soul at the blessed moment of your sacrifice. Don't imagine that from that moment there was already a real interior immolation in you. You had merely the desire, a certain efficacious desire to fulfill it, but it was only a beginning. Now that the great moment has passed and our Lord has embraced you in His most holy love and His most adorable sacrifice, your soul ought to be more vigorous. The immense grace of the sacrifice of our Lord should develop and bring forth fruit in your soul.

I desire with all my heart that our adorable Master will complete your interior sacrifice so that you will remain like a dead victim in the hands of that High Priest who will thus present you to His heavenly Father. You will then have no other task than to remain in that spirit of love which makes Jesus act on and in you, and everything will help you to procure the perfection and consummation of His designs in respect to your soul.

[Let The Spirit of Jesus Flow into All Your Actions]

Do not be astonished, dear friend, that our good Master did not wish to exterminate your self entirely in your interior. Feel certain nevertheless that He has established His grace in you, like a most abundant fountain. You have only to facilitate the flow, not by natural activity, but by allowing that divine source of the wounded Heart of our divine Master,

176

which was pierced and sacrificed for us on the Cross, to pour itself out into your soul.

Always keep your soul and its powers well disposed and faithful so that the Spirit of Jesus, who is that inexhaustible source, may flow into all your actions and motions, becoming their principle, a principle of sacrifice and immolation to His divine love.

That death and destruction must extend to your entire interior condition. There should not be left in you any desire, plan, idea of greatness, of distinction, of exaltation and satisfaction, not even in spiritual things; no satisfaction in love and divine grace, not even in that death and, sacrifice and in that life of God in you.

[*Be in God's Hands Like a Toy in the Hands of a Child*]

Your soul should forget itself and fade away; it should stand aside as if it were an indifferent, a worthless object. Do not strive for, speculate about, or desire anything for the purpose of attaining eminence in the supernatural order; but be faithful, giving yourself to our Lord and following Him according to the promptings of His grace. Be in His hands like the toy in the hands of a child. Let Him do with and in you whatever He wishes, and do not ask why or how He does it.

You are nothing. Let Him do with this nothing all He sees fit and proper. Keep this thought of your absolute nothingness before your mind in all circumstances. It should prevent you from attracting the attention of others to your self. Let men judge, examine, praise or blame your conduct; let them love, esteem, hate, despise you, or be indifferent toward you. Your soul, in all circumstances, should remain in lowliness before God, praising, adoring, blessing Him, and trying to be sacrificed to Him in all things and in all circumstances.

177

See God in everything and see Him alone, forgetting yourself more and more. Never desire praise nor have any esteem for yourself. Avoid also self-pity and self-complacency. Never occupy your mind with yourself except for the purpose of abasing, despising, humbling yourself. All your love ought to be in God and for God alone.

It is my hope that the Most Holy Virgin, our well-beloved Mother, has given you a very fine present on the day of your sacred betrothal. Do not try to find out what she has given you; but thank her with all your heart, for you may be sure that on that day she will have granted you some favor, although she saw fit to hide it from you. . . .

Pray our Lord and the Blessed Virgin that their love may be the source, the companion, the guide and the end of all that is taking place in you.

Entirely yours in the most holy and divine love. I beg Jesus and Mary to complete all things in you and consume you, and to do the same for me, your poor servant.

FRANCIS LIBERMANN, acolyte

230

The dangers of self-love. Holiness is learned from God speaking in your heart and not from books. Let God act as He pleases. Avoid curiosity in spiritual matters.

Letter Four   *Rome, September, 1840*   *Vol. 2, p. 209*

Praised be Jesus and Mary

Dear Confrere:

I have but little to tell you, for I believe that you are more in need of God's words than of human words and I am afraid that you might stop at the latter. Please, note what I should like to impress upon you: your instruction concerning divine things and your interior life should come from our Lord alone, and it is to Him that all the powers of your soul ought to be directed at all times.

[*Beware of Your Self-Love*]

It is my wish that you would listen attentively to His adorable voice as directed toward Him in a spirit of constant prayer and make all the activity of your will consist in following Him with love, peace, docility, and confidence. Listen carefully to our Lord, dear brother, and do it with deep humility. The reason why I say this is not that I notice more self-love than usual in you or more than I find in many others; but I want to warn you so that you will be on your guard against your self-love and may not permit it to overcome you after all the favors you have received from our Lord. Pardon me for entertaining such fears and don't yield to anxiety. I don't say these things because of what I have discovered in you, but because of what I have witnessed in others who fell into evil ways because of their detestable pride.

Dear brother, walk with love and confidence in the ways of our Lord, but always fear and tremble. So many others have fallen; why would it be impossible for you to fall likewise except through an extraordinary help of God? Have a constant fear of the desire to be somebody, of self-complacency at the sight of God's gifts to you, and be not afraid of being held in low esteem by others.

[*Learn Holiness from God Within You and Not From Men*]

I said that the activity of your will ought to consist in following with peace, love and great humility all the suggestions of the divine Master. It is in God that you should

179

look for instruction even in the [spiritual] things that men
and books tell you. Listen with peace and docility to the
things you hear from men, but at the same time listen to
and meditate on God's word within you. Keep your soul
prostrate before God and surrendered to our Lord while
listening to men or reading a book. Receive His divine teaching and inspirations, and the promptings of His most holy
love, and follow them faithfully without violent natural
efforts.

If men tell you things that are very good in themselves,
but our Lord does not see fit to make you relish them, don't
worry. Remain peacefully in His presence and neither despise nor reject those things; but also do not accept them
and don't force your soul. Obey the words of men when our
divine Master desires your obedience; but meanwhile keep
your eyes constantly turned to the divine Love of your
soul, to Him who dwells in you and orders all things in you
as your sovereign Lord.

You see therefore that you ought to avoid excess in everything. Don't despise men but listen to them. Even consult
them when this will help you in loving God. Follow their
advice when it is proper to do so, but in all these circumstances see, consider, listen to, love, admire and relish
only Jesus who lives and speaks in your soul, even when you
hear human words spoken by Him through others.

Every time words come from Him He will make you
relish them and appreciate them interiorly unless your self-
love or some other faults prevent it. I don't want to decide
the practical question you have asked me in this respect,
for our Lord does not tell me anything about it. It is well
to fear illusions regarding such things, and it is always
safest.

[*Let God Act with You as He Pleases. Avoid Curiosity*]

Admire the goodness of Jesus who prompts desires and then prevents you from fulfilling them. Be in His Hands like a toy in the hands of a child. If it pleases the divine Master to play this sort of game with you, let Him do it and always approach Him with peace, joy and love.

In regard to [your hints] about your future vocation, I don't see any reason why I should know about it. It is proper that you avoid curiosity with respect to what you tell me, but it is even more important that I avoid curiosity in asking you questions. Otherwise my words will be useless and you will not hear our Lord in the things I say to you. When our Lord urges you to inform me, do so. I don't object to it, but before He prompts you I see no need for it . . . .

Adieu, dear brother. Be always and in all things entirely devoted to Jesus and Mary, and live only through their love, in which I am,

Your very poor servant,

Francis Libermann, acolyte

231

How Jesus establishes the reign of His divine will in us.

Letter Five   **Strasbourg, January 31, 1841**   *Vol. 2, p. 447*

J. M. J.

Dear Confrere:

[*The Reign of the Divine Will*]

May the divine will of Jesus be always your will in all things. Be confident, dear friend; our divine Master makes you feel the need of letting His will be the sole master in your soul. He will not be wanting to you in the execution of this design which is so advantageous to your soul.

You are already aware of the authority which that holy and adorable will exercises in you. Rejoice, then, from the bottom of your heart but, at the same time, humble and annihilate yourself because of His adorable goodness. Don't imagine, however, that Jesus' divine and adorable will is soon to win complete and perfect mastery over you. Time will be needed, struggles, crosses, miseries, much obscurity, renunciations, troubles of all sorts in your interior life, and many external contradictions and humiliations. Hence, my friend, strive energetically for that great perfection of divine love in your soul, but don't imagine that you have reached the end of your struggles. Since you desire crosses, I shall tell you something about them.

But first a word about the perfect establishment of the divine will in our own. Our will is something that is most intimate in us; submitting and abandoning it entirely to our Lord in order that He may vivify and rule it is most difficult and the acme of divine love. To produce this effect most perfectly, our divine Master ordinarily, and even almost always, digs down to the utmost depths of our soul. He uproots everything that belongs to our own love and our own life in order to substitute for them His own divine life and love.

[*God First Establishes the Reign of His Will Through a Powerful Grace of Enlightenment*]

To achieve this, He usually employs two kinds of methods. The first of these is direct, and although it very often contains things that are costly to us, it is pleasing and easy, for we are not deprived of divine light. In this case God's graces draw us, enlighten us in regard to our conduct, and make us see our imperfections and our faults. We become disgusted with ourselves and we are prompted to cast ourselves recklessly on the bosom of our adorable Lord to be, as it were, wholly absorbed in and by Him.

In this way the action of grace is powerful, produces great things in our souls and attaches us firmly to our Lord. The good it accomplishes is immense. It purifies our souls and detaches them from all that is foreign to grace; it destroys our faults, imperfections, and failings that spring from our flesh and severs the soul's relations with this source of corruption. Our wretched flesh remains inclined to evil but our will is purified; it no longer follows the same lower tendencies and even abhors the flesh. Nevertheless, this focus of corruption continues to send its evil vapors into the soul, but the soul does its best to dissipate and reject them. It clings to Jesus, submitting and abandoning itself to Him in order that He may live and reign in it by His divine will and by following His inspirations while rejecting what is contrary to them.

This, dear friend, is what causes you to be troubled: you see in yourself what you think is resistance to the divine will. It is a good thing to fear much, but you should never allow yourself to become anxious to the extent of losing your freedom of mind and the peace and steadiness with which you ought to walk in and before our Lord. What you should do is to be on guard, to distrust yourself and to fear because your evil tendencies tend to penetrate into your will, with which they are closely connected. They will be repelled only through the power of the divine will.

If you are unfaithful you deserve to be whipped. And if it were to please our Lord to make you realize that you are and have nothing of yourself, but that He is and wants to be everything in you, He might give you free rein [to follow your own ideas]. It would not take long in that case before you would suffer defeat. Proceed therefore without presumption, without self-love and self-esteem, but with perfect interior humility, in the presence of Him who alone desires to be great in you. Love Him, dear friend: love Him ardently, greatly, generously and perfectly, but humbly. Bow deeply before Him who is all greatness in His little servants; bow deeply before Him in all humility but also with great love.

[*Great Darkness Follows this Enlightenment*]

The second method which our Lord uses to rule over our wills is indirect. It leads us along a painful and sorrowful road in which our Lord leaves us in great darkness. It then seems that our will has to do everything by its own powers and that the divine All is no longer everything in the soul; and yet this is not so. I need not enter into details regarding this situation, for you are not in this state. It will come at a later date, I hope, for it is only under such conditions that the perfect life and the perfect rule of the divine will are at work in our souls.

The first assault of our Sovereign Master, one in which He is victorious, is that in which He casts out of our soul all that is foreign to Him, even affections that do not come from the flesh. A soul in this spiritual condition has its defects apart from those that spring from its wretched companion, corrupt nature. The divine Master has then to fashion such a soul and its powers, expel from it all that is improper—that is, everything that is not suitable to His indwelling and is contrary to His divine life and absolute reign in the soul. He uses then that second method to accomplish that great perfection of the soul and leads it by that very painful road. Thus, the acme of divine love, the perfect reign of God's will, is attained before the soul has passed through that ordeal.

[*Be Prepared for Crosses*]

All this goes to show that you will probably meet with crosses and they may not be so far away as you might imagine. Do not readily ask for crosses, but abandon yourself to the guidance of the Master. Follow Him step by step, never wishing to rush ahead of Him or to anticipate things. When we anticipate things we are not always successful, for when crosses come too early, we do not always bear them in the proper way. Hence we should follow the march of our divine Master in all things.

My own affairs seem to proceed rather well, thanks to the goodness of our Lord. The plan of our small enterprise for the benefit of the Negroes seems to get into shape. The bishop will ordain me between now and Christmas; at least this seems probable. If it pleases our Lord, I shall be a subdeacon on the Feast of Holy Trinity, and deacon during the holidays. However, let us wait and see what God's will is. . . .

Adieu, dear brother. Let us give ourselves completely to the love of Jesus and Mary and live in that love, in which I am

Your poor brother

FRANCIS LIBERMANN, acolyte

232

If you want to join us, be ready to be despised and condemned. Do not come merely out of charity toward me.

Letter Six   *La Neuville, September 18, 1841*   *Vol. 3, p. 37*

[Dear Confrere:][1]

Please, keep in mind that we ought to expect much contradiction; and there is already a beginning of opposition,

---

[1]Only a fragment of this letter has been preserved.

I am greatly vilified and moreover, our little undertaking is still scarcely known. On the other hand, all beginnings of this sort invite great contempt, and great obstacles are placed in their way; we should expect every kind of difficulty.

There is one thing I can tell you—namely, that I have no other hope for the success of our enterprise than my trust in our Lord and in His Blessed Mother. This hope is greatly strengthened by the remembrance of everything He has already done for us. But I cannot give you an absolute guarantee regarding the stability of our enterprise. You should be satisfied with confidence in God as I am, and ought to be ready to reap the contempt and mockery of certain persons who do not know us and perhaps also of some who know you. And if it should please our Lord to give free rein to our enemies, you ought to be ready to be humiliated and condemned because you undertook such a risky thing and failed.

I felt a great repugnance in inviting you to come and join us, for I was afraid that you might be prompted to accept because of charity toward me. In such a case your intentions and desires would not have been sufficiently pure. This would have caused me great grief, for it would have been an occasion of scandal for you. I assure you that I prayed to our Lord to keep you from me if a wrong motive were the reason for your joining us.

I see now with great joy that you did not act upon such a sentiment and that you prefer to wait a little—or could it be that this delay was suggested by your director?

Adieu, dear confrere.

> In the charity of Jesus
> and Mary
>
> FATHER FRANCIS LIBERMANN

233

Your vocation does not seem to lie in the secular priesthood. Explain your situation to your spiritual director.

Letter Seven   *Amiens, July 29, 1842*   *Vol. 3, p. 193*

Jesus, Mary, Joseph

Dear Confrere:

I have waited a long time before replying to you because of my illness; and when my indisposition was over I had many other things to attend to. May your charity not lessen because of my negligence.

[*The Secular Priesthood Does Not Seem to be Your Vocation*]

I foresaw the difficulties of which you speak, I believe, and it has always been my opinion, that our Lord does not want you in the world. If you remain much longer in it, one of two things will probably happen: either you will become fickle and superficial, a thing to which your temperament inclines you, or you will become tense.

There is no doubt that it would be best for you to withdraw from the world. You should pray to Mary, your good Mother, begging her not to let you languish much longer in the world. It would be wise to reflect upon your attraction. I do not see that you ought to use more prudence than others who have a less strong attraction for the interior and retired life than you, and who would be advised to follow God's attraction without delay, especially when it is also realized that they have no aptitude for ministry in the world. . . .

I sincerely believe that if you followed the inclinations of your nature, you would be able to work in the world in spite of a certain timidity you would experience. But, when I consider the state of your soul and the interior dispositions which God wants you to have, I feel certain that your relations with the world and with external things would not be helpful to your soul nor to the souls of others. You have no aptitude for such things because of your particular spiritual state of soul. . . .

Here then is what I think about your vocation, in a general way: I believe that you ought to leave the world. We still have to find out where God wants you. In this it is your interior taste and attraction that ought to decide, unless divine Providence guides you by some extraordinary means. I believe that we ought not to count upon such extraordinary signs, although they are the best; for special vocations ordinarily are decided only by attraction, a certain taste or desire of the heart [for a particular kind of work.] . . .

Take courage and don't allow the world to get hold of you. Do not grow weak in the divine love of Jesus. Mary, our well-beloved Mother, will not permit it. On the other hand avoid tenseness and over-eagerness; feel always the freedom of children of God. Construct a temple to our divine Master in the depths of your soul and remain in repose near Him without excessive strain.

[*Explain Your Situation to Your Spiritual Director*]

I believe that you ought to explain to your director that you feel constant uneasiness and embarrassment, that you run the danger of yielding to tenseness and overeagerness or to laxness and fickleness. You should tell him your tastes and distastes, your interior attractions, your greater aptitude for an order of things that is different from that which exists in the world, the little good and perhaps even a certain evil you do in the ministry in the world, and the glory you could give to God if you were withdrawn from the world.

If, in spite of that, your director refuses to make a decision, remain peacefully in the arms of Jesus and Mary and wait quietly and lovingly until you are delivered from the world.

I see only one reason of prudence that may stop him from deciding your case, namely your uncle the archbishop. On the other hand, at present I am inclined to think that he will not raise any difficulties.[1]

In regard to your director, I think that you would do well to keep him for a while, because of the critical time during which you have to decide your vocation. Nevertheless, if you see that your stay in the world will harm you, choose another director. You could perhaps propose two or three to him and he could then choose from them the one he wants to be your director.

I leave you in the arms of Mary, and I shall not cease to pray for you. I hope that we shall finally attain our desire, not that you should come here and join us, or should go to some other place, but that Jesus' will may be fulfilled in you by means of the true attraction and taste He will wish to give you along with the facility of following it.

Remain in the peace of Jesus and Mary and grow constantly in their most holy love, in which I am

Your poor servant,

FRANCIS LIBERMANN
Priest of the Holy Heart of Mary

---

[1] The three preceding paragraphs have been transferred from the preceding passage to this location.

234

Gently accept the bishop's refusal of permission to join us at this time. Avoid both laxity and excessive rigor. Confidently place yourself at the Lord's disposal.

Letter Eight   La Neuville, November 1, 1842   Vol. 3, p. 328

Praised be Jesus and His Cross

Dear Confrere:

[Humbly Accept the Delay in the Permission to Join Us]

Let us love and adore our good Master for anything He wishes to do with us.

I was not surprised when I learned that the bishop had refused to give you permission to leave his diocese, although I had hoped that the Holy Virgin would hear your prayers and help you, and then all difficulties would have been removed. Well, it seems that God wants you to be crucified a little longer in the world. Submit to His divine will and do it in all gentleness and humility, accepting everything that Jesus may desire. Have patience; the time determined by God's providence will come and you will find yourself where you are supposed to be . . .

[Avoid Both a Worldly Spirit and Excessive Rigidity]

While you are still living in the world, there are two opposite shoals that you should try to avoid. One is to let yourself be carried away gradually by the worldly spirit and to follow the ways and habits of the world. The second is to become excessively tense and rigorous; you might even become scrupulous, led by the fear of becoming lax.

Keep a free mind and heart and act externally with a certain indifference, being merely on your guard against developing a liking for the things of the world. Be on your guard against vanity and indifferent to the praises of men. Conduct yourself with gentleness, seriousness and reserve, and do this without making a display of it. Be neither timorous nor daring, neither too slow nor hasty. Remain peaceful and calm in your activity, gently preserving a peaceful spirit and attention in all your doings. I mean, remain master over your interior and over your external actions; remain lord over your own mind. Practice equanimity in all circumstances and actions.

Let your conduct be animated by love of God alone, a love that makes you cling gently and peacefully to the divine Master. You will then not allow yourself to be affected and moved by the things of the world, either by favoring or opposing them. Those who live in the world should despise worldliness and be indifferent to its ways rather than hate, fear or abhor the world. The extreme horror or fear which Jesus gives you toward the world seems to me to be one of the most evident proofs that He wants you in a religious community. It is also a grace the good Lord bestows upon you. Desiring to keep you in the world a little longer, He wishes to preserve you unstained by it. It is better to have an excessive horror for it than to have a liking for it.

Attend social dinners as little as possible. Let them be for you what a beating is for a dog: he avoids it the best he can, and when he sees the club raised above him, he drags himself over the floor with evident signs of dislike and fear.

I strongly advise you to practice the virtues of religious: the love of retreat, silence, peacefulness, retirement from the world except when your ministry requires your presence; finally, the practice of poverty in the matter of furniture, although you should not make this too evident to others, for

191

they might criticize you and trouble you and you might then be led to yield to their criticism.

Be gentle and simple in your dealings with people. Don't be effusive in your compliments and don't make a great fuss, but be polite and considerate in a simple and gentle way, with the intention of winning their souls for our Lord.

Read Holy Scripture assiduously. You have a taste for it and it cannot but do you good. Nevertheless, you ought not to use the time necessary for your work on extra reading of Scripture. . . .

[*Place Yourself at the Lord's Disposal*]

Just one more word then. Put yourself at the disposal of our Lord; put your confidence in Mary and wait with gentleness, patience, love and humility for the fulfillment of God's will in your regard. If our Lord wants you to go somewhere else than with us, He will lead you there. In the meantime remain in peace and serve Him faithfully. The accomplishment of God's designs for you are determined by the circumstances willed by His Providence and the new desires that well up in your heart. . . .

> Entirely yours in the holy charity
> of our good and beloved Mother,

FATHER FRANCIS LIBERMANN

235

There is too much of nature itself in your eagerness to become a religious. God wants to purify your attraction. Sundry counsels.

Letter Nine   *La Neuville, January 8, 1843*   *Vol. 4, p. 75*

J. M. J.

Dear Confrere:

[*Your Own Will is Too Much Involved in Your Desire to Join a Religious Order*]

I believe that our Lord bestowed a great grace on you by delaying the execution of your plans to embrace the religious life. It was necessary that your will should be broken a little. Your desires were not sufficiently docile to the divine good pleasure of Jesus. You realized that the divine Master wanted to guide you; you knew what attitude He wanted you to adopt and the perfect love toward Him which He wished you to attain. He also gave you a certain impulse to enable you to reach this goal; but your own will was too much mingled with it, as is usual with persons who are in your condition.

You had an ardent desire to belong entirely to that good Master who was drawing you, and you made violent efforts in this direction. But there were circumstances that blocked the attainment of your goal, or rather, they prevented you from using the means which you yourself considered most suitable to preserve union with the Well-Beloved of your heart, and you fought those obstacles in head-on assaults.

Those obstacles deprived you of the means you thought would directly lead you to the perfection you so much desired, by uniting you perfectly with Him who alone is the light and strength of your soul. You thus conceived great horror for those obstacles, but in this horror were found purely natural elements of a natural craving for perfection. This horror in turn disturbed your mind, at least to a certain extent, for your trouble of mind also sprang in part from a natural love of perfection. That love was and almost always is accompanied by hastiness, by a feverish desire to attain the desired goal, by impatience and the fear of seeing the object of your desires evade your grasp. Hastiness and over-eagerness are the products of nature; on the other hand, grace uncontaminated by nature produces peace and surrender to Jesus and His divine good pleasure, together with great confidence.

Your fear and horror for those obstacles caused a mental strain and rigidity, and you clung desperately to the means which you thought to be necessary for attaining a true union with Jesus. You wanted to adhere to Him in the midst of those obstacles, by means of natural effort and strain; you held in horror and abomination everything that seemed to put an obstacle to your desires.

[*God Wants to Purify Your Attraction*]

It seems to me that it is this which was at the root of your trouble. I did not dare to explain this to you at an earlier date because I feared that God's own moment had not yet arrived, and I trusted that our Lord would sooner or later enlighten you in this respect. I have preferred to wait rather than to forestall that assistance of our Lord. This, then, is the reason why I believe that He is giving you a great grace when he keeps you a little longer in the world in spite of the great desires He gives you for withdrawing from the world. Wait then most peacefully; that time will come, perhaps even earlier than you think.

The thing for you to do is to labor in the works of the ministry with peace, humility and love. Submit to the divine guidance of Jesus. Aim in all simplicity at belonging completely to Him, in your present situation, waiting until He enables you to follow the attraction He inspires.

He wants you where you are at present. He will sustain you in this situation, and when you have drawn from it all the benefit He desires you to have, He will draw you out of it. This benefit consists in wholly abandoning yourself into His Hands, in having a love that is pure and free from all self-centered considerations, in reposing your soul in Jesus alone, in becoming independent of your own interest, even those that are spiritual, in living a life of sacrifice and constant self-offering in His presence.

[*Sundry Counsels*]

Don't hurry when saying Mass but also don't cling rigorously to the length of time you are taking now. Once you are accustomed to the ceremonies, you will habitually use a half-hour for Mass. Perform the ceremonies as it were mechanically unless you have particular sentiments, and keep your soul united to Jesus; remain mentally prostrate before God's throne, offering yourself while you offer the Sacred Victim.

Work for the poor of your parish, and do not bother the bishop any more for another appointment. Allow our good Master to do what He pleases, and remain flexible in His hands. He gives you attractions and then puts obstacles in their way, because He wishes to break you and make you pliable in His hands; abandon yourself to divine guidance.

Entirely yours in the holy love of Jesus and Mary,

FATHER FRANCIS LIBERMANN

236

Confidence in God. No systematization of the spiritual life. Despite your faults, God remains the same for you. Attitude toward the world.

Letter Ten   *La Neuville, January 10, 1844*   *Vol. 6, p. 11*

Dear Confrere:

[*Confidence in God*]

I am glad to see that you are more calm and peaceful than formerly. The good Master will gradually return your soul to a normal condition under the influence of His grace, after those disturbances that were occasioned by a situation opposed to your tastes and attraction. . . .

It has always been my opinion that God called you to labor for the salvation of souls but also that at the beginning you needed work that was calm and peaceful and that required few relations with the world. This kind of work will gradually increase and your interior powers will simultaneously develop in an atmosphere of retreat which is needed for your interior peace. Strain and violent efforts of zeal will never do you any good.

You are right in saying that you should be neither too sensitive nor too fearful. When God's Spirit is in us we ought to possess interior freedom that is sweet and peaceful. We are then aware of our faults and we know what virtues are wanting to us, but we remain in our poverty before our Lord, full of confidence in Him. In this way we gradually learn to live by faith and to purify our views, as is so well expressed by Saint Ignatius. . . .

LETTERS TO ETIENNE CLAIR

[*Avoid Systematization in the Direction of Souls*]

In regard to the direction of souls, adopt as a fundamental principle that we should avoid impeding or constricting excessively the ones we direct. Let us not prescribe too many rules to them. We ought not to follow any determined system of spirituality; otherwise we will do harm to souls. If your director had constricted you excessively in his direction, if he had forced you too much to follow certain principles, he might perhaps have done you much more harm.

I consider it a point of capital importance in the matter of direction that we leave great freedom to the action of grace. We should distinguish between true and false attraction, and prevent souls from rejecting true attractions as well as going beyond them.

[*Despite Your Faults, Our Lord Remains the Same for You*]

When you have regained peace, you will see that you did not really suffer any loss [through faulty direction]. You will indeed be wanting in some virtues, or at least you will not have them in a perfect degree, but in this you will be like the rest of men. The pursuit and cultivation of virtue is the work of a lifetime; you will notice at least that your past state did not leave you any vices and that it was the occasion for very small losses only. Now, if you had been unfaithful by your own fault, you would have lost much. No! dear friend, console yourself! That was a state of trial in which God put you in order to show that you are not worth much, that you are full of sin, vices, and darkness. You have committed faults, as happens to everyone in that condition, but our Lord remains always the same in your regard.

[Attitude Toward the World]

It remains a source of joy for me when I see that you preserve a horror for worldliness. I was afraid that during the transition from a state of tenseness and strenuous striving to that of interior freedom, you might fall a prey to worldliness. You will lose that feeling of horror for the world later when you have no longer to fear anything from that quarter, and that feeling will be replaced by an attitude of indifference.

Belong to God alone, dear confrere, but at the same time preserve liberty of mind. Make use of creatures, have relations with them, but as if not using them and not having relations with them. This you will be able to achieve through God's mercy.

Entirely yours in the holy charity of your well-beloved Mother,

FATHER FRANCIS LIBERMANN

237

In May 1844 Father Clair entered Libermann's novitiate. Soon after his profession he began to long for his parents and Libermann had to point out to him that a priest "must be about his Father's business."

Letter Eleven   *La Neuville, June 26, 1845*   *Vol. 7, p. 223*

J. M. J.

Dear Confrere:

Your letter arrived while I was on a journey; that is why I have not replied to it before this date. . . .

It is not unnatural for families to ask that their sons or brothers who are priests should live close to them. They act in this according to nature and in a sense they are not doing anything that is wrong. But the priest is a man who is sacrificed to God, who belongs to God alone. He has no longer "father or mother or any genealogy." It is true happiness for a priest to be away from all that concerns nature. We have in us a grace and a virtue that is entirely heavenly, angelic, divine; and we have at the same time a nature that is earthly, low, sensible, corrupted. As long as we are in the midst of things to which our lower nature is inclined, I mean our evil nature, we become natural men; but to the extent that we associate with the things that belong to the higher order in virtue of grace, through our priesthood, we are divine men.

A sponge fills with water when we place it in contact with water; it loses the water and becomes dry when we expose it to the sun. Again, put salt in something that is humid and the watery element which it contains will become predominant and the salt will become watery; put it in the sun and now heat will predominate and the salt will become hard like a stone.

In regard to your attachment to your parents and your longing for them, you ought to keep always engraved in the depths of your soul the reply of our Lord: "Did you not know that I must be about my Father's business?"

It has always been my opinion, as it is that of Father Place, that you should prepare your mother for your departure [for the missions]. It belongs to you to do this gradually; you know her; you know the best means and know them better than I. . . .

I leave you with Jesus and Mary and am, in their most holy charity,

Your most devoted,

FRANCIS LIBERMANN
Priest of the Holy Heart of Mary

238

For a religious, the voice of God speaks through his superiors and not through outsiders.

Letter Twelve   *September 3, 1845*   *Vol. 7, p. 284*

Dear Confrere:

I shall reply frankly, in accordance with your wishes, to the questions you have addressed to me in your latest letter. As long as you had that incertitude, I had to keep silence; but now that you want to make a decision, I shall state clearly what I think about it.

[*For You, as a Religious, Only Your Superior is the Voice of God*]

You tell me that [your uncle] the bishop is the voice of Providence for you. I personally think that he is that no longer, for by the very fact that you entered a congregation, he ceased to have that relation with you. Obedience alone is your guide and the bishop has become a stranger to you. True, his counsel, his ideas ought to make your superior examine things, for the bishop is a wise, devout man and he is worthy of respect because of his episcopal character. But it is not up to you personally to take his advice into consideration so as to embarrass your superiors.

As long as you were the master of your own will, you had to conduct yourself by your own reason, and your reason had to seek light from that enlightened man [the bishop] whom divine Providence seemed to have given you for that purpose. But now that you belong to a congregation, you do not have, or at least you should no longer have, a will of your own; the will of your superiors is for you the will of God. To think or act otherwise would be to overthrow the principles of religious life.

In your present condition, therefore, your reason no longer needs to follow its own light to guide your conduct and hence needs no longer to find a counselor to guide it. One thing is enough for you: that you act according to obedience and according to the spirit of your rules. In virtue of the same principle you are wrong in asking advice from everyone who happens to come along. You should not ask advice of anyone regarding anything that pertains to your vocation and the spirit proper to it. Once you belong to a congregation, these consultations with strangers are contrary to the rules of obedience and good order; they can even at times do harm to congregations.

Moreover, in regard to you particularly, going for advice to various persons is dangerous, and it will cause you very great perplexity. You are in need of consistency of conduct; obedience will do you good and will enable you to rise above the incertitude to which your nature inclines you.

I feel certain that the bishop would be glad to see you take a definite stand. He himself has said that the reason why he took a hand in your affairs was that you were always so irresolute. Speak positively and clearly, and don't constantly indulge in asking him advice regarding things which you ought no longer to examine or judge, things that concern the internal affairs of the Congregation, such as being employed by your superior for one function or another, or being sent to this place or that.

It is my opinion that you should not write to the bishop that you intend to wait for him at Lyons, since he is expected to go there very soon. When he is there tell him positively that you belong to the Congregation, that you have promised to God to observe the rules of obedience as perfectly as possible, and that, therefore, you ask him to let you live as a good religious, a thing you have not done until now.

[*If the Bishop Disagrees with Your Superiors, He Should Address Himself to Them and Not to You*]

Tell him that if His Excellency has some objection to the decision which your superiors have made in your regard, it is to your superior and not to you that he ought to address himself; that you are firmly resolved not to doubt or examine any more what your superiors will ask you to do; that, beside your duty in virtue of religious obedience, such conduct is necessary in order that you may at long last get rid of your ceaseless perplexities.

Father de Brandt is accompanying the bishop; show him this letter and if you wish ask his advice. All the bishop told you to make you stay [at home] was said by him not in his capacity of bishop or counselor but because he is your cousin. He grieves at the sight of the sorrow which your departure would cause to your mother; this is all! But I am sure that if he had seen that you were firmly resolved, he would not have told you those things.

The bishop is too devout, too wise and too filled with the proper administrative and religious spirit, and too well acquainted with [the requirements of] community life, to give you such advice. If the members of all congregations followed your method, in two weeks all their houses would be in disorder.

The great veneration and gratitude which I owe to the bishop and which I feel in my heart, prevent me from explaining myself to him. I would above all fear to cause him pain. Hence I am unable to act, and yet what is happening to you is a disorder which could have pernicious results if it were known in the Congregation. Only Fathers Schwindenhammer and Thévaux, beside myself, know anything about it.

Here are the things that will enable you to speak positively and clearly to the bishop. I intend to send you to

Goree at the end of next October. This island, according to what we have been told by all who have returned after having lived there, is a very healthy place. The Commander of the island said to me that it is as healthy as Paris; and a former Governor said that he had never witnessed a high rate of mortality, and everybody else says the same thing. You will not be more than three weeks' voyage from here, and by steamer even less. In the near future we will have to establish a house in the South or in Rome. If you are unable to get accustomed to Goree, we can then place you in a house in the South.

Adieu, dear confrere. Pray to Our Lady of Fourvières that she may give you light and strength to act according to God and not according to the halting ways of your faulty nature. You should return to La Neuville in September at the latest or at the beginning of October.

Entirely yours in the charity of Jesus and Mary,

FRANCIS LIBERMANN,
priest of the Holy Heart of Mary

239

God's will for you is clearly expressed through your vows, in particular that of obedience. Father Libermann's replies to the questions raised by his correspondent.

Letter Thirteen   Amiens, December 13, 1847   Vol. 9, p. 368

Dear Confrere:

I have failed to reply to your letter of November 15th because of illness. I had been ordered to leave all serious business aside. That, and not any hesitancy about the answer was the reason for the delay. . . .

I spoke to [your uncle] the bishop yesterday. There is no need for me to report the results of our conservation, for the bishop told me yesterday that he himself would do that at once. However, I want to reply to your question of November 15th.

[*For a Religious, Bound by Vows, God's Will is No Longer the Object of a Discussion*]

You want to know the will of God and therefore you ask me a number of questions which are all beside the point and should never be asked. You are in the Congregation and have made your vows in it. All those questions are thus no longer a matter for consideration, and to discuss them in your mind will merely make you a plaything of doubts and of the false lights of your imagination and your nature.

You "wish to know the will of God." You accomplish God's will when you fulfill what you have promised Him before the Angels and Saints. I would have replied to you and given you proper advice at the time when those doubts first entered your mind, but you did not ask for advice. Now you tell me categorically that you made a mistake when you embraced the religious life and that you see this clearly; hence you ask me for permission to withdraw.

I should have used my authority and forbidden you to think any more about that question, and I ought to have refused you that permission. This I would have done in the interest of your soul; but my relations with the bishop and my respect for him made it necessary for me to adjust myself to his views and to make no objections. The bishop gave you an affirmative reply through kindness, and I also said yes without a qualm, without afterthought or regret, because I was doing my duty; and yet I had the intimate conviction that what I was doing would be very harmful for your soul.

I realize that that was not the reply that you wanted. You asked my advice, [you say,] to enable you to decide the matter in accordance with divine Providence, but before receiving my reply you had recourse to the same method that you had used before. Examine all this carefully in God's presence and you will see without difficulty that throughout that time you were misled by an interior illusion.

"Am I in The Right Place?"

Let us now consider your questions one by one. I shall not directly reply to this first question, for it ought not to be asked by a man who is bound [by vows]. Let it suffice to say that you are much more in your place than you would be if you were in the world. If you had remained in it, you would have fallen into great imperfection; you might even have lost both body and soul.

"Did I Leave the Way [God Wanted Me to Take]? What Ought I to Do?"

As to the first point, my answer is *No.* As to the second, I reply: Nothing, except to renounce yourself, to learn to suffer something in body and soul for the love of God, to abandon yourself to His divine will, to obey blindly the superior whom Providence has given you, without examining his character and his ways, to forget yourself and avoid analyzing constantly your actions, desires, capabilities and your past deeds. Your great fault is that you don't know how to bear any sort of suffering. Die to yourself and don't deliver yourself, tied hands and feet, into the power of the devil. It is possible that a wounded self-love has a share in your temptation.

205

"Ought I Not to Fear That My Character, My Faults, etc. Might Cause Disedification to My Confreres?"

Yes, if you continue in the way you have been going. No, if you learn to overcome yourself, to bear something for the love of God, to live humbly, gently, poorly and charitably in the midst of your confreres. No, if you try to get out of your shell and refuse to remain shut up within yourself, if you practice kindness to all.

You repeat over and over again that you feel drawn to solitude, but I tell you now: beware of that attraction. Nothing is more misleading than an attraction, especially when it does not agree with the life in which divine Providence has placed us. Woe to him who attaches more importance to such attractions than to the ordinary duties of his life, for the devil will become his master unless God restores order in him.

You are too fond of that attraction. I believe that it would have led you to the loss of both body and soul. This is my only reason for talking in such a straightforward way to you. It is my duty to procure the salvation of all the members of the Congregation. I may never base my replies on the advantages or disadvantages that they may have for the Congregation, unless the person concerned does harm to the spiritual welfare of the others.

"Will It be Possible for Me to be a Useful Member of the Congregation?"

This does not concern either you or me. Self-love will make you say, "I want to be a useful member." Religious humility on the contrary will say: "My God, do with me what You will. I am ready to sacrifice myself to Your glory. Do with me what seems good to You."

Who are you to try to force our Lord to do something with your help? You say you have that desire. But you don't use the means to obtain the fulfillment of your desires. Moreover, a desire that is not patient and submissive to the will of God does not come from God. It will destroy things instead of building up. Ambitious and anxious desires, desires that excite your imagination so much and lead to those illusions, serve to deliver us forever into the hands of the enemy.

You tell me that your present ministry does not suit you. But is God obliged to cut out a ministry and a life for us that is tailored to all the tastes, caprices, defects and vices of our nature? You are wanting in distrust of your ideas, your tastes, the fancies of your mind and especially your attractions. These, most of the time, are warped by your natural defects, your excessive love of repose and perhaps by self-love; I say by *your excessive love of the repose* and well-being of your soul.

You ought to learn not to do something for God but to suffer everything, absolutely everything, everything without any exception, for the love of God. As long as you remain attached to your own well-being, as long as you flatter your attraction in the way you have been doing, you will be good for nothing. Once you stop being occupied with yourself and have learned to renounce yourself and to suffer everything for God, I promise you a fruitful ministry for the benefit of souls, but not before that.

You have until now lost every opportunity for doing good solely because of your interior tension. It is about time for you to begin the vigorous practice of renunciation and self-forgetfulness. You still have time. Nothing has been lost except time, and that time will not return; you cannot recapture it, but you can make use of the remembrance of past faults to correct yourself.

"Don't All Those Annoyances Make You Fear That I Shall Always Remain an Object of Perpetual Worry for You?"

I reply: If you do what I have just told you, my answer is, "No!" If, on the contrary, you always allow yourself to be propelled by your capricious mind, your imagination and your love of rest and well-being, I must answer: "Yes." But does that matter? God suffers me; why shouldn't I be willing to suffer the weaknesses, imperfections and vices of others? It belongs to you to repress those faults; you can do it, you have the obligation to do it, and I trust that you will do your best.

"The Difference Between Myself and Father Boulanger Shows That I Don't Have the Missionary Spirit."

If you haven't the spirit of a missionary, you haven't the spirit of a priest. The difference between you and Father Boulanger comes from the defects I pointed out to you just a moment ago. People consider such defects as being merely originality, eccentricity, manias. In God's eyes they are vices and infidelities. Forget yourself, renounce yourself, know how to suffer for God and stop pursuing the interior well-being of your soul. In that case the difference between you [and Father Boulanger] will disappear with the exception of your and his individual traits of character.

"If I Were in Charge of a Work I Would Acquit Myself of It as Well as Others."

Yes, if you work earnestly to renounce yourself, to suffer and get rid of your inflexibility and narrow-mindedness. No, if you do not do that.

Moreover, this is not a thing that you have to examine. Your job is to abandon yourself with simplicity and humility into the hands of our Lord. It does not belong to you to determine what should be the conditions of time, place, circumstances and the nature of the work in which He ought to employ you. You should not *talk about works and ministry,* but make yourself fit to fulfill such functions. Now it is in this that you have been wanting, because you have done nothing to counteract your evil tendencies and defects. You have loved God only to the extent that it didn't cost you anything and that He gave you satisfactions, to the extent that your love for God gratified your natural cravings. It is not by acting in such a manner that we make ourselves fit for the zealous ministry, which is a work of abnegation and devotedness.

"Grace and Nature Strongly Draw Me to a Retired Life."

This inclination is one that is rooted in your nature rather than in grace, and it is wicked. If you follow it, you will lose your soul. This inclination has caused you to commit many faults. If this inclination were supernatural, it would show itself as a facility for preserving recollectedness. Being rooted in your nature, it causes you to commit great faults, makes you the prey of many illusions. If God had permitted you to follow that inclination, it would have done you great harm in body and soul. Distrust and resist that inclination.

"I Have Reasons for Believing That a Sedentary Ministry Would be More Suitable for Me."

This is your constant and perpetual mistake. You want God to cut out a ministry for you so that it be perfectly adjusted to you. Your imagination pictures such a ministry as a restful time because it is one that suits you. Yes, it will suit all the inclinations of your lower nature and all your defects, instead of destroying those defects and making you fit to be employed by God in any function He might wish to entrust to you.

As long as you keep that illusion, you will remain in trouble and anxiety, and you will constantly long for another function, different from the one which you happen to have. Moreover, who can guarantee that by going back to where you came from you will find just the sort of work that suits all your tastes? I tell you positively that this will not happen, and any wise man will tell you the same thing.

"I Want Souls"

But is God obliged to grant you what you ask? You should practice greater submissiveness in that respect. Moreover, if you desire to save souls, make yourself worthy and capable so that you will be a faithful instrument in God's hands, and secondly learn to wait for the moment which God will choose. Meditate on all those things in God's presence. Do this calmly and humbly, and our good Master will enlighten and strengthen you, enabling you to walk in the way of peace, humility and obedience. I feel sure that you will then overcome all difficulties and will some day accomplish much good for souls. . . .

Adieu, dear confrere. May the peace of our Lord follow you always.

Entirely yours in Jesus and Mary,

FRANCIS LIBERMANN,
Priest of the Holy Heart of Mary

7. LETTERS TO FATHER MARCELLIN COLLIN

Marcellin Collin was born in 1818 at Pontivy in Brittany. He studied first at the Seminary of Saint Sulpice and then tried out the life of a Trappist at the Grande Trappe for a period of six months (1840). In 1841 he became one of Father Libermann's first novices. Ordained in 1843, he went two years later as a missionary to Reunion, from where he returned to France in 1852. After being director of Holy Ghost Seminary, he became Superior of the house of Langonnet and finally of the Mother House. He died in Paris in 1904.

240

Advice to a departing missionary. Never become angry with yourself because of your faults.

Letter One   *March 5, 1843*   *Vol. 4, p. 134*

J. M. J.

Dear Confrere:

May the holy and abundant blessings of the Most Holy Heart of Mary fill you and accompany you at all times.

I have already made some recommendations to you; let me add a few, although it is possible that in some I shall but repeat what I already told you.

[*Never Become Angry When You Commit Faults*]

Look upon yourself in God's presence as a poor man. Don't be astonished when you commit faults. Never indulge in anger against yourself on their account, but remain very quietly before our Lord in your poverty and humility while you contemplate how wretched you are. Don't be in such a hurry to get rid of your defects. Be willing to remain subject to those weaknesses as long as it pleases our Lord to leave them with you. Remain thus humbly in repose and perfectly submissive to God's good pleasure, not only in regard to what He positively sends you, but also for the things He permits to befall you.

Don't entertain esteem for yourself on account of your talents or your knowledge. Don't trust in your own lights. It is my opinion that the latter was the cause of the temptations [of stubbornness] you have lately experienced. This may have resulted from the fact that this year you enjoyed a better mental development than before and you may thus have felt a certain satisfaction and self-complacency. And this complacency may have inclined you to presumption. This in turn affected your will somewhat and it became more rigid and tenacious.

Now make sure not to yield to anxiety at the sight of those evil tendencies and your temptations. Adopt an attitude of peace and humility of mind and heart, acknowledging your poverty and wretchedness in our Lord's presence. Tend to virtue with all gentleness and peace, trying to correct your faults.

[*Such Anger is Useless and Rooted in Self-Love*]

Never forget that it takes a very long time to get rid of such faults, especially when they contain an element of pride. If you become angry with yourself, become discouraged, adopt an attitude or rigorousness against yourself and those faults, what will you gain by such a behavior? For these dispositions and attitudes are themselves the product of self-love and of a rigid will. The thing to do, on the contrary, is to be patient with those defects until you are freed from them.

212

A multitude of reasons will rise before your mind to make you become vexed with yourself and to yield to agitation. Those reasons spring from self-love, and they do not prove at all that you ought not to bear those faults with patience, gentleness, peace and humility; on the contrary! Here are some examples of reasons that could come to your mind:

"These faults displease our Lord; they prevent me from attaining the perfection proper to my state; they are obstacles to the good I should otherwise be able to accomplish; they arrest the flow of God's graces. All this points to the conclusion that I must endeavor to use the best means to overcome those faults."

True, but the best means without any doubt is that of submitting peacefully, gently and humbly to the pain you feel at the sight of your faults; we have merely to drag ourselves before the feet of our good Master and put our entire confidence in Him. If you proceed in this way, sweetening your disposition, fortifying yourself in Jesus and Mary, humbling yourself peacefully and gently in God's presence at the sight of your wretchedness, you will make infinitely more progress than if you adopt the other method. You must have noticed that this is true and that every time you adopted the method I have suggested you became the master over yourself and over your faults.

[*Humbly and Peacefully Submit to God's Will*]

When you become aware of a fault, don't reason about it, but put yourself immediately under God's hands, and do this with humility, gentleness, peace and the loving surrender which I have described. Above all, avoid bringing in extraneous reasons; such enquiries are useless in any case. For example, you mentioned that you had been ordained too soon to the priesthood, that you should have remained longer in the novitiate. Suppose for a moment that all this were true—but I tell you sincerely that those things are false—well, this would be like regretting that Adam committed original sin which was the cause of all our trouble.

Surrender yourself into God's hands and abandon yourself to His good pleasure. Be pleased not only with the things He does but even with whatever he allows to happen. Humble yourself at the sight of the evil you find in yourself and your wretchedness, but submit peacefully to God's will who permits that evil, and then put all your confidence in His goodness. He will not permit you to remain in that condition forever.

I must end this letter. I have to leave today. A letter from La Neuville informs me that the priest from Aire is at La Neuville with two postulants and that he is waiting for me.

Tell dear Father Blanpin that I have not even started my letter to him. I didn't have the time to write. I beg the Most Holy Virgin to tell him what I should have liked to express to him in my letter. She will do that much better than I.

Adieu, dear son. Your soul will always be dear to me in our Lord. Be always gentle, humble and full of confidence.

> Entirely yours in the holy love of
> Jesus and Mary,
>
> FATHER FRANCIS LIBERMANN,
> Missionary of the Holy Heart of Mary

241

Encouragement of a missionary at the painful moment of his first departure.

Letter Two   *La Neuville, March 19, 1843*   *Vol. 4, p. 145*

Dear Confrere:

I did not reply to your first letter because I thought it would not reach you before your departure. . . . I write now hoping that this letter will be forwarded to you at Bourbon [Reunion], in case you have already left.

[Be Strong Like the Master Who Sends You]

I was deeply touched at the sight of your afflictions, but at the same time I was not astonished. Don't be astonished either, and don't allow tribulation to cast you down. "This is the beginning of sorrows." Do you think that we can save souls without sufferings? Don't you recall our Lord's words: "A woman about to give birth has sorrow"?

Consider yourself blessed when you experience sorrow and pain for the love of Jesus. Don't continue to be weak like a child, but be strong like the Master who sends you. Consider yourself blessed when you experience sorrow and pain for the love of Jesus. Don't continue to be weak like a child, but be strong like the Master who sends you. Consider all the pains and sorrows He suffered to save the world. Do you want to follow another way to procure the salvation of men? No! dear confrere and son, let such a thought be far from you.

You are still a novice in dealing with men. You are not yet accustomed to suffer for the love of Him who died for you, and, not having this habit, you are vexed at the approach of those unpleasant relations and those sufferings.

Have courage, lift up your soul; walk amidst the briars and the thorns; your feet will be torn, but if you walk with courage, you will go forward and reach your destination. Be courageous, dear soul, let yourself be wounded, crushed by tribulations, afflictions, even by death anguish if necessary; but continue to march toward the goal to which the Master guides your step. March on and don't pay too much attention to sorrows and tribulations. You will suffer evils, annoyances, embarrassment, heartaches, mental troubles, humiliations of every sort. But the more you suffer the more your soul will advance in the way of holiness and also the more souls you will save.

[*God Has Chosen You as His Victim*]

Don't indulge in self-pity. Forget self! Does it matter if a poor nothing suffers sorrows and anguish, if this fosters God's glory?

Blessed, a hundred thousand times blessed are you, if your soul and body are sacrificed for the love and glory of Him who has done so much for you, who created you and, at the price of His blood, his labors, humiliations and afflictions without number, bought poor abandoned souls to whom He sends you!

My dear confrere, although my heart is broken with sorrow at the sight of all your anguish, my joy, at the same time, surpasses and almost entirely erases that pain. Who are you that the divine Master was pleased to choose you and to destine you to suffer in His Name, for His glory and His love? What a victim He chose! He immolates you, sacrifices you, penetrates to the very marrow of your bones, to the utmost depths of your soul, to tear up and crush, to sacrifice you completely to His glory. So much the better, dear confrere!

216

[*God Wants You to Sacrifice Your Desire for Solitude*]

You tell me that you look back with nostalgia at the solitude [of the novitiate.] Well! dear friend, there is no doubt about it that solitude is much more pleasant than having to deal with men. Do you recall what I once told you about that in regard to myself? Perhaps you did not then understand what I meant. You now experience the same thing, but don't allow yourself to yield to that inclination. On this earth you should not live for yourself and on your own. It is Jesus who is the lord of your soul. He disposes of it as He pleases; you should not even make any reflection in regard to the execution of His divine will. He does not want you to serve Him in solitude, in peace and sweetness. On the contrary, He wants to cast you into the midst of pains and annoyances which you will suffer in your relations with the world. Be a faithful instrument in His hands, and He will accomplish His glory through you.

You are more sensitive than others. I know that there are few who feel such pains as keenly as you do. So much the better! It enables you to suffer more for Jesus and for the souls you have to save. Don't worry about all that, then, but accept your troubles in a spirit of gentleness, peace, humility and love. Remain humbly prostrate in your littleness at the feet of our good Master. Don't allow yourself to become agitated and do not follow the suggestions of disturbing ideas.

[*No Self-Pity*]

Don't be full of self-pity. The great sensitiveness with which you feel those annoyances is not an evil but a good, for it obliges you to suffer more for the salvation of souls. It is a sword in the hands of our Supreme Priest, by which He kills His victim. But if sensibility is a good, self-pity is an evil. What you need is submissiveness, surrender to

217

God, gentleness, peace and humility of heart in the midst of the pains and contradictions you suffer on the part of men.

During your novitiate I often repeated to you what your conduct ought to be in such circumstances. Pray the divine Master to help you put those suggestions into practice. I feel sure that you will commit faults in the beginning. This should not astonish you; you will learn how to act by and by according to the rules which you now know only theoretically.

[*Listen to the Voice of Jesus, Speaking in Your Heart*]

Don't grieve because at present you find yourself, as it were, abandoned to yourself. Say to yourself, in the depths of your heart: "I am not alone but He who sent me is with me." It is about time for you to become a man. You must accustom yourself to listen to the voice of Jesus who speaks in the depths of your soul and to be molded according to that divine Model through the power and the guidance of His divine grace. Have confidence, pay attention to the divine words He addressed to His apostles at the moment of His departure. They were then in a situation similar to the one in which you are at present.

Until now you have enjoyed the sensible presence of the divine Master through the instrumentality of one who took His place and had the grace and power to guide you. Although the latter of himself is among the most wretched of men, the weakest and most incapable, he was Jesus Christ Himself for you. He had His wisdom and power; your soul was in peace and repose in the presence of that divine Master.

But now, like the Apostles, you are abandoned and obliged to address yourself to that Lord of souls only through the channel of pure faith. But this, precisely, is incomparably better. It is a reason for joy rather than for grief. Moreover, this makes your sacrifice so much greater, for you don't receive the same amount of human assistance.

[Confidence in God]

The divine Master repeats to you what He said to His beloved Apostles: "Let not your heart be troubled nor let it be afraid." Faith in His Father and in Him is enough for you. It will enable you to have Him always with you. "Fear not, little flock, for your Father has been pleased to give you a kingdom." Why and what do you fear, dear son? Jesus gave you His peace before He sent you [to the missions]; He has also left you His peace; hence your heart should not entertain any fear or anxiety. His Divine Spirit will be your Master; have confidence and abandon your soul to His guidance. . . .

Adieu, dear confrere.

Entirely yours in Jesus and Mary,

FATHER FRANCIS LIBERMANN
Missionary of the Holy Heart of Mary

242

Remain in God's presence as a victim to be immolated for the salvation of souls. Conduct aboard ship.

Letter Three   *April 1, 1843*   *Vol. 4, p. 170*

Jesus, Mary, Joseph

Dear Confrere:

[Remain in God's Presence as a Victim]

This now, I hope, is the time, more than ever, when our Lord wants to use you for the salvation of a great number of unfortunate and neglected souls. Hence I must confess that I have rejoiced in my heart while at the same time shedding tears at the news of your sufferings. Suffer, dear friend; Jesus also suffered to save the world. It is precisely when your heart is torn to pieces that you live through a most precious time. Open your heart to Jesus; prostrate yourself before Him and His heavenly Father and offer yourself to all the torments and tribulations that accompany labor for the salvation of those souls.

Let your soul be torn and broken. Let it be like the grain of wheat that is crushed so that it can be given to the hungry poor. Console yourself, beloved confrere; the more God's goodness tears up your heart, the more it will make His grace develop from it, enabling you to feed those poor souls that are so empty of God and His love.

Are you going to feel sorry because you have to suffer? Reflect how greatly your sufferings will foster God's glory and serve the salvation of those wretched souls that are the prey of the devil. Courage! Have courage dear confreres!

Deliver yourselves to sufferings, to labors and to the most intense sorrows. This thought, which I expressed to you on other occasions, should be always before your minds prompting you to remain constantly in His presence as a victim, as a target for all the darts He might wish to direct against you.

Does it matter if a wretched man suffers all his life and even for all eternity if such a thing be necessary? Are we not created for God? Are we not His property? Is He not allowed to do with His property what He pleases? It has been His wish to make you His chosen vessels, and this was not for your glory or your well-being. It was for the glory of His heavenly Father and for the increase of the spiritual riches of His holy Church. If He wishes to use you to your own disadvantage, you have no valid objection.

Remain peacefully and lovingly before Him then, and let Him tear and crush you as much as He pleases. It is sometimes He himself who makes you suffer; or He uses men to cause you grief; or certain circumstances hurt you; or you will have to suffer from the very souls whom He sends you to save. It doesn't matter. Don't reflect upon such things. Accept the pains and the sorrows whatever be their source; accept them as coming from His hand for your own sanctification and that of those He entrusts to your care. Accept as certain the principle that the more pains and interior sorrows you suffer the more souls you will save. Abandon yourself to Jesus, then, forget yourself and your own well-being, desiring that Jesus alone may be praised, glorified and loved by all creatures.

[*Conduct Aboard Ship*]

The way to conduct yourselves on board ship is very simple. Accept peacefully any pain and annoyance which some passengers may cause you. Do not show your grief; oppose no one; don't get mixed up in their disputes and wrangles of any sort. Practice indifference in the depth of your souls. At the same time, however, learn from those contacts to know the spirit and character of men, refraining at the same time from judging or condemning them. This will teach you how to deal with all, and you will gather experience for your future conduct in regard to men. . . .

In general be kind toward all. Don't talk freely nor unburden yourself to everyone with whom you come into contact. Try to be pleasing to all; console them in their pains and seek to distract them when they feel bored. Enter into the views of others when they are in accord with God. Take no notice of what is defective in what they say, for this is not the time to speak, and you would gain nothing from your criticism. As you know, prudence dictates that

221

you be in good relations with everybody. Act thus with them, and do not act or speak like one who is superior to them in mind, judgment, piety, or conduct, but be modest, humble, gentle and kind toward all.

Have recourse to God alone when you have trouble or interior trials. Seek in God alone the consolation you need, and try to console all, in a great spirit of modesty, charity, humility and simplicity; and you will gain the upper hand without anyone noticing it.

Don't argue even when they say the most foolish things. Follow your rule; remain occupied during your voyage; don't bother anyone; try to satisfy everyone and be always kindly disposed and affable, ready to listen to those who need yor advice and to render service to all. Do all this without tension, over-eagerness, or affectation; but be gentle and calm, moderate and simple. You may then feel certain that our Lord will bless you.

In regard to Father Launay, be affable in your relations with him. But don't get mixed up in his quarrel with the Prefect Apostolic and with others. Don't seek his company; even for the sake of charity do not seek him out. Be polite, reserved and moderate in your exterior conduct toward him. This is about all that I consider proper to tell you regarding those matters.

Rejoice, dear confreres and sons, because Jesus is pleased to give you a share in His holy Cross; no greater happiness could come to you. Belong entirely to Jesus through Mary and with Mary; all the rest is valueless.

Adieu, my very dear confreres and friends. I will always remain united with you in Jesus and Mary and will remember you in the Holy Sacrifice of the Mass. We finished our novena [for you], for we thought you had already left because an easterly wind has been blowing here for the last two weeks.

Adieu.

Entirely yours in Jesus and Mary,

FATHER FRANCIS LIBERMANN
missionary of the Holy Heart of Mary

243

Crosses are useful for your sanctification. God is withdrawing from you all sensible consolations to make you live a life of pure faith and perfect surrender to him.

Letter Four   *March 8, 1844*   *Vol. 6, p. 98*

Dear Confrere:

[*Crosses are Very Useful for Your Sanctification*]

Your letter filled me with compassion for your soul in its present affliction. I trust that this very pain which God's goodness sends you, or at least allows you to undergo, will be very useful for your soul. Such afflictions seem to be almost a necessity in the beginnings of religious works. A ministry that gives you so much consolation, that brings you success among the good souls whom the merciful Lord entrusts to you, the affection of those dear people and your tender love for them, all these might have done you harm if you had also enjoyed perfect interior peace of the kind you imagine and desire. Or at least your intentions in your labors might have been less pure, and your works might gradually have been spoiled without your noticing it.

Crosses, pains and interior embarrassment are precious safeguards against all such dangers. Hence submit peacefully to God's will which lets you suffer those troubles. Abandon yourself confidently to His divine good pleasure and His adorable guidance. If you adjust yourself properly to your condition you will commit less faults in your conduct. And if there are defects in it, don't worry, for God knows how weak and poor you are. He also knows the desires of your heart.

Souls that generously sacrifice themselves run no dangers. God's goodness passes over their small faults. Answer me, dear friend; do you commit those faults out of malice? Surely not. Do they show ill-will? No! I say "no" without any hesitation, although at times it might seem otherwise to you. All your faults are sudden spurts; they are weaknesses, and these very weaknesses are most often accompanied by a certain agitation which lessens their sinfulness. Now, it is certain that God readily forgives such faults and that that sort of fault does not prevent the action of grace.

[*God Wants You to Live Henceforth a Life of Pure Faith*]

In regard to the present condition of your soul, it is possible that you are a little mistaken in your appraisal of it. I really think that your interior state is about the same as when you were here; there is only less and less sensible devotion; you have gradually less feeling of God's presence.

You know, dear confrere, that you walked then in great simplicity and experienced very little sensible devotion, although there still remained a certain feeling that it existed. You no longer experienced that lively affection, but you had a slight and intimate realization of the way you stood with the divine Master. This sufficed for you and you were pleased. Although your satisfaction sprang from the fact that your soul was attached to God and you were pleased seeing that you stood well with Him, that satisfaction was not wholly pure. You were still too dependent on your feelings, on sensible emotion, and did not yet want to be without such emotions, without a feeling of security that was based on such emotions, or rather without both the feeling of security and those emotions.

You realize, then, that your soul was looking for support; it desired contentment; it did not want to live by God alone in a spirit of faith and independently of all pleasure at the sight of your interior state. But now God wants to force you to abandon your soul to Him alone. He deprives you of all support. He wants you to live in a spirit of pure faith, with a hope that is based on His goodness alone and not on an interior condition of soul of which you are conscious. He wants you to live in all simplicity and perfect charity and to labor for His glory with pure and honest intentions, refraining from using His divine graces for your own satisfaction.

You might possibly get satisfaction when reflecting upon what you find in yourself, but it will not be self-complacency at the sight of God's grace in you, and this grace will more fully animate your actions. God allows you to have consolations in your ministry, but he does not want you to experience joy in the interior grace which He gives you. Rest assured that those graces are constantly producing an increase of holiness in you.

[*Holiness Does Not Reside in Sensible Feelings*]

This sort of holiness will not be in accord with your own ideas, but it will be in conformity with God's ideas and designs regarding your soul. You form a concept of a certain type of holiness which you imagine God demands of you, and when you are unsuccessful, judging things according to your plans, you grieve. But this is your mistake, dear friend; it is not your idea of holiness that has to be realized. You battle and you torment yourself, but you will never be successful in accomplishing things according to your own views.

You imagine that your holiness ought to be something that you can feel. Now this is not so; it must, on the contrary, be an attitude of the will. You should remain before God with your will, your desire, peacefully occupied with your labors, contented and tranquil and without feeling anything. This is a state of entire privation; it is incomparably better and more perfect than a state of soul in which you feel things, although being deprived of such feelings seems to be wrong, at least in the beginning.

You do wrong in trying to put yourself in a state that conforms with your own concepts; you are trying to feel things, when you ought to live in pure faith and pure good will. Your efforts are a sort of strain; they are not a sentimental effort, for you are wanting in sentiment, but you live in a state of inertia, of incapacity, for God's goodness wants you to act in a more spiritual way and through pure faith.

You strain with your will in following the false idea you have conceived, and your mind is in the dark. Your idea of perfection is rather a phantasy; it is not really something you believe in, nor is it based on a view of your intellect. Hence what you call "remorse" ought not to be called by that name—at least this is so most of the time. It is an embarrassment of your mind that is based on a faulty phantasy or on a worry springing from the darkness of your mind.

[*Be Patient with Your Own Faults*]

Don't will so eagerly; don't strive so vehemently to reach sanctity in accordance with your concept of holiness. Be supple and flexible in God's hands and docile to the guidance of His grace. Don't take a fancy of your imagination or a movement of your will for an inspiration of grace. Walk in all simplicity and honesty. Preserve peace of soul at all times. Do your best tranquilly, without strain or tension. Leave to God the care of perfecting you in harmony with His wishes.

In the meantime bear your weaknesses with peace and patience. Avoid rigidity and tenseness as the greatest evils. Believe me, you will have better results. It is not necessary at all to have a sensible awareness of the presence of God and of your union with Him. Your will tends Godwards; this ought to suffice for you. But there is more, for your mind is united with God at times when you think it is least united with Him. Be satisfied with your present state of soul and don't seek to put yourself in the state which you imagine you should have. It is a real fault to make efforts in the latter direction. Live in peace and with confidence in God's mercy. Banish fears and strain, for these are purely on the natural level. Have great freedom in your actions, as is proper to a soul that desires to belong to God.

When you do something that is faulty, humble yourself in all peace. You worry because you feel unable to open your soul to [your Superior] Father Le Vavasseur, and you are wrong. I assure you that I felt quite certain beforehand that sooner or later you would not be able to have the same openness with your director as [with me] when you were here. If you were still with me, you would now have the same feeling toward me that you have toward him.

[It is Time for a Manly Spiritual Life]

At the beginning, when we are still in the way and state of sensibility—you were still in that state during your noviti-ate, although less toward its end—we are in a state of child-hood; we need someone's guiding hand. This is an imperfec-tion. I do not mean to say that direction, obedience and open-ing oneself to a spiritual director are an imperfection, but the need for them is an imperfection, since we then still lean on a creature. Later, when that sensibility has disappeared, when we live more by pure faith, we become men. God leads us by way of faith. Pure faith presupposes that there is no longer any sensible support of our conduct; hence we are then disposed to be deprived of everything and even of spiritual direction.

It is certain that you are now in a state that has gone beyond that of sensibility, one in which pure faith ought to reign. Remain then purely and simply attached to God, and don't worry if you have nothing on which you can lean. You have God, and God alone; this should be enough for you. It hurts, it is hard, for it seems that our whole life then becomes, as it were, a shadow. The soul seems void and apparently has no more spiritual or supernatural life. But we are greatly mistaken; our interior life has become more pure, more simple. I said "this hurts," but only in the beginning, before we have submitted and have abandoned ourselves perfectly to God.

If, when you receive this letter, you have not completely overcome yourself in this, do it immediately. Give yourself, body and soul, to God, and don't seek any more for support in a creature. The time of childhood is past; the mature age of Christian perfection must begin for you. "When I was a child, I felt as a child, I thought like a child. But now that I have become a man, I have put away the things of a child."

This is no longer the time to be carried around in the arms of a father. You must walk alone. Don't worry so easily when something is wanting to you. A child weeps when someone makes faces at him; a man does not weep even when someone beats him with a stick. Be stronger, therefore, and don't easily yield to pusillanimity. Don't think immediately that you are on the wrong road, that something is wanting to you, as soon as you are not in the state of soul that is the object of your own desire. As soon as a child is tired, he wants to be carried by his father, and if the father refuses the child weeps and grieves. A man, however, continues to march by the adult strength that animates him. Your manly strength is your faith and confidence in our Lord and His holy Mother.

Continue your spiritual direction with simplicity of heart; tell your director what may be useful for you. If there are things that trouble you excessively and you don't know how to explain them, you need not tell them, and don't worry about those things. Our Lord wants to replace all and everything. I think you will not lose anything through it.

[Abandoning All Desires and Worries, Live Only for God]

Dear friend, don't strive to be in this or that interior state; but be pliable and practice indifference in God's presence. Let Him give you what He pleases and do with you and in you what He wishes. You live in privation. This does not matter, provided your soul truly belongs to our Lord. I feel sure that your soul belongs to Him in spite of the small troubles in which you sometimes find yourself.

The same thing applies to [the study] theology and to all the rest. Don't desire anything and don't worry about anything. If you find time to study theology, do it; if not, be at ease. You must not have anything anymore on earth to sustain you, but only God, through faith and charity, and without the accompaniment of any feeling. Theology served formerly to keep you in a state of sensible repose; but sensibility is a thing of the past for you. You must now live in a state of privation, based on pure faith, pure interior charity, and without sentiment, but with complete confidence in Jesus and Mary.

Live in peace and don't make violent efforts which would only make you act against the holy will of Jesus. . . . Take care of your health . . . and don't kill yourself [through excessive work]. On the other hand, avoid worrying about your health. Commend it to the care of Jesus and Mary. . . . *Adieu,* dear Father.

Entirely yours in the charity of the Most Holy Heart of Mary,

FRANCIS LIBERMANN
priest of the Holy Heart of Mary

244

We have undertaken many works at the same time, but what can I do? God forces us.

Letter Five   *{August, 1844}*   *Vol. 6, p. 321*

Dear Confrere:

I cannot let this opportunity go by without sending you a short word for yourself, although I have nothing particular to say.

Don't be angry if I don't send you help for your poor Negroes of Bourbon. I believe that by the very fact that we are sending missionaries to Madagascar you will get more men from time to time and it may even happen that at a later date the community of Bourbon will be much more important.

Take courage and don't get angry if things do not immediately run to perfection. You must realize that I am not doing what I want. Divine Providence directs our affairs in spite of myself. For I assure you that if I had followed my own ideas, I would carefully have avoided undertaking so many things at the same time. I am afraid of this, but what can we do? Can I resist the will of God that forces me absolutely? Our poor human prudence does not extend very far.

It is possible that my fears will be changed into gratitude toward God's goodness because He has led us thus with drums beating. According to human judgment, it is imprudent to undertake everything at once, but God will provide and make up for things when He obliges me to act entirely against my own likes. Moreover, my fears are not such that I believe that great evils will result for the work. All that might happen is that we might be obliged to neglect one part, or even to abandon one, if this were necessary. God will make known His will and designs. Let us not cling stubbornly to our ideas; let's not be unbending. Things will go badly if we permit our poor human prudence to battle against Providence.

Our affairs have developed in such a way for the last two years that I don't know what to think of them; and I would consider it a crime to resist the things that are taking place. Judging from the turn things are taking, I believe that in two years' time we shall have everything concerning our missions regulated and fixed. We must allow ourselves to be led by divine Providence . . .

Adieu.

Entirely yours in the charity of the Most Holy Heart of Mary,

FRANCIS LIBERMANN

Priest of the Holy Heart of Mary

245

Worrying about your miseries impedes your progress in holiness. Consider Jesus' mercifulness.

Letter Six   *{November, 1844}*   ***Vol. 6, p. 429***

Dear Confrere:

I must write a short word to you. I learned that you have been ill; but the good Lord has not yet desired to take you, for you are still too wicked! You must finish the "eight years" [you have promised yourself]. We shall then let you go, but not before that.

[*Do Not Worry About Your Miseries*]

My dear friend, work for the glory of our good Master. Have a free mind; never yield to anxiety or trouble on account of your miseries. Every time your soul is peaceful, you will more easily overcome yourself and grow in holiness. When you are agitated you are worthless. You become mean toward yourself, toward the good Lord, and toward man. You have no reason for yielding to anxiety in the midst of your miseries, for you have all the divine Master's love in your favor, and it is to this love that you should constantly sacrifice yourself.

Be of good will; and you are, dear friend! If so, be at peace, for "peace unto men of good will." Give yourself wholeheartedly to the service of Our good Master. Do not count the number of distractions you have in your meditation; your soul belongs to God, that suffices. The flesh, that is, the sensible part of your nature, is as nothing in the balance against a will that is sincerely attached to God. Divine grace is in you. Rejoice, then, and proceed with confidence. God is fighting for you; remain in peace!

[*Jesus is Merciful*]

Some faults will, as it were, escape you now and then; the good Lord will purify you of them in other circumstances. Don't worry about them, God does not count and reckon things so rigorously when it concerns souls that desire to belong entirely to Him alone. Jesus' conduct toward you is full of mercy. Remain in His mercy, and don't fear His justice so much. Moreover, if you commit some small foolishness, you will merely have to take a few "beatings" in Purgatory, but not many, for the divine Master will purify you before you leave this earth.

Don't be a coward and don't entertain so much fear for the "beatings" that will purify you. Avoid committing faults, but if you fail through weakness, don't worry.

Always consider Jesus merciful rather than severe. This will be profitable to your soul. Mary, after all, our good Mother, ought to be of great assistance to you. Avoid rigidity, try to be gentle in your interior at all times. Don't be harsh; always lean to the side of mercy and gentleness. This is what you should attend to, for you have a strong inclination to the opposite and herein lies your great fault.

We are all well here. Father Le Vavasseur will give you the news, good and bad.

Don't be angry because we have undertaken the mission of Guinea, which has cost us so dearly. God desired it. Keep quiet, adore Him, bless Him, and don't reason about it. He will repay us a hundredfold for what we have lost and will give us the means to save Guinea. . . .

Adieu, dear confrere.

> Entirely yours in the charity of the Most Holy Heart of Mary,
>
> FRANCIS LIBERMANN,
> Priest of the Holy Heart of Mary

246

Jesus loves you despite your faults. The reproaches you experience do not come from Him but from yourself. Do not try to "break your character." Purity of intention. Mental prayer and union with God. Relations with your confreres.

Letter Seven   **January 29, 1845**   ***Vol. 7, p. 34***

J. M. J.

Dear Confrere;

[*God Wants You to Be Patient with Your Imperfections*]

Your letter of May 1, which I received not very long ago, touched me most deeply. There is one piece of general advice I must give you: accustom yourself to living at peace with your enemy. Let me explain. You have a troublesome character, a temperament that torments you. Don't put it into your head that it is absolutely necessary for you to get rid of it, but convince yourself that it is God's will that you should live with that enemy. Submit peacefully to this divine will, bear yourself with patience and gentleness. Don't yield to sadness, pain, or disappointment. When your temperament has shown the tip of its ear or even sometimes has shown its whole head, making you act harshly, humble yourself, regain your peace of mind, and forget all about it. Be convinced that your sentiments of unyielding harshness are not as wicked as you imagine. This harshness is a trait of your temperament in spite of yourself. You are impelled that way before you have the time to make a contrary act of the will. Once your interior is stirred up, you need time to restore your balance. All violent efforts are fruitless. In such moments you have nothing to do except to remain humbly submissive to God's will which permits you to remain in that condition.

[*Jesus Loves You in Spite of Your Faults*]

You may rest assured, dear son, that if you submit humbly to the divine Will which permits you to groan under the weight of your imperfections, if you join to it peace and confidence in the goodness of Jesus, you can be certain that the good Lord will be pleased with you.

What a joy you gave me comparing me with the divine Master! Yes, certainly, when every week [in the novitiate] you returned to me to tell me all the faults that you had committed through frailty, my heart was full of tender compassion for you, and all those faults did not shock me in the least. I knew that you had once more forgotten yourself, that they were frailties which in turn aroused your will to give yourself entirely to God. How much more then does the divine love of Jesus go out to you with all tenderness. If such a thing were possible, His love would increase on the occasion of those frailties.

Our Lord knows better than anyone else how extremely weak we are. Be at peace therefore, dear friend, and feel certain that your soul is agreeable to Jesus. Don't torment yourself; you are not saddening His divine Heart. At least you did it much less frequently than you imagine, for most of the time your will has no share in the wickedness of your lower self, and if it does take part in it, it is usually because it is taken by surprise.

What can you do? You have a very bad temperament. You must live in peace and with humble submission to God in this respect. You want to belong to God; you do belong to Him and will later be more truly attached to Him. Always revive your courage; work, sacrifice yourself for the glory of the Master.

Don't be dissatisfied with your lot; the imperfection of your nature is compensated for by greater interior graces which you do not notice, graces which are fruitful in spite of the wickedness of your character. This wickedness will serve to keep you poor and small at the feet of our Lord. It is like the fertilizer we put on plants to make them produce more.

[*Your Feeling of Remorse Does Not Come From God*]

You are wrong thinking that the remorse of which you speak is our Lord's reproach to you. No! dear confrere. Jesus does not speak so harshly to your soul. He loves it too much for that. The very harshness of the reproach shows that it is your wicked nature that is its source, and its voice is raucous. I beg you, for the love of God, don't listen to that so-called reproach. Boldly and fearlessly despise that voice; turn away your mind from considering it. I take upon myself all the evil that might result from this; I myself want to bear responsibility for it before God. Don't take the voice of the wolf for that of the lamb. Be convinced that those reproaches are not remorse or inspirations of the Holy Spirit. I will answer for that with my head if necessary. Here is the proof:

1. As I have just told you, those interior clamors have the same sound, they are of the same kind as your temperament.

2. They never give you courage; you will never, or at least almost never, be able to follow them.

3. Those interior activities do not lead you to God. They cause you to be occupied with yourself and with all sorts of things, and they excite your imagination, whereas the voice of our good Master is sweet and peaceful; it inspires courage

for the accomplishment of what it proposes and directs the soul Godwards.

You consider that "your state is a punishment." This is a serious error. Don't reason about that; be content with belonging to God and sacrificing yourself for His glory. Suffer your miseries as I have told you above, and keep your soul in peace. I repeat and repeat again what I have already said: Our Lord Himself must be the director of your soul. This is true not only for you but it is true for every apostolic man.

Consult, however, [your superior] Father Le Vavasseur in regard to your interior life. Don't do it in order to find consolation, but sacrifice yourself to the divine Master. Consult him in order to avoid acting presumptuously and so that you may preserve simplicity.

[*Do Not Try to "Break Your Character"*]

I must return to what I said a moment ago. Don't talk about "breaking your character, crushing the hardness of your character." We don't break iron; we soften it in the fire. The line of conduct I have traced for you is the only one to follow: It softens your harshness and rigorousness to the extent that the good Lord desires it. Hence don't be too much in a hurry to get rid of that fault. Don't desire it with excessive eagerness and don't put too much ardor in that tendency. This would do more harm than good; it would make you lose peace, interior humility, submission to the divine will and confidence in God.

You may sigh gently under the weight of your chains, but be patient. When you are alone with our Lord, don't make any reproaches to yourself, have no remorse, turn your mind away from your faults and give yourself peacefully to God's love with confidence, humility and surrender to Him.

I repeat once more that those reproaches spring from your own nature, from your particular character, sometimes even from self-love. Despise them and speak trustfully with our Lord instead of speaking harshly and anxiously with yourself.

If you were called to render an account of your state of soul at this moment, you would not be in as bad a condition as you imagine. The crude imperfections that are found in you are not voluntary; moreover, they are purified by interior grace to a greater extent than you think.

[*Purity of Intention*]

In respect to purity of intention, I have only a few words to say to you. Self-love, self-interest, self-complacency in your actions: these are enemies which you can overcome only by despising them. The more you take such sentiments to heart the more they will trouble you. They are enemies which will die only at our own death. You must suffer them with peace and humility. Reject them by despising them, by indifference, by looking on them as out of place. They will gradually diminish and finally disappear almost entirely, though not altogether.

[*Mental Prayer Should Not be Forced*]

Mental prayer is an important affair and yet quite simple. You must make your method of mental prayer as simple as possible. You need not make numerous considerations. Do not seek to execute every detail of the method of Saint-Sulpice; you would not succeed. What, then, ought your mental prayer to be? It should consist in a simple, calm and fully confident repose in our Lord's presence; this is all. Don't seek to make many reflections or to produce numerous affections. Absolutely nothing you do during mental prayer should be "forced." Remain before Jesus like a poor child before its father; nothing more. Don't seek to utter to Him the sentiments you have or would like to have; don't make efforts to express your needs to Him. Remain before Him in all your poverty and weakness. Put yourself at His disposal in order that He may do with you whatever He pleases.

Look upon yourself, in His presence, as a thing that belongs to Him, as a thing of which He can dispose to the whole extent of His wishes. And you should do this without effort and without many words, whether interior or exterior. It should be a habitual attitude of the soul, which remains constantly in His presence and which, during meditation, is isolated from everything else for the purpose of showing the divine Savior what it is to Him. This manifestation must be done without labor or strain. Remain before Him with the will of being at His disposal. Content yourself with casting a glance toward Him from time to time for that intention. When distractions assail you, try from time to time to dismiss them gently and without anxiety, by casting a peaceful glance toward Him to whom you belong.

[*Union with God During the Day*]

In the course of the day act likewise. From time to time cast a glance without effort but with the intention of belonging to Him, and accompany it by the awareness of your poverty and wretchedness. But all this must be done tranquilly with the peaceful desire of belonging to Him in spite of your wretchedness. Don't seek more than that.

In seeking contact with our good Master act similarly, allowing Him to direct you; do not prescribe anything to Him; do not formulate plans, imagining that things ought to be this way or that. Be content with being in His presence, at His disposal, and abandon yourself to His guidance like a blind man, without seeking too much to talk to Him or to hear Him speak to you. Be at His disposal, abandoned to His direction, placing all your trust in Him alone.

[*Relations with Your Confreres*]

Continue to act toward your superior as you have been doing. Don't be afraid. I will not listen to everything he will tell me in order that he may be discharged of his function. I know him as well as you do. It is perhaps because of your difficulties with Father Blanpin that he has wished to be discharged of the superiorship. He did not tell me anything about that, but this might be the case. Do all you can to give him the consolation of having peace in the community.

Dear Father Blanpin is a child of the good Lord; he is extremely simple and very good. It is your character that is the source of all that trouble. However, don't torment yourself on that account; this will not last. Have as few relations with him as possible. Nevertheless, do not avoid him, and don't make it appear to him that you are shunning his company. Try in every way to be kind to him. You cannot imagine what pain a good, fervent soul suffers from such opposition. This is a time of temptation for him; it will pass and he will be very good. . . .

Entirely yours in the charity of the Most Holy Heart of Mary,

FRANCIS LIBERMANN,

Priest of the Holy Heart of Mary

247

I must confess that I have made a mistake. But, do not expect that everything can be perfect, not even in a religious congregation.

Letter Eight   *January 28, 1846*   *Vol. 8, p. 40*

J. M. J.

Dear Confrere:

I begin where you leave off. You are distressed because I don't write to you. . . . Don't suspect that I am forgetting you; far from it! . . . Fine! I prefer to see you cast yourself into God's arms, forgetting all that is dear to you, and then to receive consolation for the forgetfulness of which you thought I had been guilty, but I can assure you that my heart is very close to you.

[*I Must Confess That I Made a Mistake*]

Now let me immediately speak about the grievous wound I have inflicted upon you by sending you poor Father Plessis. You two (Father Le Vavasseur and yourself) are trying to crush my heart and you are right. I deserve it, for I am very guilty. But what can I do? I made a mistake when I accepted that kind of person and am still wondering why I did it. Father Plessis was better then than he is now; he was regular and had sensible fervor, but I could and should have foreseen what would happen. I thought of it, reflected upon it and felt it. I am truly without excuse before God. I am perfectly in agreement with you if you wish to send him back to me; I shall then have the opportunity to expiate my fault.

Your letters hurt me greatly, but the violent pain they caused me was a great consolation for me. I committed a fault; I deserve to suffer, and I must offer something by way of expiation.

If I sent Father Plessis to Bourbon it was because I thought that Father Le Vavasseur was the man most capable of managing him. But it was my mistake, for instead of that he himself became discouraged and imagined all sorts of things against us. And you, my little man, entertained the same thoughts. But set your mind at rest, my dear confrere; things are going much better here than you think.

You can rest asured that we will never accept any one into the Congregation whom we do not consider to have solid virtue, devotedness and ability to acquire the religious spirit. We shall make frequent mistakes, but this occurs in all congregations. . . .

[*Do Not Expect Perfection in a Religious Congregation*]

Your views regarding the administration and the direction of a congregation are as impractical as mine are with respect to the politics of Louis Phillippe. If I had followed the plan you gave in your letters—and I mean both of you— the Congregation would already be dead and buried. Leave me the freedom to act. You should presume that our Lord will grant me the grace of His divine light for the administration of the work of the Most Holy Heart of His dear Mother. I may be unfaithful and might be caught occasionally, but don't believe that God will abandon me to such an extent to my blindness that I shall upset and destroy the hopes of a work that is dear to Him.

You are bad philosophers. You conclude from the particular to the universal. You reason: one unworthy or incapable candidate was accepted; therefore everything is lost; therefore I am careless. . . . Now, note well that we are

242

still in an unsettled condition of affairs. We have not yet
the personnel that is required to conduct our Society with the
complete regularity we should like; and we are still without
the material resources that will be needed. So why not wait
a little? Give us the chance to get settled; but you are
terribly impatient!

You cannot conceive, dear friend, how difficult the beginnings of works such as ours are! What solicitude, what
troubles we have had to pass through to obtain what we
now possess!

Don't be so severe in your judgments, dear confreres.
If you had been in my place, you might have committed
greater faults and more numerous ones than I am guilty of.
I am truly tempted to think that this would be the case,
judging from the rigor and inflexibility which you want us
to use. I am longing for the time when the good Lord will
give me a Council. You cannot imagine how hard and
painful it is to be obliged to do everything yourself. . . .

I want to add another observation, although it is a
repetition of one I have made before; I mean that you are
judging things a little too much from a highly speculative
standpoint. You have such an optimistic view about religious
life that its realization will not be found in any religious
society. In practice it is impossible for a community to be
composed of men who are perfect according to your
standards. . . .

Adieu, dear confreres. Although you have both given me
a scolding, I love you just the same and with a most profound and lively charity. May the peace, the strength and
the love of our Lord Jesus Christ fill your souls.

Entirely yours in His divine love and in the love of
His Holy Mother,

FRANCIS LIBERMANN,

Priest of the Holy Heart of Mary

243

248

Discouragement is unworthy of a servant of God. Such a feeling is disagreeable to God. Remember that we are not doing our work but His.

Letter Nine   *{1847}*   *Vol. 9, p. 62*

J. M. J.

Dear Confrere and Son:

Give me a strong scolding because I have not written to you for so long a time. However, if you had been here you would have understood that I was not at fault.

During my absence of five months I was not able to write, and at my return I was overwhelmed by urgent business and had to attend the new arrivals, who numbered forty. Then there were the Brothers. Each of them wanted to speak to me about his spiritual affairs. All this was of great importance, for I had to know whether things had gone on all right during so long an absence . . . Then there was the affair of buying the abbey of Notre Dame du Gard. . . .

[It is Unworthy of a Servant of God to Yield to Discouragement]

And now let's come to your own business. It would seem that you and your confreres in Bourbon have yielded to discouragement. This has pained me greatly. Our Lord has sent me many afflictions in the work He has put in my care, but I can assure you that none has been more painful to me than seeing you suffer pains and anxieties. There is nothing bad in suffering pains and even anxieties in the service of God.

These trials are given for your sanctification, to make you more flexible in His hands, more humble, more detached from yourselves and more confident in God. But to yield to those anxieties and to allow them to agitate you and cast you down is not worthy of servants of God. What else have we to do on this earth except to put ourselves, body and soul, into God's hands so that He may dispose of them as He sees fit and that we may be wholly sacrificed to His glory?

[Any Movement of the Soul Which Tends to Discourage or Trouble Us is Disagreeable to God]

Let's have no other thought in mind except that of walking in the way traced for us by God's providence and endeavoring to foster His glory and save souls. If we wish to be faithful instruments in His hands, we should not be occupied with ourselves. Let's stop worrying about our own person, and walk with simplicity before Him, doing the work that lies before us with peace and confidence. Let us never occupy our minds with the future nor torment ourselves about the past. Let us now, in the present moment, put our soul into God's hands in all peace, humility and gentleness, having no other desire than that of abandoning our lot into God's hands, sacrificing ourselves to His divine will every moment of our life.

God's goodness will often try us. Let us be docile, peaceful, and humble in His hands. Let us not yield to sadness nor permit our imagination to disturb us. When we allow sadness and our imagination to trouble us, we not only do wrong but we do harm to our soul and to the souls of others, and we very often compromise God's own work. In general, any movement of our soul that tends to discourage us or give us trouble is disagreeable to God. If we yield to it, we open wide the gates of our soul to the devil. He will not fail to profit by it to destroy us.

[*We Are Doing God's Work, Not Our Own*]

Your discouragement in our present circumstances causes me embarrassment. . . . I intended to send you men, but I don't dare to present them to the Government for fear that your discouragement might afterwards oblige me to change my plans. I hope that this will not happen. . . . In any case don't yield to discouragement. Place everything in God's hands. It is not our work we are doing but His. We are not seeking our own interest, but His—saving souls for Him. He has the power to give it success. If He wishes to arrest our efforts this concerns Him alone.

We should avoid judging and analyzing the conduct of our Divine Master and content ourselves with praying and waiting. My dear friend, for the love of God, be more strong-hearted, more detached, and less excitable. . . .

Entirely yours in the charity of the Holy Heart of Mary,

FRANCIS LIBERMANN

priest of the Holy Heart of Mary

249

The tendency of missionaries to neglect their religious life in favor of apostolic labors endangers many souls.

Letter Ten   Notre Dame du Gard, September 21, 1851
Vol. 13, p. 293

Dear Confrere:

Before replying to your letters of July 16, I shall say a word about the affairs that occupy us here at present.

Yesterday, September 20, we held the last meeting of the Council. The whole day we discussed the general situation of the Congregation and the measures that ought to be taken to consolidate it and especially to maintain it in the Spirit of God and in sound discipline.

[*Missionaries Easily Tend to Sacrifice Religious Life to Apostolic Work*]

We have reached a moment when there is a pressing need for taking serious measures to insure the good of the Congregation. If we had taken such measures before this time, it might have been too early. Taking them later might prove to be too late. We have to safeguard ourselves against an imminent danger that is inherent in all missionary work. It is a danger that threatens every community, every missionary at a particular stage of his labors. Being full of eagerness and being prompted by a zeal inspired by God, they want to devote themselves totally to the work in which they are engaged. They are tempted to sacrifice to it the Rule, submission to the orders of superiors, and the community spirit.

If we were to yield to such a temptation, it would mean that after a few years the Congregation would be dislocated in all its joints. God knows what would become of the holy enterprise which He in His wisdom has entrusted to us, a work for which we have already made and are still making great sacrifices.

[*They Become Totally Absorbed in Their Work and Lose All Religious Spirit*]

The missionary, the superior, and the ecclesiastical head of a mission, each in his own sphere, see only the work with which they are charged, the good that lies before them, and they launch themselves into the field of battle with all the ardor of their zeal. They become totally absorbed in their particular work and forget that they belong to a body of men who must march together. They free themselves too easily of the bonds with which God bound them together.

In this way there are as many isolated men as there are missionaries. The gains that were temporarily made by them will eventually be counterbalanced by hundredfold losses.

The missionaries behold souls to be saved and work to be done, but community life seems to them to be an impediment, and they get rid of it. They think that by living holily, according to the spirit of the community and in the observance of the Rules, they will not do as much good or save as many souls as if they had freedom of action. So they follow their eager desires and sacrifice community life. There is then no longer any regularity, no more interior spirit, no more relation of obedience with superiors than is consonant with their ease. At least there is no longer perfect obedience, and the bonds between communities and the Superior General and the Mother House are broken.

[By Weakening the Bond of the Congregation, They Cause Great Harm to Souls]

They think they are inspired by zeal, but in reality they follow the impetuous urge of their nature. They console themselves for the loss of their interior spirit and community life by the consideration of the good they have done for souls they wanted to save, and fail to take account of the evil they are doing to themselves and to others. They accomplish a small amount of good and do evil on a large scale because they weaken the bonds of the Congregation, destroy all hope for its perseverance in fervor, and deprive it of the mighty power that springs from a united march and a strong discipline.

A dislocated body cannot move. It exists only for suffering. What purpose could be served by the Congregation if it were reduced to that state by the imprudent zeal of its members? How many souls will not be lost because of such imprudence that sacrifices everything for a present advantage? When a missionary lets himself be guided by such effervescent zeal that is not directed by the Spirit of God, he exposes himself to losing thousands of souls in order to save one.

It is our duty therefore to occupy ourselves seriously with the vital question of the general discipline of the Congregation. We must carefully watch the ardor that devours you who are in Bourbon, the ardor that destroys regularity in Mauritius, an ardor that is also felt in Guinea. We have resolved to be on our guard against the egoism of individual missions, communities and missionaries. When they are interested only in the work in which they are directly engaged, they sacrifice everything for it, and this, if you examine it well, is clearly selfishness.

[*As a Superior, You have the Duty to Secure the Observance of the Rule*]

I am not at all making reproaches to you. Father François will tell you that I have always been satisfied with the community of Bourbon. I know that you have always done all that was possible in the circumstances in which you were placed. But I want to put you on your guard, you and your dear confreres, against the natural tendency of a missionary and the future dangers that will result.

Try then to do all in your power to maintain the good that already exists among you and to better conditions. I believe that your present situation is more favorable to community life than the previous one. You need no longer worry about what the civil authorities might say, nor need you worry too much about the opposition of the clergy. The only precaution you have to take is to come to an understanding with the bishop. He will understand very well that we are not permitted to infringe on our Rules. . . .

Watch over the effervescent ardor of Father François! Don't let him kill himself and don't let him set aside the Rules and obedience. I approve your prudent conduct in regard to his fasting. Father François should fast only to the extent that his health is not endangered.

Entirely yours in Jesus and Mary,

Francis Libermann, Superior

8. LETTERS TO FATHER STANISLAS ARRAGON

Stanislas Arragon was born on May 6th, 1819 at Chapareillan in the Diocese of Grenoble. He entered Father Libermann's novitiate in September, 1843, and was ordained the same year. Together with Father Tisserant he left for the island of San Domingo (Haiti) in 1845. After the failure of this mission, he was transferred to the mission of Guinea on Africa's west coast. He died at sea on his return voyage to France in 1855.

Father Arragon was a man with a most violent temper, little self-control, and a penchant for extreme measures. Advising a confrere about the "real savage" who was going to be stationed with him, Libermann wrote: "Trying to make Father Arragon a man of moderation, polished and amiable in his measures would be like trying to build castles on the clouds. It would be easier to stop the sun in its course."[1] Hence it is not surprising that Libermann on occasion had to be quite firm and use rather severe language in his letters to this recalcitrant priest. Yet he loved Father Arragon and knew how to handle him "firmly" and "without allowing him to meddle in things that do not concern him."

250

Father Libermann explains that the acceptance of a mission in Australia was not undertaken lightly and should not be a reason for dissatisfaction among the African missionaries.

---

[1]N.D. Vol. 8, p. 113.

LETTERS TO CLERGY AND RELIGIOUS

Letter One　　　　*{December, 1845}*　　　　***Vol. 7, p. 403***

Dear Confrere:

Let me begin with the thing that has given you so much grief. I thank the Lord because you experienced grief at the news that we had accepted to work in New Holland [Australia]. For it shows how attached you are to the poor Negroes. Persevere in your attachment to the work undertaken for the salvation of those who are the most neglected among men. . . .

We had strong reasons for accepting that distant mission, so strong in fact that all here agreed upon undertaking it. The situation of Guinea was extremely uncertain; there was a possibility of abandoning Bourbon; Haiti was in a desperate condition; and Madagascar was out of the question, because we did not want to risk another disaster.

I know very well that our conduct should be based entirely on confidence in God. We must, nevertheless, not neglect the means which Providence offers us for the stability of the Congregation. We must have the same confidence that God will send us enough men to support the missions confided to us. Provided we don't act lightly, we can count on God and our hopes will not be confounded. . . .

Don't worry. Guinea will, I hope, always be our cherished mission. It has cost us too much not to be dear to us. . . .

I agree with your remark about what Father Briot said to the effect that the Europeans who live on the coast are as much "neglected souls" as our Negroes. Very well! Let's do ministry for them. Let us not allow them to perish when we are able to help them. But do not forget that this is only an accessory ministry. . . .

[No signature]

251

Furious about the acceptance of the new mission in Australia and the appointment of a superior he did not like, Father Arragon wrote a most violent and abusive letter to Libermann. The Venerable replied in a severe yet fatherly reprimand couched in the following terms.

Letter Two   *May 8, 1846*   *Vol. 8, p. 142*

J. M. J.

Dear Confrere:

I received your terrible letter of March 25th. If I didn't know you, that letter would have caused me the most profound sorrow. I shall, nevertheless, tell you all that is in my mind regarding it and do it in all simplicity.

1. [*Your Lack of Self-Control Endangers the Mission*]

If you continue to act in the way you have been doing, you will wreck the mission, no matter what else you do. Or, at least, you will nullify the natural talents, the zeal and the graces God has bestowed upon you, and you will be a curse to your confreres. You will merely discourage them and be an obstacle to them in their works. That is why I beg you for the love of Jesus and Mary, use moderation and don't follow the promptings of your fiery nature.

Let me now take one by one the remarks you have made in your letter and reply to them.

I want to say first in a general way that you plunge into activities with excessive eagerness and excitement. Realize that the Spirit of God is not in such behavior. Stop and ask yourself whether the radical way in which you judge things is in harmony with the mind of God. If I were

253

ninety and had fifty years of experience behind me, I wouldn't dare to speak about things in the categorical way you do.

There is presumption in talking that way. And yet I feel certain that it is not presumption that makes you speak that way. God knows that I eagerly desire that you make observations regarding everything and I want you to do it in a spirit of obedience. But I wish you would express yourself with more calm and moderation. Though being morally certain that there is no presumption in it, this element will enter into it and there is danger that it has already mingled somewhat with your remarks.

2. [*Do Not Write Letters When You Are Furious*]

Your language is too abrupt, harsh, excited, and bitter. For the love of God don't write any more when you are in such a state of excitement. Calm yourself and let wisdom be your guide when you express yourself in writing. Consider and judge for a moment: You tell me you were ready to form an agreement with your confreres for the sake of choosing another superior and refusing the one I am sending you. Read and examine the Rules and see whether they permit such a thing. Consult the Rules of every congregation and order in the world and tell me: Do you expect to find any that allow that sort of thing?

Examine yourself in God's presence and ask yourself if you are acting according to the Spirit of Our Lord, according to the Gospel. Let us suppose that I am the worst of men, that I am, moreover, what you think I am, that is, that I have no confidence in any of you, wouldn't you have to submit to God's will in virtue of obedience? Otherwise what would become of the virtues that should be practiced in the Congregation? What would become of union, charity, religious cordiality, if a member could safely act in that independent way?

3. [*I Formally Order You to Accept the Superior I Have Sent to You*]

You accuse me of not having confidence in anyone of you. This is completely untrue. Is it right to maintain that I have no confidence in a missionary because he is not named superior or prefect apostolic? I certainly have sufficient trust in Father Bessieux, for I am naming him superior to take the place of Father Briot. I certainly have enough confidence in you since I have named you first assistant for a post from which the superior will most probably be absent for a long time.

I must confess that your last letter causes me anxiety. You have a terrible antipathy toward Father Gravière. If you continue to behave as you have done, God alone knows what the result might be. Why not recollect yourself, let grace act in you, be faithful to it and don't surrender to the wicked promptings of your fiery nature. Be docile like a child. Treat Father Gravière with respect, and the affection that are due to a superior, to a representative of God. Your language about him is abominable. Suppose he does make mistakes, suppose the works suffer because of his mistakes, suppose much harm is done on that account, does this concern you? You will not have to give an account to God for that.

Calm yourself and don't upset everything by your impetuosity and excitement. Moreover, the matter is settled and it was decided even before I received your letters about it. Should you now break all the rules of religious life and bring disorder into the community because I didn't follow your opinion or have made a mistake?

I command you, therefore, in the name of Our Lord Jesus Christ to accept Father Gravière with affability, charity,

with the sentiments you owe to superiors.[1] Why would
you wish to discourage him? He has already experienced
enough repugnance toward accepting that mission. He is
severe but just. He is active, wide awake, and knows how
to make decisions. I want you to write immediately to me
and assure me that you will behave properly toward him.
Do all you can to encourage him, to preserve peace and union
with him and among all your confreres.

4. [*Any Observations You May Have to Make Should be Presented with Humility and Without Anger*]

You wanted me either not to name a prefect apostolic
or to give the nomination to Father Bessieux. But it doesn't
belong to you to act as judge in that matter. As bound by
obedience, you should submit to the will of God in respect
to the superior who is given you.

If you have observations to make, do it modestly, calmly
and with submission to God. I love and sincerely respect
Father Bessieux, but I did not think it proper to present
him as a candidate for the function of prefect apostolic. You
should assume that I have examined the question in God's
presence.

You object and tell me that Father Gravière did not
stay long enough in the novitiate. Granted—but the circumstances were so pressing, so extreme, that I felt obliged to
go beyond the Rules and make an exception. Believe me,
such a procedure is as painful to me as to you. Your reproach revives vividly the pains I felt when I saw myself
obliged to take that extreme step. I am determined never
again to send anyone to the missions before he has finished
his novitiate. My heart bled when I felt obliged to transgress
the ordinary rules.

---

[1] This is the only example of a command in the name of **obedience**
found in Libermann's correspondence.

You reason endlessly, regulate, settle affairs, because you don't realize what it means to administer the Congregation, and lack experience. Hence don't denounce my conduct the way you have done. I can't render you an account of it, but believe that I am not acting inconsiderately.

You are doing wrong, dear confrere. If Father Gravière is insufficiently acquainted with the Rule, you should encourage him by your good example and thus make him adhere to it. Watch yourself never to make observations to him when you are excited. Calm yourself and speak to him with gentleness and modesty. You may and must instruct me regarding his conduct, especially in regard to the Rule. Do this, it is your duty. But, I pray you, never do it in an excited way, for you will put me in a quandary because I will not be able to judge whether your observations are right or wrong.

5. [*We Do Not Have to Accept Your Advice About Affairs That Do Not Concern You*]

You state that I pay no attention to your advice. I don't know what advice you are talking about. I have always been careful to act taking account of your ideas. I cannot act otherwise than seeking information about the condition of the country where you live and I have always urged you to give me details.

I think you are speaking about Australia, but your advice cannot make any change in that project. You have conceived the idea and you continue to repeat that that new mission will cause a loss to the mission in Guinea. What can I do to eliminate that thought from your mind? I don't see any connection between the Australian mission and the ruin of that of Guinea. I have already told you and will continue to repeat that Guinea will be our first mission and that we will take the very best care of it. You may be sure that you will more quickly become discouraged about that mission than myself. If I were to send to Guinea ten missionaries instead of the seven which you now number, would you achieve more at the present moment? Would you find work for them?

Hence let me act. The general administration rests on my shoulders. You did not receive the grace of state to argue about that matter. You state that we are giving to the mission of Guinea a direction that is diametrically opposed to the conviction of the missionaries. This is totally false. On the contrary, we have adopted all your views and are completely in agreement regarding the way we should proceed.

You have expressed the desire that we ought not to accept Australia, but that has nothing to do with the direction of the mission of Guinea. You have your own reasons which seem serious to you in your opposition to Australia. But to us those reasons seem valueless while ours are grave. Would you have wished me to follow your advice in a matter that in no manner regards your mission, and to discard my own view? But in so doing, I would also have discarded that of all our confreres who are at La Neuville. Suppose that we had considered your view to be wiser than that of all of us, we would not have been able to follow your advice because you are not acquainted with the Australian situation.

Hence do not permit your mind to be darkened with violent ideas. I am ten times more attached to Guinea than you are and am more interested than you in its success. I am better acquainted with the situation, have more experience than you have, and I see no way in which the good of Guinea is compromised. Moreover, even if you were more capable of deciding such things than I am, you had no right to rebel against a decision that had been taken so conscientiously.

6. [*Overwhelmed with Work, I am Unable to Write as Often as I Should Like*]

You make the reproach that I am not writing to you. First of all, the majority of your letters did not require any reply. They were instructions that were useful to us and I wish you would continue to send such information. If I were not overwhelmed with work, I would reply to every single one of your letters, but I have no one to help me in the administration and so am forced to limit myself to the necessary. Have pity on me then. Am I not suffering enough already because I am unable to converse with you as much as I would like? There is really no need to prod me to action in this matter, but what can I do? I simply am unable to do what I would like. Be patient. As soon as I am able to entrust the direction of the novitiate to someone else, I will find more time to send encouraging letters to the missionaries. I have always replied to all letters which required an answer or when it was useful. In all probability my letters do not reach you as fast as you would wish, because of the slow means of transportation. I have sent you more than eight letters.

7. [*No Decision Has Yet Been Made About Our Jurisdiction*]

You reproach me also for not having instructed you regarding the [question of the extent of our] jurisdiction. I did so in a letter as much as I was able and I have told you that I would act for that purpose. Nothing has yet been decided. I shall go to Rome in order to determine that personally. I have even told you in one letter not to build yet in Dakar until that business is arranged. You have begun to build because you did not receive my letter in time, but I was unable to write you earlier. As soon as the doubt arose

I wanted to stop that work. Decisions about jurisdiction are not made in one day. You must practice patience. It is a necessary virtue for a missionary.

8. [*I Do Not Want "to Send My Missionaries to Their Deaths"*]

You tell me that the Government is deceiving me. That is false. I know the state of affairs in that regard. You say that "I want once more to send my missionaries to their death, but that this time they will refuse to go." You do wrong in saying this to a man who loves you more tenderly than you have been loved by your father and mother, and who would prefer to die himself rather than to see you die. You add: "They will not go." I know that, speaking absolutely, they may not be obliged to go there, but you commit a fault by stating such a thing. I tell you also that they will not go. I have told Father Gravière to examine the matter thoroughly. I write the same thing to you and the others and tell you not to go [to the proposed new post] if that country is unhealthy.

This is my rule of conduct, or rather these are the principles that guide my conduct with the Government. We can march without the Government, but we cannot march against it. If the Government is against us, the mission will soon be ruined. Hence we must treat it with consideration and prudence and yet act in all things according to the Rule, that is, through the orders issued by the spiritual authorities.

9. [*I Do Not "Despise Our Missionaries"*]

You say something horrible in your third observation: "Take care lest your missionaries whom you and your grave councillors despise, despise you in their turn." But, dear friend, why allow anger to guide you? In regard to Father

260

Schwindenhammer to whom you allude, he is perfectly inno-
cent of all that your impetuosity prompts you to say. I beg
you, calm yourself, for you offend God. Moreover, when I am
in Rome, I shall give an account of our conduct in respect
to the Government and feel sure that it will be approved. If
they disapprove, I will obey the orders that are given to
me. . . .

I am grieved because of what you say about Father
Schwindenhammer. He sacrifices himself for the Congregation, he spends himself for it, he is as much interested in
its welfare as I am myself. I add that he has a very good
spirit, that he knows the spirit of the Congregation, that he
is a pious and reliable priest. I cannot understand why you
have allowed yourself to become so aroused in his regard. It
is not he who has been instrumental in determining the acceptance of Australia. And if he had done that, he would
have done a good thing.

10. [*Control Your Imagination and Your Temper*]

Hence let that question of Australia alone. You are permitting your imagination to be fooled by idle fancies. If I
had fifteen missionaries at my disposal, I would not send
three more men to Guinea. That work must first be well
started and put on a solid foundation. Only then will its
needs become clear, and I will send you the confreres that
are needed.

As regards Father Gravière, you are exaggerating things
and your violence could do harm to your relations with him.
It is not at all Father Schwindenhammer who has given me
advice in this regard. It is solely because of the embarrassment of that moment that I had to take that step prema-
turely. It still grieves me now, but it was necessary, absolutely necessary to take this step. Moreover, you should
in no way seek to control my conduct, for you do not know

the state of affairs. Try to console your superiors when they are in a difficult situation, instead of grieving them even more by reproaching them for things they feel most sorry they had to do.

Be careful in your relations with Mohammedans. Do not speak against Mohammed. Do not use brusque methods. You would risk ruining exerything. Follow the method you chose at the start, namely, that of winning their confidence.

I shall pray with all my heart to our Lord that He may grant you peace, moderation, docility and charity. Do not become discouraged because you have given free rein to your temperament. Regain peace and God will be with you.

Best regards in the charity of Jesus and Mary.

Entirely yours,

FATHER FRANCIS LIBERMANN

252

Libermann expresses his sorrow for having had to speak so forcefully in the preceding letter. Gentleness and consideration in the relations with confreres. Prudence and moderation in dealing with government officials.

Letter Three   *September 13, 1846*   *Vol. 8, p. 288*

Dear Confrere:

[*I am Sorry I Had to be So Outspoken in My Preceding Letters*]

My last letter must have caused you profound grief. I tell you truthfully that my heart was oppressed after it had been mailed. I have felt the same sorrow every time my mind reverted to it. I am doing nothing for God's glory while you sacrifice yourself, and I then come along and afflict you in the midst of your labors by a letter that would distress you! Yes, this thought oppresses and afflicts me.

However, it was necessary, for I was afraid that there would be disorder and trouble in the mission. Foreseeing the loss of souls that would result from that disorder, I saw myself forced to act. I earnestly beg you, dear confrere, be a little more moderate, and preserve peace among our confreres and good order in the mission.

Do not worry about the future. The things I have arranged in Rome and which, according to the Cardinal, should be effective will, I hope, put the Mission in good condition and will serve as a remedy for all the fears you have shown in your terrible and famous letter.

[*Be Gentle and Considerate with Your Confreres*]

Work therefore at all times with zeal and fervor. Never yield to discouragement; be always gentle and calm, humble and peaceful with your confreres. You can always count on my most tender affection for you. Try to be less abrupt, less rigid. Watch over your self-love when you are successful and arm yourself against discouragement in times of failure. . . .

Your scrape with Father Lossedat is ugly. You acted too brusquely. Try to win him back. Treat your confreres with consideration, do not hurt their sensibility. Be indulgent toward them when they have real defects, even when they commit true faults. You ask whether you were right or whether it was Father Lossedat who did the right thing. Father Schwindenhammer has given me an analysis of it. I am not able to give a precise answer to that. But I can tell you that Father Lossedat felt certain that he was right. However, due to agitation and grief he upheld something

which he knew well was not so. Do you now see how
important it is to handle your confreres with consideration?
Very great evils result from a want of forbearance and a
lack of union with them. . . .

[Moderation and Prudence in Dealing with the Government]

Regarding your relations with government officials and
commercial agents, you as a missionary should avoid yielding to impatience. You are all terrible men; you understand
nothing about the business and the administration of a
mission. You will do great harm to it and create many
difficulties and obstacles if you follow the promptings of
your fiery spirit. But if you act with prudence and moderation you will greatly lessen the difficulties. Being impatient,
you all repeat that it would have been preferable to refuse
the proposals of the Ministry.[1] This shows that you know
neither men nor things. You may be sure that if we had not
accepted those proposals, far from being free in our religious
work, we would have suffered great restrictions. We would
have run the risk of losing the mission.

Relations with government officials will be necessary as
long as we are on the coast. They are found everywhere and
have the power in their hands; they can impede and even
nullify all our efforts. If we had refused the help they offered,
it is certain that they would have been most distrustful of
us and you would have met with great opposition on their
part.

Since they are representatives of a political government,
they could easily have found good reasons for putting obstacles in your way. But now they are supposed to trust us
and you should do your best to eliminate any reasons for
distrust that might still remain. Conduct full of moderation

---

[1] The Government had offered aid and protection to the missionaries.

and prudence will win their confidence. You shouldn't be surprised that they act harshly and cause you trouble. They are soldiers; most of them have no religion and are prejudiced against you. Act in a way that will give you freedom for your ministry. Act with gentleness and prudence. Don't give in to anger because of the faults they may commit against you, however great, or whatever the nature of their failings. . . .

May the peace of Our Lord be with you.

Entirely yours in Jesus and Mary,

FRANCIS LIBERMANN
priest of the Holy Heart of Mary

253

Religious regularity. Be slow to judge, submissive to your bishop, and moderate in your views.

Letter Four   Amiens, November 19, 1847   Vol. 9, p. 320

Dear Confrere:

I am worried because I don't receive any news from you. It is now six months since I received word from you . . . Yet it seems that you have recovered from your illness. So let me have news in the near future. . . .

[*Religious Regularity is Important*]

According to Bishop Truffet's letter the community is doing well. The Rules are observed and the confreres attend peacefully to their religious exercises and their studies while waiting before they engage in active ministry. I think that time will come soon for you to spread out; your community will be smaller but in a year or so we shall increase it sending you new confreres. Regularity and the spirit of piety are most important in your community, for it is there that we shall send those who have just finished their novitiate. It will be like a second novitiate for them while they are becoming acclimatized. This kind of second novitiate will be very useful, for they will be able to make an immediate preparation for their struggles amidst particular dangers and arm themselves with the virtues that will be specially needful.

Take the necessary precautions to insure the preservation of the spirit that now animates the community. It is possible that there might be relaxation during the bishop's missionary journeys. You should all persevere in a life of recollection and piety. . . .

[*Watch over Your Judgments*]

I trust that you are living in agreement with Bishop Truffet. Let me make an observation in that respect. . . . Watch over your judgments. You are young and inexperienced. You will be prompted to judge according to appearances and the way you have dealt with persons until now. Bishop Truffet is a type of man that differs completely from that of most men we have dealt with. Although I myself have not received any education, I know that his type is totally different from mine. The difference in ordinary conduct which in me results from my lack of education has its source in him in his particular turn of mind and his character, as well as in the great energy and superiority of his mind. His mind is vigorous and is strongly colored by his imagination, but the latter does not prevent him from making safe and correct judgments. . . .

Grace and the sublime character of the episcopacy have no doubt caused a development of his character and his ways

266

and given him an increased power for doing good. Because of a lack of understanding and on account of your fiery temperament and your disposition to discouragement, you may have yielded to excitement and done wrong. There might be occasions for this, for a man with such a clear-cut and definite character as is possessed by Bishop Truffet has always some defects that are not fully controlled. Such vigorous and eminent minds easily fall into error and exaggeration.

[*Try to Submit Peacefully to Your Bishop and to be Moderate*]

You would do wrong if you yielded to vexation on that account. Calm your mind. Remain humble and submit peacefully to things you think you could legitimately object to. Remember that he is the superior of the mission. He is the bishop, he is responsible before God, not only for his actions but also for yours. He has received a special grace for that mission. Follow him with simplicity and renounce your own judgment. God will reward you for it. Union between all the missionaries will be the stronger and more perfect good will be accomplished.

If your soul suffers, and I know you have to put up with certain things, if your ideas differ from those of Bishop Truffet, . . . it will be for your own benefit. You have an ardent mind; but suffering will serve to rein in your impetuosity and abruptness. Learn to become moderate in adopting an opinion, to defend it peacefully, to relinquish it with humility, and thus to conform your judgment to that of others, especially to the judgments of your superior. I don't know whether those remarks are in order. In any case they are useful.

Your mother sent five hundred francs for you. She is somewhat troubled because she did not receive any news from you for such a length of time. I put that sum to the account of your mission. Write to your parents. . . .

Adieu, my dear confrere. May the peace of our Lord Jesus Christ be with you!

Entirely yours in Jesus and Mary,

FRANCIS LIBERMANN,
Missionary of the Holy Heart of Mary

9. LETTERS TO FATHER CHARLES BLANPIN

Charles Blanpin was born at Ligny-lès-Rely, in the Diocese of Arras, on May 10th, 1817. He studied first at St. Sulpice and then entered as a deacon in Father Libermann's novitiate in 1842. Ordained to the priesthood in the same year, he left in 1843 for Reunion with Father Collin. Having lost the use of his voice, he returned to France in the Spring of 1846. He was cured at the Shrine of *Mater Admirabilis,* Trinità dei Monti, Rome, on November 7th of the same year, and returned to Reunion in 1847. In 1856 he went to the island of Mauritius, where he labored seven years. After four years in Bordeaux, he was appointed to Martinique in 1867. He died there in 1890.

254

You have been sent to sanctify souls and not for your own satisfaction. Always retain control of your emotions. Brotherly love.

Letter One   Feast of St. Joseph, 1843   Vol. 4, p. 150

May Jesus and His holy love reign in your soul!

Dear Confrere:

I would have liked to reach you by letter before your departure, . . . but you are now probably on the high seas. . . . We are so certain that you have left the port that we are going to start the novena of prayers [for a safe journey].

[*You Have Been Sent for the Sanctification of Souls and Not for Your Own Satisfaction*]

Be full of confidence in God's goodness; He will not abandon you. You have met already the kind of difficulties that always accompany our first contact with men. Don't worry on account of the pains they cause you. You were not sent there for your own pleasure but for the salvation of souls. You must labor for their salvation and sanctification in spite of the sufferings that are attached to such work. Our good Lord deigned to save men by dying a most cruel death for them. Consider yourself fortunate when you can suffer some trouble inflicted by men, for it is a sign of God's good pleasure in regard to your labors.

Avoid worry and don't become harsh toward them. . . . When men are mean toward us, we should treat them with great kindness and suffer them with patience. When we have to act and combat their evil ways, we should avoid any trace of ill humor and self-love in our reproof, for such evidence will produce an evil impression on the minds of the persons concerned. . . .

[*Always Retain Control of Self and of Your Emotions*]

Tell Father Collin that it is most important for both of you to be always masters over yourselves and your emotions in your relations with others. If you suffer grief, humiliation and the like, don't allow those feelings to lord it over you. Be their master in the presence of God and in the presence of men. Before God, in the sense that you are not the slaves of those sentiments and that they do not make you act against His will, but in a way that is uniform and submissive to His adorable guidance. Before men, in the sense that your emotions should be so controlled by you so that they do not unduly influence your senses. Be masters over yourselves in such a way that people will not know what is going in you. Still less should you act explicitly with the design of showing what is going on in you. Being thus masters over yourselves and acting as if you were not stirred up by a lively emotion, follow God's will and you will procure His glory.

Practice equanimity, uniformity of disposition at all times. With such a conduct you will go far and very soon you will be masters of everything the good Lord wants to make subject to you for His glory. If, on the contrary, you give rein to your emotions, you will do many foolish things and men will be your lords and masters as it were.

[*Brotherly Love*]

Live together like children of God, in all gentleness and peace. Suffer each other's small and great defects, act in harmony and union. You are serving the same Master and seek only His glory. You are employed in the same work. The same spirit of charity animates both of you. Don't be men but angels of Jesus Christ. You act as men and not as angels every time you yield to ill humor, even if you do not manifest your sentiments to the other. You have gone to that country to preach the Gospel of peace to men who do not know this peace. You are therefore messengers of peace; live as such. May the peace of Our Lord fill your souls. If your characters are not perfectly suitable to each other, it is not a motive for not loving each other tenderly or not bearing each other wholeheartedly. He who can't bear the brother's faults of character is a mere man; he still has the imperfection of Old Adam. God's grace prompts us to suffer all things. "Charity is patient, kind" etc. Love each other, then, my dear confreres and sons. Love each other in the love of the Divine Master and our Beloved Mother.

May the grace of Our Lord Jesus Christ accomplish in you what my heart and yours so ardently desire—that you love in all gentleness and perfection. He who loves fulfills the whole law of Jesus Christ. If you don't love each other, you who are victims immolated on the same altar to the glory of Jesus, how can you love others? Love each other, therefore, in spite of your different natural tendencies which lead to impatience as soon as something contrary occurs. Then the peace of Our Lord which surpasses all understanding will fill your hearts and consume them in divine love. . . .

I visited your home eight days ago and preached in your church which was as full as an egg . . . . I had dinner with your grandmother . . . I had to promise your mother that I would come back to preach the Stations of the Cross . . . . Your mother is very well at present . . . .

Adieu, dear confrere.

> Entirely yours in Jesus and Mary,
> FATHER FRANCIS LIBERMANN,
> missionary of the Holy Heart of Mary

255

To counteract certain dangers inherent in your ministry, avoid familiarity and practice self-restraint.

Letter Two   **March 8, 1844**   *Vol. 6, p. 105*

J. M. J.

Dear Confrere:

I must begin with a temporal matter. Don't worry any more about your dear mother; everything is going well. Your poor mother has given me much grief and sorrow.[1] I went twice to see her and used every means to win her confidence, but it was all in vain . . . . I then resolved to wait for the moment of God's Providence. The good Lord must have

---

[1]Mrs. Blanpin was a wealthy widow, pious but very scrupulous, and suspicious of becoming a victim of fortune hunters.

heard your prayers! . . . . I left her in a state of consolation and she was relatively calm, but she will never be perfectly at peace with herself . . . .

It seems that it has pleased Our Lord to try you by illness. This has not frightened me; it was due to the change of climate . . . I strongly disapprove the conduct of all of you who worked so hard from the very beginning. Those who go suddenly to an entirely different climate should take care of themselves and proceed slowly at first . . . .

Watchfulness is in order everywhere. "Watch and pray" said Our Lord. I am not surprised hearing about those dangers you speak of, although I didn't expect that they would be so great. Watch and pray, dear friend. The shepherd who runs after his sheep follows them to the precipice but takes care not to fall into it, for he then loses both himself and the sheep. Be reserved in your external behavior, avoid any semblance of familiarity with such people, while remaining gentle and charitable. Don't invite familiarity on their part. They are naturally inclined to become familiar. They notice the Fathers' kindness toward all the Negroes; they have confidence in you, become affectionate and find it easy to open their heart to you; they find consolation in you just as they suffer rebuts from others. So be reserved in your conduct with them.

Safeguard also internal reserve. I mean, you should not relish the affection of those good people or let your heart dwell in the pleasure it feels in your pious relations with them. Dangers will always be present, but prayer and confidence in God will enable you to conquer. Moreover, the most holy and pure Heart of our good Mother will watch over you. Listen to Father Le Vavasseur [your superior]. He knows all the dangers you will meet with and is better able to give advice than I am. Don't be anxious. Our Lord and His good Mother will watch over your reputation. Use the precautions which Father Le Vavasseur suggests and then be calm. Try to practice recollection without striving too energetically for it. Such over-eagerness and contention in a missionary cannot last. Place your confidence in Our Lady at all times . . . .

Entirely yours in the charity of the most Holy Heart of Mary,

FATHER FRANCIS LIBERMANN

256

We must patiently endure the troubles resulting from the character of our confreres. They serve to sanctify us.

Letter Three   *November 9, 1844*   *Vol. 6, p. 413*

Dear Confrere:

I have just received your report about the mission you preached at Colimaçons. We rejoice with all our heart because God's goodness deigns to bless your work. . . . Have courage and put your confidence in God. He will bless your works more and more. . . .

[*The Faults of Your Confrere Serve to Make You Grow in Holiness*]

Good Father Collin has a quite unique character. I know that from the beginning you did not see eye to eye, but there is considerable good in this. It gives you an occasion for practising virtue, and God's grace will help you to grow in the spirit of our good Master. Nothing else serves your spiritual formation as well as that exercise.

Moreover, your annoyance with him will not last forever. Once you are freed from it, your soul will have twice as much repose and holy freedom as it had before. You your-self realize well the great good that will result for you, for you call it a treasure from which you wish to draw profit. You are quite right in calling it a treasure: you cannot imagine all the goods that result from it. Be like a victim constantly offered on the altar; sacrifice, immolate yourself, immolate your self-love. That temptation which exists between you and Father Collin is the hammer in the hands of God by which He wishes to break up all that is defective in your souls. It is a flail which, by striking the ear of corn and shaking it violently, separates the grain from the straw.

[*Try to Control Yourself*]

Remain humbly prostrate before God. Acknowledge your miseries and weakness and walk always with courage in the way of God. That temptation must also be the occasion for patience, longanimity and forbearance with the neighbor. You know that "patience has a perfect work." It will also teach you self-control, to be moderate and reserved. It will oblige you to have frequent recourse to God and to humble your-self before Him, to see what you really are.

All this is very good and largely compensates for the faults of weakness and frailty which self-love, sensitivity or briskness cause you to commit. That is why the Divine Savior, in His great love for you, has preferred to expose you to the danger of those passing faults rather than deprive you of the good that will result for your soul. I can say the same about our dear Father Collin. He most probably grieves because of the faults he commits through frailty and would like to live in perfect harmony with you. Here you see the results of a difference in characters: souls of good will are tried and establish themselves in solid piety. They work, commit faults, but by and by gain mastery over themselves.

I feel certain that it is not pride or contempt that makes Father Collin take those apparently haughty airs. The real reason is that he is irritated by your way of acting and talking and also because of your different characters. He makes efforts to overcome himself but doesn't seem to be always successful. I expect to hear a jeremiad from him also. He will certainly complain spontaneously in his next letter.

[*Suffer with Love and Confidence in Jesus*]

You should suffer your temptation patiently and avoid displeasure with yourself. Try to remain in a spirit of gentleness and confidence in Our Lord and Our Lady and preserve peace. Remain very humble, but aim at this peacefully and in the presence of the good Master. Suffer with love, distract your mind from thoughts about your confrere, quiet your imagination and don't readily think that you consent to those outbursts. All this takes place in the senses and imagination; generally it is not real nor is there consent. It is a cross, a misery. Bear it as a cross and humble yourself on that occasion as in any other trouble.

Don't be afraid because of your unfaithfulness. Jesus will make up for all that is wanting to you. Labor for the salvation of souls for and through the love of Jesus and Mary. When people come to you, receive them in Jesus' name. He will do what you are unable to accomplish.

[*Be Like a Child with Jesus and Mary*]

Regarding meditation, abandon yourself to the good Master; remain in peace in His presence. When you have distractions, quietly return your mind to your prayer, gently raising it to Jesus and Mary. Don't feel ill at ease with so good a Father and so good a mother. Approach them as a child, with sweet affection, cast a glance to Jesus and

276

Mary and then remain in His presence. Have confidence and courage! Nothing you complain about contains any danger for your soul.

Your mother is a saintly woman; she is deeply attached to God, . . . [but pursued by fortune hunters]. How unhappy are those who possess the goods of this world! But don't let all that trouble you, dear friend. Have confidence; your mother will sanctify herself in spite of everything. She has made great progress. The thing that grieves me is that people who are interested in money cause her so much trouble and agitation. However, things are improving in this respect.

Entirely yours in Jesus and Mary,
FATHER FRANCIS LIBERMANN

257

Our defects can help us to become more firmly established in the way of God. He makes use of a troublesome confrere to overcome your self-love. Jesus is our All.

Letter Four   *{January, 1845}*   *Vol. 7, p. 40*

Dear Confrere:

Your mother spent three days with us. I invited her to the dedication of our chapel and I asked her to pray for our poor Negroes, so that she might in some way share in the labors of her son. I did my best to make things as pleasant for her as possible. I was glad to see that she was more calm and peaceful than I have seen her at any other time. She is a holy woman who would be very happy if she had peace of soul. She would enjoy that peace if people didn't annoy her. . . . She has left very satisfied and perfectly at peace. . . .

[*Our Defects Can Help Us to Become More Firmly Established in God's Love*]

Now let me say a word for yourself. The good Lord puts you through a trial. Don't worry because of all the temptations you have undergone. Go with confidence to Mary: her motherly heart will not abandon you. Don't be surprised that the enemy torments you. It would be surprising if he did not. Feel sure he will not be successful. Profit by your state of affliction and remain in humility before God.

We know for certain that we are poor and weak and that we have defects. We know we aren't good for anything but doing evil. This we know through faith, but this is not the same as having experimental knowledge of it. We have to pass through a state of wretchedness to make us realize profoundly that we are nothing. We are entering the way of holiness. I assure you, dear friend, that I don't know anyone who arrived at solid and stable perfection without passing first through the crises you have experienced. I'll say more: the miseries you mention are insignificant in comparison with the things I have seen in very privileged souls who, after their sorry experience, advance with giant steps. Be courageous therefore, dear friend, and full of confidence in God and in Our Lady.

The thing that should ordinarily be done in such a state is to remain in one's poverty before God, in a spirit of humility and submission to His will which leaves us in our weakness and misery. Be convinced that what you went through was but a passing squall. Troubles, agitations and temptations of this kind occur only at a certain stage of the spiritual life. They last some time according to God's designs and, after that, one is firmly established in the way of God.

[*God Uses Your Confrere to Help You Overcome Your Self-Love*]

Moreover, your difficulty was due to a special circumstance, the difference between your temperament and that of Father Collin. I guess that he will continue to find exercise for his teasing mind! He often annoys you without really intending it and even against his will. Feel certain that that difference between your temperaments was but an occasion. You had to suffer and would have suffered in any case, but God's goodness made use of a confrere for that purpose. At the root of your trouble there is probably a certain amount of self-love, a certain over-sensitivity and a spirit of contradiction. Don't be surprised to find such evil sentiments in you. They are in all of us. When God in His goodness keeps those poisonous springs closed, we are then at peace, but when He allows them to be stirred up for the sake of our spiritual progress, they produce an awful stench.

Be patient, dear friend! Those evil times will pass and your soul will regain peace, a stable peace, founded on firm renunciation. Be patient with yourself while waiting for better times. Once you enjoy the company of other confreres—and I hope this will be soon—you will be separated from Father Collin. You will have less relations with him and things will go better; you will be more tranquil.

Don't envy the lot of Father de Regnier.[1] Your turn has not yet arrived. You will have to labor and suffer and sanctify yourself. Surrender your soul to Jesus and Mary. . . .

[*Jesus is Our All*]

I shall give you news in two or three months. Be brave, dear friend. Suffer your temptation with peace, gentleness,

---

[1] One of the victims of the first missionary expedition in West Africa.

humility and perfect submission to God's will. Jesus is with you; be in peace. Sacrifice yourself constantly to His glory. Live like a servant, belong to Him. Be constantly at His disposal that He may do with you all that He pleases. What have we on earth and what do we seek for in heaven if not our sweet Jesus and the fulfillment of His divine will?

We are nothing; we cannot do anything; we are worth nothing. We belong to Jesus; this is all our glory and our only happiness. Well, dear friend, if our good Lord Jesus accepts you in spite of all your miseries, and takes and leads you as His beloved child, are you not blessed upon earth? Abandon yourself to the good Savior. Give yourself to His good and lovable Mother and suffer in peace for love of Jesus.

Adieu, dear confrere and son. Write to me more often than I write to you.

Entirely yours in the living and pure charity of the most Holy Heart of our Mother,

FRANCIS LIBERMANN

priest of the Holy Heart of Mary

258

Disregard any worries caused by your temporal posses-sions. I greatly admire your mother. Your sufferings are the result of your love of God, mine come from my sins.

Letter Five   *{April, 1845}*   *Vol. 7, p. 144*

Dear Son and Confrere:

I can give you only a short word in reply to your letter, for I want to give it to our confreres who are at Toulon [ready to embark for Bourbon]. I hope that it will reach them still in time.

[*Do Not Worry About Your Temporal Goods*]

Don't worry because I might have trouble on account of your temporal goods. I have always said that we are never more at ease than when we have nothing. However, since those goods were given you by God's Providence and He desires that I take care of their administration, I have to shoulder that task. I am accustomed to suffer afflictions on the part of men; this is my life. Yes, dear confrere, it is my life, for when I have no trouble, I don't serve God and do nothing for Him. . . .

Neither should you grieve because you possess those goods. God, in His goodness, has wished to make them serve for our own sustenance. True, if that resource had been wanting, He would have given us another. Nevertheless, since God willed that you should give us that help, rejoice before Him and know that He will reward you, giving you the hundredfold by His grace. . . .

[*Your Mother is a Holy Woman*]

Your mother is very well. We agree perfectly. She doesn't want to hear about business and interest. I can't tell you how attached I am to that good holy lady. She continues to consider herself the most wretched of creatures. I admire her devotedness to God, her spirit of sacrifice and her humility.

You can't imagine how wretched I feel when I compare myself with her. I am hoping that I shall soon be able to pay her my annual visit. She urges me to come and would like to see me. This shows that things are going well. She suffered constant annoyance from her relatives and the

Reverend pastor who wished her to make a will in their favor and they said things to make her feel sorry that she had let you go away. They said I was doing everything to get hold of her property and yours and that those goods belonged to her relatives. I knew this was going on, though she didn't tell me. I gathered it from a number of circumstances. But she has since told me explicitly. The pastor now understands the state of affairs and leaves her alone so that she enjoys great peace....

[*You Suffer Because of God's Love, I Suffer Because I Am a Sinner*]

Don't complain because you can give so little time to mental prayer and to study. Blessed is the missionary whose time is absorbed by work for the salvation of souls. You are much more to be congratulated than pitied. You have a great happiness which I don't have. I too haven't a moment during the whole day to occupy myself with my wretched soul, nor have I time for study. What keeps me busy? Letters! And these never serve directly for the salvation of souls.

But your life is occupied with saving souls. Mine with making arrangements. I am like the secretary of a great banker. The secretary is good at arithmetic, he puts order into accounts, deals with millions in his calculations, makes brilliant commercial speculations, but all that is in the purely speculative order so far as he is concerned. Others collect the profits which he has calculated and the benefit of his speculations. He leaves his office and sometimes hasn't a penny in his pocket. This is my situation. I calculate, speculate, make plans for your gains. And I have empty pockets. I shall be happy on Judgment Day if I obtain the Lord's mercy. You, on the contrary, save souls. What a blessing!

Be at peace therefore. Don't worry if you aren't able to make your meditation properly and if you suffer some trouble. Make sure only that you are faithful to God in your exercises prescribed by the Rule. You suffer for the love of God, and I suffer migraine, that is all! Your pains belong to your apostolic work and result from them. I suffer because I am a sinner. Suffer with patience and with love. . . .

Don't be surprised at the things that are taking place in you. You are not yet fully formed. You will become more calm by and by.

Adieu, dear confrere.

Entirely yours in Jesus and Mary,

FRANCIS LIBERMANN
Priest of the Holy Heart of Mary

259

Your affliction (the loss of the power of speech) is a punishment for my sins. Offer your trouble for the salvation of souls and your own spiritual growth.

Letter Six   *La Neuville, September 6, 1845*   *Vol. 7, p. 296*

Beloved Confrere:

[*My Sins Fall on Every Member of the Congregation*]

I cannot write more than a couple of words. . . . Yet I would have liked to write at greater length to console you who are so dear to me in the charity of our good Master. No doubt you are in need of that consolation. I wish I could be with you for one hour at least every week, to help you carry the cross which God's goodness has laid on your shoulders.

Dear son, my heart is suffering with you. If at least I were able to give you some relief! I have prayed frequently to the Blessed Virgin to do this for me. But I fear that the prayers of a wretch like me are not heard. Pardon me for my spiritual poverty and my sins. Do you have to suffer on their account? Yes, dear friend, and this is what grieves me most when I see what a poor man I am. Yes, certainly, the sins I commit indirectly fall on every member of our dear Congregation and on its works. "God does not hear sinners," yet I have to pray ceaselessly and be heard for everything that concerns our holy and admirable work.

I often pray Our Lord that He may deign to punish me alone for my sins and may hear my prayers as if I were most agreeable to His eyes. Oh! let Him overwhelm and destroy me if need be, provided my wickedness does not affect the souls of you whom He loves with a love of predilection, nor the works He has entrusted to us.

*[Offer Your Troubles for the Souls Entrusted to You and
Your Own Spiritual Growth]*

Regarding yourself, remain humble and peaceful in His presence and count on His mercy. Offer your pains and troubles for the souls to whom you would like to speak about His divine love and are unable to do so. I assure you that you will be more pleasing to the Heavenly Father and will do more for souls than if you were speaking to them. Once your speech is given back to you, the good you will accomplish will be so much greater. Moreover, the good you will do during this time of silence which God's goodness imposes upon you will be more useful to your own soul, for you will become more firmly established in humility and habitual submission to God's will. . . .

Your good mother now enjoys perfect peace. It is so important for her to 'preserve it at all costs. . . .

Entirely yours in Jesus and Mary,

FRANCIS LIBERMANN
Priest of the Holy Heart of Mary

260

Preparation for Holy Mass. Self-will. Do not judge, do not condemn.

Letter Seven   *La Neuville, March 20, 1846*   *Vol. 8, p. 85*

Dear Confrere:

I have waited a few days before replying because I had to pay due respect to my beloved companion, my migraine. You act in harmony with the designs of our good Master by spending a few days in the home of your family. Don't you recall that when the Apostles returned from their mission, Jesus said to them: "Rest a while." Well, the Lord has told you the same thing through my mouth. Now let me deal with the various items in the order you mention them in your letter.

1. *The Holy Sacrifice of the Mass*

I remember what that holy man, Father Desgenettes, who assisted me, said to me at my first Mass in the Church of Our Lady of Victories: "My good friend, you are now in the third Heaven as you stand at the altar. When you will have said it as often as I have, you will be more cold." I understood then what was taking place in his soul. You see then that the holiest among men can experience the same things as yourself. Hence there is no reason for worry.

Use the following means to counteract your "coldness." Try always to take some time for a suitable preparation and use it to put your soul at Our Lord's disposal that He may do with it what He pleases. Keep your soul peacefully and humbly before Him during that preparation. While going to the altar, preserve this disposition of humility and readiness to be sacrificed. At the altar, if your preparation has produced a suitable disposition, try to retain it and remain in it. If you have a pious thought so much the better. Be guided by it. If, on the contrary, you experience nothing, be content with remaining in your nothingness and poverty before God, ready to offer yourself and sacrifice yourself with Jesus to His Father. You may also give yourself to Mary, that she may offer you with Jesus to His Father. This thought suffices and it is not even necessary that it be always present to your mind. It suffices that you have it at the bottom of your heart, in your desire and intention. Having this desire, you need not fear that [Holy Mass will become a matter of] routine.

During the day, preserve that disposition, for the priest must at all times be what Jesus is at the altar and what he is there together with Jesus—a victim immolated to God, immolated to His divine will. Remain in a spirit of surrender to God throughout the day and in an attitude of perfect submission to His good pleasure. Stay, like a very small child, in the hands of Mary who offers and sacrifices you to God's will. This divine will must be everything for you at any cost. . . .

2. Self-Will

I don't worry much about that. I feel certain that the evil is not as great as you imagine. I know your soul, its strength and its weakness and I am certain that the picture you paint is not quite correct. You have all that is required for being truly obedient. I think that the independence of which you complain is more a question of lack of attention than independence of your will. And your repugnance for obedience when things were not to your liking, was rather a matter of irritation toward Father Collin.

In any case we shall clear up all that when we talk together. I feel certain that all this will quiet down and pass away. Don't reason about it. Have no fear. Put your confidence in Mary and be at peace. You will see that once we shall have discussed these matters for a few weeks, everything will clear up and you will no longer see things in such dark colors.

3. *Judgments*

Here is what you ought to do. Remember that Our Lord said: *"Nolite judicare, nolite condemnare."* There are two points in this text. He says, *"Nolite,"* we should *not will* such things, we must refrain from willing to judge others. Once you are involved in dealing with men, you will easily notice how wicked the world is. Quite often it is impossible not to notice the evil that is found in our neighbor. In such a case one deals with such a thought as one does with bad thoughts; one tries to think of something else.

When the evil does not leap to the eye, let us not look for it nor scrutinize it, but pay no attention to it. Of course, there are exceptions when we need to know those things in order to guide our conduct accordingly. When we act this way, we have nothing to fear; we fulfill the word of the Master, *"nolite,"* our will is not in it.

The second point is *"condemnare."* When we have noticed some evil in our fellow-man, we are displeased, we get vexed and are angry with him. In that case we condemn. We should calm ourselves and refuse to consent to this. *"Nolite."* This we learn gradually. I am not astonished that

287

such things took place in you. You had been walking in all simplicity, with so much thoughtlessness that you saw something good even when there was evil.

But when you acquired experience of the world, your eyes were opened and hence you readily judged and condemned the world. You will correct that little by little and overcome it in the long run.

It was even a good thing that this happened to you, for you might have adopted the ways of those people because of your excessive simplicity and your want of attention. However, I did not fear this, because I knew for sure that Mary would watch over you. You had to run that risk. Now you are out of danger, because you are more inclined to judge people than to imitate them. May Jesus and Mary be blessed for it, not because of the evil that might be contained in those judgments but because of the good that has resulted from it for your dear soul.

[Sundry Counsels]

Don't be astonished, dear son, that your heart is sometimes invaded by sadness. This is because of your illness and no serious evils will result. I have often remarked this phenomenon in many persons who were naturally very jolly and gay. As soon as they were cured of their indisposition, their gaiety returned. Another occasion for your sadness is your present situation. You need distraction. That is why I decided to take you with me in my travels. Moreover, when you are with us we shall do our best to provide distraction for you....

Remain [with your family] as you have promised until Passion Week, and come to us after that. You realize we can't do without you on Palm Sunday. How can we find chanters for the Passion if you aren't there? I also think you would become bored if you were to stay longer. Here we shall try to distract you and this is easier here than where you are....

I am angry with you because you are afraid you are bothering me. Does a child bother and importune his mother when he embraces her? Now it is only in such a way that you bother me when you tell me about what concerns your soul.

Your love for your mother is of a more sensitive nature than your love of Jesus. The reason is that you see her with your senses and you hadn't seen her for a long time. But your love for her is not, nor should it be, as strong in reality as your love for Jesus, nor should you prefer her to the love of Jesus.

Be always prepared from the bottom of your heart to sacrifice your natural love as soon as your love for Jesus requires it and in any circumstance. Don't worry about the rest....

Entirely yours in Jesus and Mary,

FRANCIS LIBERMANN
Priest of the Holy Heart of Mary

261

Rejoice that you are able to suffer something for Jesus. In your loneliness, throw yourself into the arms of Mary.

Letter Eight　　*Rome, August 4, 1846*　　*Vol. 8, p. 205*

J. M. J.

Dear Confrere:

Your letter arrived here eight days after you mailed it. I reply now when in all probability you have already made use of [the curative waters of] Eaux-Bonnes.

[*Rejoice That You Have Something to Suffer*]

Poor son! Your sensitive soul is made for the cross. It is true, you will always have to suffer as long as you are in this world but you know that at the end there is the heavenly glory. The cross is the shortest and straightest way to that goal. It is Jacob's ladder on which the angels of the earth—the children of God—must ascend to their Heavenly Father, and where angels of Heaven descend to lend their help to their earthly brothers, in the painful labor of ascent. Dull souls who seem to have no other sensations than those of animals, have no pains in this world. Nothing annoys or pains them as long as they have fodder. Must we envy their lot? We should envy them as little and perhaps even less than we should envy the lot of beasts.

Rejoice, then, in the midst of your sufferings of mind and heart. You should perhaps have more reason for grieving if you did not have those sufferings than now that you have them. We are not here in a lasting city. All things pass away, they pass with the rapidity of lightning. Blessed are those who suffer. They will not cling to this fleeting world and will constantly tend to a world that does not pass, the heavenly father-land where Jesus expects us with the radiating glory of His sacred Cross.

[*Throw Yourself in the Arms of Mary*]

Your sensibility is certainly a gift of God and at the same time a source of pains of body and mind. God's love for us is the reason why He makes us pass through that crucible. I wish I could have been with you to encourage and sustain you in your moments of grief. But no! Jesus wishes you to be alone with Him for a few days. He wants to be your only Consoler. Be patient, gentle, humble and peaceful in His presence. When you experience feelings of sadness, throw yourself like a child in Mary's arms. It is our glory to belong to Jesus crucified, to be the child of the Heart of Mary which was constantly pierced by the sword of sorrow. It is our glory to be children of sorrow.

The thing that grieves me most is to see you alone. But I feel certain that the good Lord Jesus will give you courage and that Mary will be with you. Try therefore to keep yourself occupied without tiring yourself out. Vary your occupation and interrupt it with walks and distractions. Avoid anxiety about your health. If you are getting better, blessed be God. If things do not improve, let us also bless the Lord. Remember also that, most of the time, the effect of the waters does not show itself immediately.

Put your lot into the hands of Mary, be with her like a little child with his mother. If he is hurt, he immediately goes and shows the wound to his mother. He is much less occupied with being healed than with the desire of showing his pain to his mother in order that she may pity him and caress him. The mother caresses him and dresses his wound, and the little one, without worrying about his cure, is contented and tranquil. His mother gives him a kiss. She says a loving word to him and he is satisfied. Remain in that way with your good Mother and suffer with love all that Jesus is pleased to let you suffer.

As regards myself, I am in very good health in the midst of the most intense heat. Nothing is wanting except La Neuville. We shall get there also, please God. . . .

Adieu, dear confrere and son. Write me often.

Entirely yours in Jesus and Mary,

FATHER FRANCIS LIBERMANN

262

The miraculous cure obtained through Mary should serve to sanctify your soul. Do not lose your simplicity in the midst of all the curiosity you are causing.

Letter Nine   La Neuville, November 28, 1846   Vol. 8, p. 357

Beloved Confrere:

Our joy and our consolation is very great. Your second letter, which has just arrived, confirms more and more the grace God has given you. I feel sure that that exterior grace of the first rank which God has granted you through the hands of his most holy Mother, who is also ours, will have its repercussions in the depths of your soul. That miraculous cure [of your throat] is a grace of the first rank, which is given to produce the sanctification of your soul.[1] I know that in this circumstance God has merciful intentions for others, but you come first and have the first share in His favors. That grace, therefore, will resound in your soul and make you a holy child of Mary. Your words show me that you have the determination to serve God better than ever. It is Mary who will guide you and, I hope, she will make you perfectly pleasing in His eyes. She has restored to you the use of your voice in order that you may please Him. I don't doubt that she is speaking loudly in your heart.

I see in your letter what I had expected. Everybody wishes to see you and hear you speak. It's hard for you to refuse to satisfy the pious curiosity of those good people. Be on your guard, however, and don't allow their importunities to lead to the dissipation of your own piety. Proceed with

---

[1]For the story of this cure see Libermann, *Letters to Religious Sisters and Aspirants,* Pittsburgh 1962, p. 52.

simplicity, for you know, dear child of the Heart of Mary, that simplicity is pleasing to Mary. She should be your inheritance. At the same time, and while acting with gentle and kind simplicity, try to preserve moderation and peace. Keep your soul gentle and peaceful in order that the grace and favor you have received from God may produce in you the sanctification which God's goodness intends to impart through it. . . .

Adieu, dear confrere.

> Entirely yours in the most lovable and merciful Heart of Mary,
>
> FRANCIS LIBERMANN,
> priest of the Holy Heart of Mary

263

Shortly after his cure, Father Blanpin suddenly underwent a great change. Hitherto as simple and unassuming as a child, he now wanted to be independent and his own master. This changed disposition, coupled with his extreme sensitivity, made him suspicious of Father Libermann and resent authority. As soon as he had sailed again for Reunion, Libermann wrote him a letter in which he pointed out the dangers of uncontrolled sensitivity.

Letter Ten   *Amiens, October 22, 1847*   *Vol. 9, p. 294*

Dear Confrere:

It was with a heavy heart that I assisted at your departure. I returned with your good mother, she with tears in her eyes and I, silent, because it grieved me to see you leave with sorrow in your heart. And if I was saddened before, so also seeing you agitated, I was anxious at the thought that you were sailing with grief in your soul. What a sad voyage you must have made! . . . Your letter written on the high seas seems to bear marks of that sorrow. A letter of Father Jerome reassured me a little. For he told me that you were full of charity and kindness toward the others. That showed that you were regaining your cheerfulness. Well, I have placed you in the hands of Our Lady.

It is my hope that once arrived in Bourbon, your sorrow will have gone. According to the letters I have received from Father Le Vavasseur, he was impatiently waiting for you and eagerly longed for your arrival. That gives me hopes that he will act toward you in a way to please you. On your part, I feel sure that you will do all you can to control yourself in painful moments. It is my opinion that from now on your life will have its burden of sufferings. Your natural sensitiveness will always cause you some trouble, but that sensitiveness, so often and so easily bruised, is a source of holiness for you. I feel sure that with the help of our good Mother you will profit by it. Recall our conversations on that subject.

[*The Dangers of Excessive Sensitivity*]

Excessive sensitiveness brings about sadness and irritation. It would be dangerous in others, but you are a privileged child of Mary. Those who have character like yours usually come out even or double. It can lead to the highest sanctity but sometimes it prompts a person to lose everything. The bad feature about such a character is that emotional impressions run ahead of reason. They are violent, painful, crucifying; they generate sadness; they arouse the person not only against the object that caused the impression, but create a disposition of great irritability.

Moreover, those impressions excite the imagination of such persons carrying it away and giving it an extraordinary effervescence. That is very bad, but even worse is the fact that the sensitiveness arouses the imagination and that the latter, in its turn, increases the sensitivity. Not only do such persons then suffer a heartbreak and moral evil, but there are rash and unreasonable judgments, great exaggerations, judgments against both persons and things and consequently powerful illusions.

Since self-love dwells in us, as soon as such impressions occur, this self-love is aroused. It becomes a partner in the disturbance, takes the lead and direction of the entire revolt and upsets everything in the end. Self-love increases the illusions, makes the irritation unbending and vivid. From this, finally, follow chronic irritations, positive repugnances and calculated opposition.

This, my dear friend, is the portrait I sometimes paint to myself of what is taking place in you, at least in part. It would give me anxiety if it concerned anyone else, for such a condition can have dire consequences when the person is not very faithful to grace. But Mary is with you and it is not possible that you will fall. You may, of course, become guilty of a passing infidelity, but these do not lead to those evil consequences.

[*I Myself Am Also Very Sensitive*]

There have been moments lately when I myself was [excessively] pained, namely, at the time when your agitation was most severe. I consider it my duty, dear friend, to accuse myself before you as of a very great fault though I have already confessed it in the sacred tribunal as soon as I had returned from Paris. I hope that God has pardoned me.

I have the more reason for being sorry because of that excessive sensibility that was so unreasonable on my part, for I fear it took place because your bruised sensitivity—which your heart was unable to control—was directed against me.

295

Those phantoms of suspicion that came over and over again before your harassed imagination pictured me to your eyes in ways that horrified me. I have my moments of weakness. You should pardon me for them; they did not last long.

I already suffered when I saw the gradual diminution of your friendship for me. This made me desolate, for I assure you that I loved you with all my heart and as always in spite of all that. I sorrowed later and suffered inexpressible pains, seeing that you had conceived suspicions in my regard, but I was never irritated. For I have this advantage over you that, though being as sensitive to moral pains as you are, I experience no irritation or disturbance in the imagination . . . .

In any case, forget all that, I beg of you. I would have asked you to do this a long time ago, but I felt great sorrow for having afflicted your heart perhaps on account of a certain self-love. But God, I trust, has pardoned me and you also.

I saw your good mother toward the end of the holidays. I saw her at Aire. She is at peace, leaving aside the small annoyances she suffers in her family. As long as her conscience is at ease, she can bear all sorts of pains . . . .

Adieu, dear confrere. Write to me and tell me how you are doing. Rest assured that I am and always will be

> Your most affectionate friend in
> Jesus and Mary,
>
> Francis Libermann
> priest of the Holy Heart of Mary

264

Trials and sufferings are to be expected by anyone who wants to share in the work of the Savior.

Letter Eleven   *February 20, 1851*   *Vol. 13, p. 37*

Dear Confrere:

I have suffered with you greatly on account of the troubles and contradictions you have had to endure since the departure of good Father Le Vavasseur. How painful those contradictions must have been to you who are so straightforward especially because they were underhand. I have frequently thought of you and said to myself that Mary, our beloved Mother, will lighten those burdens and will not permit you to become discouraged. Well, you are now at the end of your miseries. I feel confident that the good Lord will give you henceforth as much consolation as men have sought to give you pain. That shows us what the life of missionaries is in this world.

Sorrow is their daily bread. God uses it to sanctify them and render them capable of saving souls.

Jesus came into this world to save souls and it is in sorrow that He has engendered all the elect. His servants, who through the designs of His love are associated in that holy and great work, must have a share in His suffering and His ignominies in order that they may have a true share in His work. It is only through sorrow that we can save souls, because Jesus, the great Savior, has not wished to accomplish His work in any other way. Again, the enemy of souls will always cause suffering to those who have come to snatch them away from him in the name of Jesus.

That is why it is a great glory for us to suffer persecution. I have said that I hoped that the good Lord would console you. But do not fear. In the midst of all those consolations, He will not allow you to be without tribulations, for a servant, a helper of Jesus cannot be without sufferings. However, those sufferings are repaid a hundredfold by the happiness attached to them for the souls chosen by Jesus and Mary.

You are going to receive a new confrere in the person of little Father François! You will see that he is full of piety, gentleness, energy and that he has all kinds of good qualities that will make him a pleasant and edifying companion. . . .

Adieu, dear confrere. May the peace of Jesus and Mary fill your heart.

Entirely yours in their holy charity,

FRANCIS LIBERMANN, Superior

10. LETTERS TO JOSEPH LOSSEDAT

Joseph Marie Lossedat was born at Culnhat, near Clermont, September 24th, 1820. He entered Father Libermann's novitiate as a deacon in 1843 and was ordained a priest the same year. He went to the mission of San Domingo (Haiti) in 1844. When this mission failed, he went to Africa in 1845. Forced to return to France by illness in 1853, he spent two years in Europe before being reappointed to Africa. After laboring for thirty years in Goree and Dakar, he returned again to France and died at Chevilly on May 30th, 1887.

265

Libermann's letter of encouragement to two deacons of the Seminary of Montferrand who wanted to join his congregation.

Letter One   La Neuville, February 12, 1843   Vol. 4, p. 106

J. M. J.

To my beloved brothers Lossedat and Thévaux, greetings, peace and blessing in Our Lord Jesus Christ, our Sovereign Master, and in Mary, our good mother.

[Do Not Try To Bargain with God]

I rejoice with my whole heart, dear confreres, because our Lord Jesus Christ has deigned to inspire you with such good sentiments and prompt the desire to work for the salvation of the most abandoned souls. It is my hope that He will fulfill His holy designs in your regard, will give you the strength to accomplish His holy will in everything, and make you reach the perfection of the apostolic spirit.

It is not a small matter to attain to the spirit that is necessary for so great and beautiful a vocation. Endeavor to die to yourselves and to all that is earthly, and to give yourselves entirely to our divine Master, and He will give you the grace of attaining at least in part to the holiness of your vocation. Don't go half-way but surrender completely. When we bargain with Him, we must expect Him to do likewise and we shall gain nothing by it. If, on the contrary, we act with generosity and surrender completely to Him, Jesus accepts our offering with the fullness of His divine love and complacency and He gives Himself also completely to us.

[*Expect Crosses If You Wish to be True Missionaries*]

If you wish to be perfect missionaries, you must be ready to live by privations, troubles, humiliations and crosses of every sort. Recall constantly that Saint Paul, wishing to prove that he was just as much an apostle as Saint Peter, Saint John and the others, gave as a major proof that he had suffered so much in labors for the glory of His Master. Henceforth, then, you must devote yourselves to suffer all pains, humiliations and troubles in the peace and joy of God's love. You must consider yourselves victims chosen by Our Lord to be sacrificed for the greater glory of His heavenly Father.

Maintain your souls in a state of perpetual peace in the presence of the Sovereign Priest who has to immolate you. Let not your will resist at any time when there is question of suffering. Be like motionless victims, bound and shackled before Him, and allow that divine Priest to do absolutely everything that is pleasing to His heavenly Father.

At present, you have but little suffering because the time of your apostolate has not yet arrived, but the time will come. You will have to tear yourselves away from your parents and will meet with other small pains. Accept them in the meantime as an investment for the future. What you must do at present is to lose sight of your self-interest, your well-being, satisfaction and pleasure. Live like Jesus when He was on earth. He did not satisfy Himself; He never sought Himself, His own glory or greatness. He acted as if He had no personal interests. All He wished was to be immolated to the glory of His Father. That must be your life also.

As regards the realization of such a life, for the present you must be satisfied with desires. However, even now you can and must try to forget yourselves, to accept lovingly all the troubles that come your way and those little sufferings which are never wanting. Lead a humble, gentle, peaceful life. Forget yourself and let others forget you. From now on no one should be able to offend you any more, for you have put all your interest into the hands of your Master. You have no more personal interests; only the interests of your Master ought to concern you.

[Be Gentle and Humble]

Be gentle toward everybody. Accustom yourself to the practice of gentleness. It is a perfect virtue and is acquired perfectly only at the expense of all our natural affections and interests. Accustom yourselves to preserve in your souls a peace that is full of gentleness and humility. Don't worry or become anxious at the sight of your faults or anything else. When you see something in you that is faulty, humble yourselves in all peace before Jesus your Master. Get the habit of remaining in your lowliness and poverty in the presence of the divine Master, knowing well that you have nothing in yourselves that is worth anything. Live in peace and humility of heart before Him, with firm confidence that He will not abandon you in your wretchedness.

Never consider yourselves to be worth anything. Even in the midst of the greatest blessings, preserve your spirit of poverty. Whenever your thoughts turn toward yourselves, let it be to behold how poor you are. Do this with gentleness and confidence in God. Never appear before Our Lord except in an attitude and spirit of lowliness and of peaceful surrender to His divine goodness, with full confidence and humble love.

[*Realize That You are Not Sacrificing Very Much*]

Get the habit of directing your souls to God with a peaceful and gentle movement of the heart, but let it always be accompanied with a realization of your littleness, incapacity and worthlessness. At the same time, desire to sacrifice everything, yourselves included, to His love. If you have all those sentiments, and even if some day you will have the happiness of sacrificing yourselves entirely, say to yourselves that you have merely given to God all that belongs to Him and that your sacrifice did not amount to very much.

Don't imagine that you are doing great things by giving yourselves entirely to God, for all its happiness is for yourselves. All the glory ought to be for God; and the humiliation, oblivion and confusion for you. What advantage accrues to the Most Holy Trinity to have one more little worm? What favor are we doing to Him by giving Him a nothingness which belongs to Him even before we think of it? Woe to us if we do not belong to Him, for we refuse Him what is His. Poor miserable creatures that we are! We imagine that we are doing admirable things, when our God of mercy grants us the supreme happiness of being chosen to belong to Him. We dare believe that we are giving something as soon as we have merely the desire to sacrifice ourselves for Him.

LETTERS TO JOSEPH LOSSEDAT

[*Jesus Has Chosen You to be His Willing Victims*]

Esteem yourselves very fortunate, therefore, my dear confreres, because Jesus, the King of heaven and earth, has chosen you for His victims. You are not doing anything to raise you in honor and glory. The glory belongs to Him and your role is to remain in your nothingness before Him, full of admiration because He has deigned to cast His eyes on you and consider your poverty.

O chosen vessels! If you are faithful, Jesus will use you for the salvation of many. But He will sacrifice you. He will teach you how you must suffer for His glory. Be faithful, therefore, and follow every impulse which Jesus wishes to give to your souls. Live by Him and in Him, keeping in mind your poverty, nothingness and incapacity. Don't say: "I am going to save many souls." It is Jesus who will decide that. He is the Lord who can at will foster His glory by means of the poorest instrument as well as by the richest. His Father made out of nothing this whole beautiful universe and the creatures of heaven. If nothingness has been the starting point for such a magnificence, a poor man can also serve as His instrument for the diffusion of His grace. However, it is He who will do it and not you. Say rather: "I will be a poor man before Jesus, in order that He may do with me and in me everything He wants. I will be docile, humble and abandoned to His hands, full of confidence, in order that He may do everything He wishes."

The nothing, you see, did not resist the Creator. We are more wretched than nothingness, for we constantly resist Him. What an admirable thing this is that Jesus deigns even now to occupy Himself with us! It is a great thing for us to be perfectly docile to Him and never to resist Him in anything. There isn't one saint in Heaven who never resisted Him in anything. Mary alone has that glory. That is why she is the supreme wonder. At least, try to resist as little as you can; be docile and pliable, in order that He may fit you for His great work and use you afterwards according to His good pleasure.

[*Summary*]

I am quite lengthy. Well, if you learn by it the three things I wished to inculcate, the pain you took in reading this long letter will be well rewarded: 1. Forget your own interests and love suffering; submit to the divine will in all trials. 2. Constantly humble yourselves in Our Lord's presence; preserve a low opinion of yourselves and realize your incapacity and nullity; humble yourselves peacefully and quietly and be at the same time full of confidence and love. 3. Live an interior life, abandon yourselves to Our Lord. Do all that without contention, without violent and sensible efforts.

I pray our divine Master to fulfill all these things in your souls and I am, in His holy love and that of His most holy Mother,

Your most poor servant,

FATHER FRANCIS LIBERMANN

266

Gently endeavor to overcome the resistance which your parents offer to your departure.

Letter Two   La Neuville, August 13, 1843   Vol. 4, p. 306

J. M. J.

Dear Confrere:

[*Jesus Too Had to Leave His Mother When He Went to Preach*]

Your letter touched me profoundly. I fully realize the pain you feel and your present embarrassment. Be faithful, give your soul to Jesus and place all your confidence in Him alone and in His most holy Mother. Think of the conduct of the divine Master. He too had to leave His holy Mother to go about preaching and, besides that, to be crucified. It is true that Mary did not oppose His design. On the contrary, she desired to be with Him and make her own sacrifice. Nevertheless, He gives us the example if we wish our souls to be perfect.

It is most difficult and painful to have to offer resistance to persons who are dear to us and to whom we cause sorrow. But when the glory of our Heavenly Father is at stake, we must repeat after our divine Master, "Who is my mother and who are my brethren?"

Try to arrange things as gently as possible in order to soften the pain which your departure will cause your father. You could perhaps tell him that you want to come here at least to consider things better for one year and that, if the good Lord doesn't ask you to go to the missions, you will not go. A year is a long time. It gives time to reflect. Perhaps by proposing things that way, you will pacify him a little.

[Do Not Delay Your Departure]

I don't think that the short time of vacation will console your father and give him better dispositions, and I see no advantage in your staying with him until the end of the holidays. I urge you to follow the counsel of your director in this respect. Asking many people for advice is not good.

It is a consolation to consider the reasons that are advanced against your vocation, for it shows you that the only obstacles are flesh and blood. If you prolong your stay at home, you may have to engage in more severe battles. A kind of compassion for the sorrows of your family will prompt even some priests to take sides with them, and things will become more difficult for you. The only thing I can say is, follow exactly the advice of Father Gamon. If you do, you will have peace and assurance. I don't know your situation well enough. I am too far away to be able to give you detailed advice.

Our novitiate will open on the eighth of September. It is possible that six of our missionaries will have left for Guinea by that time. Or they might still be here; this will be decided this week. We will not forget you in our prayers. You belong to us and share in the charity of Our Lord Jesus Christ who must reign among us.

[*Sundry Counsels*]

I urge you to live in your own home in your usual way, without cutting down your customary activities or acting otherwise than the other members of your family. Acting differently might annoy your parents even more.

Don't seek, don't ask [your parents] for the goods of this world. What we need is divine gifts and grace, not earthly goods. Don't reply to everything that is said against your designs for God's glory. Let the world express its views. Reply in a non-committal or evasive manner. Turn the conversation to some other topic. Say that it is useless to discuss such matters.

If the pastor or any other person wishes to pay for your journey, accept, for we have presently heavy expenses for our missionaries who are ready to leave. . . .

I put you in the hands of Mary, our good and amiable Mother. I am very busy because I expect the visit of Bishop Barron, the Vicar Apostolic of Guinea, who is going to spend a few days with us. He is on his way.

Adieu, dear confrere.

> Your poor servant in Jesus and Mary
> and in their holy charity,
>
> FATHER FRANCIS LIBERMANN,
> missionary of the Holy Heart of Mary

*Soon after being sent to Haiti, Father Lossedat became
ill and experienced strong feelings against the way his superior (Father Tisserant) tried to solve the Haitian schism.
Libermann sent him an encouraging and clarifying letter.*

Letter Three   Amiens, September 17, 1844   Vol. 6, p. 340

Dear Confrere:

[Rejoice That You Have Fully Returned to God]

Well, my dear confrere, your soul has passed through the
crucible! Pains and crosses are the portion of those whom
God wishes to sanctify. Be faithful, dear friend, and God's
goodness will save you and use you for the good of many.
You need courage. You say you have grown lax. This doesn't
surprise me, although my heart grieves over it. You have
fallen under the influence of a climate that is quite new for
you; it has affected your temperament and brought about
that evil effect.

You have had yellow fever in your body before becoming
acclimatized to that country; and your soul has passed
through the fever of laxness, interior pains, anxieties, bitter-
ness, and distrust, in order that you might become firmly
established in virtue, acclimatized in holy humility and self-
renunciation in the midst of your apostolic labors. Rejoice
because you have now fully returned to God and His divine
service. Adjust yourself to the situation of things in that
country, I mean, sanctify yourself in the midst of all the
evil that surrounds you.

[Avoid Prejudices Against Your Superior]

I have noticed in your letter that peace reigns in your
soul. Try to preserve it, and guard against possible trouble

and agitation. It was probably the want of confidence in Father Tisserant that lay at the source of the evil from which you have suffered. This want of confidence usually prompts judgments about the conduct and the intentions of others; and these foster a spirit of opposition. I shall speak of all this to our dear confrere and shall then be better able to advise you. In the meanwhile, remain in peace. Discard your prejudices against him. Don't fret over that. What is past is past.

Several of our confreres have experienced that temptation in my regard. They are now totally cured of it. At the moment of temptation, we judge things improperly, we see everything upside down. After a while the mind becomes more calm; feelings of opposition cease; the soul returns to peace and our prejudices disappear.

I am sorry you didn't tell me positively what was the object of your prejudice, I mean what was the imprudence you reproached him with. I should then have understood things better. But no matter, calm yourself and put everything into the hands of the divine Master. It is possible that what caused the trouble was a certain natural ardor or a too lively desire to do good, a certain impatience in procuring it. Seeing the obstacles Father Tisserant refused to remove, you began judging him. If we want to accomplish true good, we must practice heroic patience. A premature ardor causes the loss of everything.

Secondly, you saw around you frightening moral evils and your soul was saddened by that sight. It was overwhelmed, became discouraged, yielded to trouble, to anxiety and irritation. This interior irritation coupled with those feelings may have inspired sentiments of opposition and distrust. Then there were your relations with the persons you mention who were not favorably disposed toward Father Tisserant. . . .

LETTERS TO JOSEPH LOSSEDAT

[Superiors Can Err, But That Does Not Entitle You to Go Your Own Way]

Suppose even that Father Tisserant's conduct was reprehensible, you should express your opinion in a peaceful way and then leave things alone. You can't be sure that you are right and he is wrong. But you have a certitude of faith that you are doing right by obeying. Suppose you are certain that he errs, it is not certain even then that God doesn't wish to bless his way of acting. You have seen that his work has actually been blessed for, in spite of all obstacles, he has been accepted.

Remember that in order to succeed in an enterprise several means can be employed. If the means you conceive or those suggested by others are good, those chosen by Father Tisserant could also be good. Yours may be better, but those of Father Tisserant could also be successful. We should realize that in a mission as difficult as that of Haiti, it is necessary to count on God alone. This, I feel sure, is what Father Tisserant is doing. Of course, he can make a mistake: God will make up for it. It does not belong to an inferior to correct the conduct of the superior. You will see, dear confrere, how God's blessing will be on you, if you are well united together.

You are both in a difficult situation. It is impossible for Father Tisserant to follow all our sentiments and opinions. There are as many opinions as there are men. Every man must act "according to the wisdom he has been given." Father Tisserant will have to answer before God for the mission; he must act according to what he believes is right before God.

The lack of agreement must have done harm. But don't worry, dear confrere; you had to pass through your apprenticeship. One always spends such a time more or less at one's own expense. Your apprenticeship has not cost you much; your sickness has remedied everything. If I tell you all this, it is not because I wish to convince you, but to put you on your guard.

[*Be Gentle and Patient with Sinners*]

Avoid being bitter with sinners. Expand your soul when you meet with sinners. To become angry at the sight of their most abominable sins is absolutely contrary to the conduct of Our Lord. You know well that He reproved this conduct of the Jews. Our zeal must be gentle and full of patience, kindness and compassion. It is in this alone that the apostolic spirit is found.

Be full of deference for the priests who are not doing their duty. You should try to win them and not become embittered against them. When we become displeased, we merit God's punishment. What would we do if God's goodness did not overwhelm us with graces? Be gentle toward sinners, gentle toward yourself, humble and peaceful in God's presence, patient amidst all the evils that surround you. You will see, God will help you.

I fear that you might be a little discouraged on account of the difficulties. Don't be too much in a hurry to accomplish good. Patience is of the highest importance in apostolic works. When we are in a hurry we necessarily get discouraged, for we always experience great obstacles.

Adieu, my dear confrere. Be strong. Wait for the return of Father Tisserant and the confreres he will take with him. This will be better than all the reflections I make to you.

Entirely yours in the holy Heart of Mary.

Father Francis Libermann
Missionary of the Holy Heart of Mary

268

Encouragement of an isolated missionary in an extremely difficult situation.

Letter Four   La Neuville, November 7, 1844   Vol. 6, p. 409

Dear confrere:

[*In Your Isolation, Let Christ be Your Strength*]

I am eager to write to you, for it is such a long time since you received news from us and you must be worried. I am overwhelmed with work, but I cannot leave you without news.

Have courage, dear confrere. God's goodness is trying us; but it lifts us up, strengthens us and will never abandon us. Good Father Tisserant has just suffered a very dangerous illness, but he is now out of danger. . . . It hurts me to see you alone for so long a time. Mary strengthens you and encourages you! Yes, indeed, a victim should not consider its own interests any more, but be courageous. "The Lord is my strength," this should be your motto. Courage then, my friend, Jesus and Mary are with you. The more pain and crosses you have at the present, the more you can count on consolations at a later time when you will reap the fruits of your labor.

[*Apostolic Beginnings are Always Difficult*]

Don't judge matters according to the actual conditions of things. All beginnings are difficult and offer little foundation for hope. When the apostles began their preaching in Jerusalem, the situation seemed desperate: the priests and the mighty ones resisted them; it looked as everything would fall into ruins; the Christians were dispersed. Nevertheless, they

311

did not lose their apostolic vigor. By and by they began once more, and then they met with wonderful success. O my beloved confrere, be an apostle! It is not by fiery zeal that everything must be gained. We must join to it patience, gentleness, constancy and fidelity in remaining humble and loving in God's presence, in the midst of pains, resistance and contradiction. Apostolic longanimity is a powerful weapon for the salvation of souls. It is hard; we have to be perfect victims in order to practice it perfectly. Be such a victim; put your confidence in Jesus and Mary. That patience, that constancy and longanimity guarantee that the source of our zeal is in God. Avoid agitation, dear friend, do not indulge in animosity against those who contradict you and against great sinners, and you will act according to the Spirit of God. Everytime you experience excitement of mind and agitation in yourself, distrust it, restore calm, and bring your soul back to Our Lord.

Be full of confidence. God's goodness will not abandon you. You will see before long that good will be accomplished in Haiti. Don't base yourself on the present condition of things and the present dispositions of the inhabitants. With God's help everything will change for the better. You will see piety revived in a great number, and order re-established. The Haitian government will be consolidated little by little and peace will return. Some bad individuals will squawk here and there; but they will have little influence; religion will recover its lustre.

[*Avoid Becoming Involved in Politics*]

Moreover, if troubles begin again, a thing which I hope will not come to pass, this will not prevent you from doing great good. Avoid mixing into political affairs. "Let the dead bury their dead," that is, let the men of the world busy themselves with wordly affairs. Try in all your relations to calm the minds. Take no sides in agitations that may take place. Content yourself with your ministry. Save souls; bring them the happiness of God's grace and establish them in virtue and piety, as much as depends on you. If you cannot do all the good you would like to do, be patient and wait until God's moment has come. It will come, my dear friend; this is sure; and it may not be far off. . . .

Here everybody is well. . . . I would like to have you here for the dedication of our chapel which will soon be finished, . . . but we must not seek satisfactions on this miserable earth. Crosses and pains are things through which we save souls. We shall think of you on that day. . . .

Adieu, my dear confrere.

> Entirely yours in the holy love of the Immaculate Heart of Mary,
>
> FRANCIS LIBERMANN
> priest of the Holy Heart of Mary

269

Do not become discouraged. Tolerate anything rather than preventing the appointment of a bishop by antagonizing anyone.

Letter Five   *{November 27, 1844}*   *Vol. 6, p. 455*

Dear Confrere:

[Do Not Become Discouraged]

The news you sent me about Haiti doesn't worry me. Be more and more convinced that if we want to do good we must expect to meet all sorts of opposition. I feel certain that good will be accomplished in Haiti. Don't yield to discouragement; be patient and you'll see that God's mercy will shine upon that country that is ruined by bad priests.[1] At present you aren't doing anything remarkable. You cannot do much because you are alone, but you are preparing the terrain. Be patient therefore. Wait peacefully for God's own moment which is not far off. . . . In six weeks time I hope to be able to send you a confrere. . . .

[*Tolerate Anything Rather Than Preventing the Appointment of a Bishop*]

Be very moderate, I beg you, dear confrere. Don't cause any rows. If you can manage things in such a way that a bishop can be appointed in Haiti, the country will be saved. But if you anger people, if you act in a way that arouses suspicion, you will estrange them and retard or prevent perhaps forever the appointment of a bishop. What an evil that would be! Tolerate any kind of abuse rather than putting obstacles in the way of the nomination of a bishop. I take the responsibility for any fault that, you fear, may result from acting with gentleness and moderation.

That is all right now. I returned to Paris with a violent migraine and a bad head cold. I don't know how I have been able to gather my wits enough to write you this letter!

Adieu, dear confrere. I don't forget you. Remember always that you must be a victim immolated to the glory of God. A victim does not get angry; a victim does not become impatient. Do you hear that? You laugh no doubt, but since I see you in such good humor, I want to add: a victim never gets discouraged. Be humble and peaceful in God's presence and before Mary.

Entirely yours in the charity of the most holy Heart of our good Mother,

FRANCIS LIBERMANN
priest of the Holy Heart of Mary

---

[1] At the time Haiti was in schism and the last refuge of ecclesiastical misfits.

270

Reinforcements are coming. The work of an apostle resembles that of a farmer.

Letter Six   Orphanage, December 15, 1844   Vol. 6, p. 484

J. M. J.

Dear Confrere:

[*Reinforcements Will Soon Arrive*]

I write just a couple of words, for I want my letter to leave by the next boat and give you the consoling news as soon as possible. You will soon see the arrival of Father [George] Paddington and of one of our most fervent novices, a man who will rejoice your heart. I can't send Father Thévaux yet but hope to be able to do so a little later. He is all afire with the desire to go to Haiti. The name of the novice is Father [Maurice] Bouchet, who was the most fervent seminarian of Saint Sulpice at one time. Are you pleased? You smile! But this isn't all. If possible we shall send you two others and perhaps even three. . . .

Well, does this renew your courage? Why get discouraged at the sight of the difficulties and yield to thoughts of despair regarding the salvation of a country, because you have not yet been able to do anything for it. My dear friend, the time has not yet come! You and Father Tisserant had merely the task of preparing the terrain. If I were but one short moment with you, I would make fun of you. Look at the great apostle who is all upset! I now dare to laugh at you, because I announce good news which will make you cheerful. If I still noticed a knitted brow, I would take a more serious tone.

[*An Apostle Labors in Sorrows Before the Harvest Comes*]

Allow me to make a comparison to show you that you have done wrong in yielding to the temptation [of discouragement]. The farmer who cultivates his field during the winter does the hardest work of the year. He perspires and gets tired without seeing any fruit of his labors. The soil is black and rough and there is not one blade of green in sight. This is the situation in which you are at present. Have courage and patience! God's hand will not be shortened in Haiti. All the considerations that trouble you are worthless. It is from the almightly power of God and your fidelity to grace that you must expect everything, and not from the political measures taken by the Government.

When Spring comes along, the farmer sees but little green; he waits with patience. The grass grows a little; then bad weeds mingle with the crop and give him a lot more trouble and pain. This time will come a little later for you. Don't be afraid, the time for the harvest will come. Have courage, patience and pray! Calm yourself! When the confreres have joined you the dangers you now fear will disappear and your soul will enjoy peace.

Be faithful; God knew that you would have to suffer. It is not in vain that He gave you the desire to sacrifice yourself for His glory. Well! This is what is beginning to come about. But be convinced that this is the "beginning of sorrows." Remember, dear friends, that no good is ever produced without great sorrows. It is necessary to tear up the soil to make it produce fruits. You are now all "torn up"; soon you will produce, but you will realize that it is not you, but the divine Master alone [who produces fruitfulness]. You will then have greater confidence in Him and will not count on your own efforts.

Remain in peace. You have merely to obey and try to do good. I hope to be able to write to you at length on this subject and the conduct you should adopt toward the inhabitants of Haiti . . . . I cannot write more, for I haven't any paper. I am obliged to use this ugly sheet, for I cannot find anything else here and everybody is at the High Mass of the orphans.

Entirely yours,

FRANCIS LIBERMANN
priest of the Holy Heart of Mary

271

Encouragement in a difficult situation. Be flexible. The trials you are undergoing serve to purify your soul.

Letter Seven   La Neuville, December 27, 1844   Vol. 6, p. 505

Dear Confrere:

It must be a pleasant surprise for you to hear that I've changed my mind and am sending you Father Briot instead of Father Bouchet. . . . [He will be sailing on January 2.] Have courage, dear confrere, and the good Lord will help you.

[*You Are Like Someone Who Tries to
Rescue a Drowning Man*]

The poor mission of Haiti resembles a drowning man. Evil men want it to sink deeper and deeper and lose everything. But you, a poor servant of God, are like the person who, seeing the drowning man, runs to his rescue. He comes to the edge of the water but doesn't dare to jump in, for he is afraid. So he stays at the edge and tries to save the drowning man. He grabs him by the hair. He feels happy to be able to help, but soon tires of holding up the man, for he is unable to draw the poor fellow out of the water. He hasn't enough strength to pull him out, particularly because the poor fellow is stuck in the mud and the weeds. The rescuer nevertheless prevents him from drowning. For some time he shouts, worries, calls for help, and feels discouraged. He weeps, groans, is ready to abandon the poor man, but what then? The man would be lost, and the good-hearted rescuer would forever bewail the fact that he had lacked courage and had not persevered a little longer until help would arrive.

If on the contrary he has enough courage to wait, he turns this way and that. He adopts different postures to enable him to keep hold of the drowning man. He prays and puts his confidence [in God]. And at long last he gets help and, aided by God's help, they are now able to draw the man out of the water. He is half dead but gradually revives. The poor man so courageously sustained is very tired but he is saved, and the rescuer rejoices and is happy.

[Do Not Hold Too Tenaciously to Your Own Opinions]

Don't be weak, dear friend. Don't lose hold. Put your confidence in God and in the long run your difficulties will disappear. Don't fret so much because of the existing abuses. These can't be cured overnight, for they are inveterate. You must advance step by step. Father Tisserant's authority is not yet sufficiently established to permit him to act energetically. Moreover, his authority is too recent. Be patient. You will see that you will gain ground little by little. After all, from now on you will have confreres with you, and they are good. This will give you great help in your personal difficulties. . . .

I assure you that if I were in your place, I would content myself with expressing my opinion peacefully and would then follow the opinion of others rather than my own, if mine did not seem right. On the other hand, I beg you, don't worry about the past; be calm and peaceful . . .

LETTERS TO JOSEPH LOSSEDAT

[*The Trials You are Passing Through Serve to Purify Your Soul*]

If you worry much about the past, you will let interior troubles get hold of you and lead you to discouragement. Let Our Lord act and remain in repose. Don't be astonished that you have had temptations. They were necessary to educate you in a solid apostolic spirit. It would have been impossible for you not to be tempted. You will see, dear confrere, that good will result from it for your soul. I have never known any soul that was solidly established in the love of God that did not first pass through the kind of pains you have experienced.

Be convinced that the moral disorders in Haiti and the conduct of Father Tisserant were merely an occasion. What can we do? We are but poor fellows, full of pride and imperfections. There is a time in the spiritual life when we all must pass through the trials you have suffered and which, I hope, are coming to an end. Peace comes after that and we are then little by little settled in solid piety. Feel reassured about your past and present conditions.

Aim at profiting by it to remain in your poverty in God's presence. Learn little by little to be gentle and humble of heart. It is in this alone that you will find rest.

I am sure that if you had been here, you would have felt the same afflictions and the same distrust. Don't imagine that they were caused by the conduct of Father Tisserant. They spring from your own nature and the condition of your soul. The soul passes through various states before it reaches perfection. You were, and perhaps are even now, somewhat in the state in which God purifies you more and more. Don't you know that when someone sweeps a chimney, he scrapes it very strongly and tears off pieces from it because of his violent strokes. Our souls are black like chimneys. They need cleaning. You have undergone a strong cleaning and

319

this doesn't frighten me. On the contrary, it will all be to the good; when you recover peace you will be the more humble and devoted to God.

This is very consoling for you. God has purified you through pain, anxiety, agitation, and temptations. He always acts in this way. Why? "In order that we may bear more fruit."

You may have committed certain faults—this always happens in that sort of trial—but our good Master knows how to appreciate your good will which belonged to Him alone. Recall the parable of the vine which expresses so well what I had wished to say. The bad branch is cast off, the vinedresser puts it away and leaves it alone. This is the condition of a number of bad priests whom God suffers without grieving them. They are running to their perdition. But regarding the other, the good branch, Our Lord says: "The Father will purge it." This shows you what God's goodness expects from you. Let him cut and fashion you. Entrust yourself to God and try to become more and more attached to Him. Despise all those little miseries that occur in your soul, and place yourself humbly at the feet of Our Lord in order that He may crush you as much as He wishes.

Have courage, dear friend. You have enough interior pains and troubles. Lift up your soul. It is not an evil, be sure of that. It was necessary for you to pass through that trial. Once more, if you had been here, the good Lord would have made *me* the object of your trouble. It is myself you would have distrusted. For these things are not founded on reason. You merely undergo a trial, a state through which your soul must pass.

I have seen absolutely the same kind of trials and even stronger ones in chosen souls which, after passing through all that foolishness, are doing wonders for souls. Have courage then, dear confrere. All that has happened in you

LETTERS TO JOSEPH LOSSEDAT

In all probability you have felt one of those emotions from the moment of your arrival at Goree. Don't let it control you. No doubt, the people you have to deal with are crude and hard to handle. But this precisely is our reason for going to them. We must sacrifice ourselves for God's glory. We will overcome all obstacles if we practice patience. Patience, animated by confidence in God, is a great and admirable virtue.

Be brave, dear confrere, in doing two things. First, arrest the emotion either of repugnance or excitement from the very start. Secondly, be patient and suffer pains and difficulties. I feel certain that if you have the courage to practice those two things, you will be an instrument in God's hands for the salvation of a great many souls. Everything depends on that. You have in you everything that is needed to be an excellent missionary. It is that twofold courage you should try to acquire. All the particular virtues for your own sanctification, all the virtues related to community life for the good of your confreres, all the apostolic virtues for the salvation of souls, depend on your courage. It is therefore your big affair to acquire that courage. All the pains you may have to endure are not too high a price to pay for it. How great is my wish to be with you for one year to help you in that arduous task! But our good Mother will do this better than I . . . .

Adieu, dear confrere. Belong entirely to our good Lord.

Entirely yours in Jesus and Mary,

FRANCIS LIBERMANN

273

In this masterful letter Father Libermann explains the principles which should guide superiors in their dealings with their subordinates.

Letter Nine   **April 15, 1846**   **Vol. 8, p. 109**

Dear Confrere:

I wrote to you a few days before I received your letter of March 4th. I think that letter will disappoint you, for you won't realize that I merely replied to the first word you wrote to me before your last letter and you will grieve because I didn't reply to your questions. I know you and you, well, I believe that you know me. So, you realize, dear confrere, that I am very eager to console you in all your troubles and wish to do it as quickly as possible. I would very much want to be with you at least for a whole year, but this is not according to God's wishes. He does not want me in the missions. I would have written to you earlier, but my absence prevented it. . . .

[*Confidence in God*]

I am well aware of the fact that your mission is a difficult one. Yet it is my opinion that you are exaggerating certain difficulties because of the trouble you are experiencing. Let us put our confidence in God. Don't think that Mary will abandon you. I feel sure that there are grave difficulties which you have not even noticed and which I consider to be most serious. However, they do not frighten me.

Our Lord is with us. With His help we will overcome all obstacles. Let's go on and do what our weakness permits. It belongs to Him to bless our works and He will bless them. It belongs to Him to straighten out our foolish mistakes and He will do it.

LETTERS TO JOSEPH LOSSEDAT

[*Divine Providence Makes Allowance for Human Frailties*]

We make perfect designs and want those perfect ideals to be executed to the full. That, however, is not and never has been the way of God's providence. God wants all beginnings to be weak and imperfect. He does not want everything to run smoothly from the very start. We must submit to God's will, do things the best we can, and then leave the rest to His care. Hence, I urge you to remain very peaceful about the faults that will be committed. And don't worry when things don't develop according to what you think ought to be done to insure their success.

I feel sure that very often your ideas will be right and true. However, when you get excited about things, when you grieve and are troubled, more evil than good will result. It is proper to the highest wisdom, even mere human wisdom, in such cases to sacrifice a part of one's own views and to do the best you can with the means available. When you see that your confreres don't share your views, even when it is evident that they are not choosing the better course, it is preferable not to cling too much to your own ideas and not to contradict them.

Allow everyone to follow his own ideas and accomplish the good in his own way and encourage them in doing so. This method will make them yield the maximum they can produce. They would have accomplished more if they had had other ideas but that can't be helped. They don't have those ideas. If you try to force them to adopt your own ideas, in general much less good will be accomplished. They will be upset and might even become discouraged.

[*Beware of Imposing Your Personal Ideas on Others*]

It is difficult to realize the importance of tolerance. We can't expect men to have identical views. When we are intolerant we arrest the good, we are always in trouble, we

325

deprive ourselves of the necessary rest, discourage others and often discourage ourselves. On the contrary, if we let everyone act according to his personal ideas, according to his character, mentality and his whole make-up, great good will be accomplished.

It is true that many will commit faults and imprudences, but in due time they will get experience and each will perfect himself in his own way. This then is a very important principle and one that is universally applicable: We must always be on our guard against expecting or demanding perfection. It's good for us to know how things should be to attain success. We should know what conduct should be adopted and the best means to attain the best results. But it is even more important to be able to modify our plans, to yield and accommodate ourselves to persons, to things, and to the circumstances in which we are placed.

Feel certain that you'll never be able to execute things according to your wishes. It is a vain ambition to aim at a result that perfectly fulfills what we conceive and desire. It is of the utmost importance to adjust and accommodate ourselves to everything, if we wish to attain success. Otherwise we shall get crushed in our struggle with the difficulties that arise from persons and things.

I know and have always been aware of the fact that you have sound judgment. However, you cling too much to your own views and especially to the method to be used in executing them. You do not know how to be flexible and to adapt yourself to the attitudes of others. You are not sufficiently tolerant regarding their behavior when that is not quite correct or suitable.

[*The Evils of Intolerance*]

This intolerance contains a threefold evil. The first concerns yourself. It will make you live continually in trouble and have constant heartbreaks. You know, dear friend, how sorry I am when I see you in trouble. I am eager to remove its cause. Learn, then, to bear the faults of your neighbor. Learn to suffer a job that is only half done, even one that is done badly. If you want to have peace of soul, if you want to be able to accomplish great and important things, you must at all costs learn to practice a certain indifference regarding the ills you are not able to cure. Be convinced, dear confrere, that you will remedy many ills if you learn to suffer them in the manner I have suggested.

The second evil consequence concerns the neighbor. As long as you don't use the method I have described, you will impede the other's march, you'll prevent him from doing all the good he is able to accomplish according to his particular way, especially if he has a weak or narrow mind. You will discourage him and perhaps cause him to commit numerous faults and imprudences.

The third evil consequence affects both yourself and the others. If you become tolerant, if you learn to yield, to bear with others, even to encourage everyone in his way, you will unavoidably acquire a certain influence over their minds. Thus you will do not only the good accomplished by yourself but also be a great help to others. On the contrary, if you can't remain quiet about the least faults you notice in your confreres, the time will come when you will be almost always in opposition to them, for you'll almost never find men who are exactly as you want them. As a result, you will not acquire any influence over their minds.

[*Encourage Each One to Perfect Himself According to His Own Way of Being*]

It is certain that I have a much greater influence over our confreres than you would be able to have. Well, what is the most powerful means which I use to guide them?

It consists in tolerating in everyone the faults which I foresee, I shall not be able to eliminate. I sometimes tolerate manners of conduct that are most improper, most crude. I especially leave everyone in his own condition and seek to perfect everyone according to his way of being.

Rest assured that nothing is ever accomplished in such matters through force, contradiction and resistance. Everything, on the contrary, is accomplished, everything is gained by means of encouragement, tolerance, gentleness and calm. I say "everything." I don't mean that one succeeds in making others lose their character and their natural way of being, or even the faults inherent in their way of being. However, we gain and obtain everything that can be gained, and we make those who would have been useless under the opposite regime, contribute their share to the good.

Let me take an example. Suppose you wished to make Father Arragon moderate, polite, friendly in his ways, you would be chasing a will-o'-the-wisp. It would be easier to stop the sun in its course. But if you treat him in a friendly fashion, if you let him act according to his character and act toward him in the way I have suggested, you will certainly produce the good effect I have described. If, on the contrary, you yield to vexation of spirit, if you show him displeasure, if you chide and reprove him, you will reap all the bad results I have mentioned.

Leave everyone then in his proper condition and way of being. God made him that way. He is ready to do everything for the good, and you should encourage him. Then each one will do this as it has been given him from above. Hence don't expect to receive comfort from men. Seek rather to console and encourage others. Remain the master of your own soul and you will be the lord of the whole world. It is in this that the superiority we must possess consists.

[*Disregard Your Own Afflictions*]

Have courage! You suffer and will continue to suffer, but those sufferings will cause your soul to expand. Believe me when I say that I suffer and will always suffer as much and probably more than you. At least, I am as sensitive to afflictions as you are, but is this a reason for yielding to discouragement? Never! No, never, with the grace of God! Should we manifest those afflictions to others? Again, no! I will never complain. Be strong and firm against yourself, and you will render great service to God. If you yourself don't learn to suffer, you will always remain below that which God expects of you.

This sums up your whole job: you must be master over yourself, suffer without paying attention to it, offer your sufferings with generosity to God. Bear and sacrifice yourself, and bear the others, in spite of their faults. You love great and beautiful things. Now here surely is a thing most beautiful, it's sublime. Ask for the grace to act in that manner.

I shall do my best to make appointments in a way that will give you peace. I might be able perhaps to arrange things so that you, either alone or in the company of Father Gravière, can explore the coast in view of a new foundation.

In any case, we shall try to arrange things for the best. When Father Gravière is in those parts, he will have greater facility to judge what is most suitable, and he is greatly interested in you.

Entirely yours in Jesus and Mary,

FRANCIS LIBERMANN
priest of the Holy Heart of Mary

329

274

Encouragement of a priest in forced inactivity. Beware of self-pity, too much hurry in doing God's work, and intolerance in dealing with government officials.

Letter Ten   *Amiens July 27, 1847*   *Vol. 9, p. 229*

Dear Confrere:

Finally we have received two or three good letters from you. I am pleased and hasten to reply. I shall limit my answer to the last letter, which is most important.

You are wrong, dear confrere, in saying that you made me sad because you desired to come back from Africa, as Father Gravière told me. I was sad in the sense that I pitied you in your afflictions but not in the sense that I was displeased with you.

The state you were in quite naturally made you wish to be with us again in Europe. However, for your own good and that of your work, I judged it better that you should stay. I found it hard to be so "cruel" and let you get bored to death in Goree. But I was unable to do anything else. Your return would have been harmful [for it would have discouraged the others]. Nevertheless, if your illness had obliged you to return, I would have received you with joy and without anxiety. Everybody would have felt that it was a matter of health.

So it was not your wish to return which worried me, but rather your stubborn silence. My last letter still needled you on that subject. I didn't know why you kept silent and thought you were angry with me because I didn't call you back. Now, at long last, I feel happy and I hope that from now on we shall not be without news from you.

LETTERS TO JOSEPH LOSSEDAT

[*Your Forced Inactivity Has Been a Major Cause of Your Troubles*]

And now let me speak in detail about the various reasons you mention for your troubles. Your first grief comes from your sickness and inaction. I dare even say that your sickness in all probability was somewhat due to your forced idleness and to the annoyance and boredom resulting from it. . . .

All this must have been for you a source of sorrow, trials and temptations. To a great extent they must have caused your illness and, in turn, your illness must have affected your morale thus aggravating your pains and sorrows. I could think of only one remedy for your trouble. . . . [to let you become active again and] undertake missionary work along the coast. Father Gravière was wrong in not letting you do this from the very beginning.

[*An Apostle Should Not be Full of Self-Pity*]

I hope that you will feel better from now on. Always, however, expect that you will have to suffer some pain. One who consecrates himself to God in a task as important as yours must expect suffering. Renew and keep your courage then and don't let tribulations cast you down, no matter where they come from.

An apostle is not a child. He is not sorry for himself and full of self-pity. He has learned to forget himself and to meet his afflictions with bowed head. His heart is strong like a rock in regard to his own sorrows, but gentle and tender like a dove toward the evils affecting others.

Recall that Jesus Christ saved the world by the sufferings of the Cross. If you want to be His follower, to be an apostle—and this you do desire—act like Him. Recall that He was very gentle toward those who crucified Him and that He forgot His own sorrows to compassionate the evils

331

of his mortal enemies. He counseled the women not to weep over Him but over Jerusalem.

[*Do Not be Too Much in a Hurry to Accomplish Things*]

The second reason for your afflictions was without any foundation. As you know now, [the mission was being reorganized]. You should not want to proceed too rapidly. Things develop slowly, but if you proceed prudently, you will invariably succeed. You can be sure that the most successful procedure is always to advance step by step without trying to hasten things. . . . Let's not run too fast lest we fall flat on our backs. We are on difficult terrain, where we should make one step and advance to the next one only when we have secured a solid footing. It is in this way that we shall advance little by little and whatever we do will be more solid. . . .

[*Be Gentle and Tolerant in Dealing with the Authorities*]

Regarding the third reason, the troubles arising from difficulties in your relations with government officials, let me give one very important piece of advice. I have always foreseen that one of my major difficulties would be to make the missionaries have pleasant relations with the officers that are on the coast. I'm convinced that it is of the utmost importance for the good of the mission that you be in agreement with those men.

For the most part they are good men but they are inflexible and authoritarian. If you don't handle them with gentleness, they will give you trouble and hinder the good you wish to accomplish. . . .

You should not be surprised when you suffer annoyances on the part of government agents. This is a necessary evil we must bear patiently. If you read the letters of St. Francis

Xavier you will see that he had to suffer much more from them than you have, even though in his time men were full of faith.

It is amidst such troubles and contradictions that God wants us to do good. We must do all we can to live in proper friendship with those who annoy us; we must be gentle and attentive in our relations with them in order to win them to ourselves. . . .

If, on the contrary, you treat them harshly and openly oppose them, they will not yield. Virtue, piety and prudence don't consist in being on good terms with those who are very kind to us, but in being able to get along with those who are mean toward us. You are all good men, that is sure, but I have no doubt that your own inflexibility has gotten into trouble with those men.

[*Never "Declare War" Against the Government*]

You say that Captain Brisset is unbending. Of course he is. I can say this without knowing him, because I know that all our army and navy officers are unyielding. The proper way to deal with them consists in never hurting their feelings. Never attack their authority by words, even when they happen to be wrong. And when you have to resist them, when your ministry demands it, act with all prudence and gentleness, taking beforehand every precaution to avoid a conflict with the authorities. Once war is declared, they will not budge. So do your best to prevent declarations of war, even when they ask you to do things that your conscience is not permitted to grant. In a word, gentleness and charity will always be most helpful. Rigor and inflexibility will be interpreted as intolerance. Once they consider you intolerant, you become useless. For those men, who are poorly instructed in religion and are prejudiced against you, the term "intolerant" is a terrible word. They are quick to apply it and put you beyond the pale of humanity. . . .

Don't become discouraged because of all those troubles. Put your confidence in God. Be gentle, moderate and patient. If the French officials are unbending, impatient and even downright wicked sometimes, it is your duty to be compassionate, and to humor them to the extent that your duties allow. Be particularly gentle in your behavior toward them when the fulfillment of your ministerial duties is involved. Avoid rigor, haughtiness and similar faults in that matter. Add to that a note of charity, of sympathy, and kind attention. This will win them if it is at all possible. . . .

Adieu! Write often.

Entirely yours in Jesus and Mary,

FRANCIS LIBERMANN
priest of the Holy Heart of Mary

INDEX OF SUBJECT MATTER